The Choice She Made
LK Wilde

Bk 2

PART ONE
LOWESTOFT

Chapter 1
April, 1930

The woman's heels click-clacked against the polished floor as she walked away. Marnie smiled; another satisfied customer. The new spring collection was selling, despite the economic woes shrouding the town. As she gazed around the shop, Marnie felt at peace. This sanctuary of frocks, fabric and fripperies shielded customers from the everyday. It was an escape. Even those with little to spend could while away their time in comfort, gazing at items they hoped one day to afford. For no one was turned away or shuffled on from their browsing. A customer might not be a customer today, but treat them right, and they might be tomorrow.

Marnie folded a piece of lace and added it to the pile on the shelf. She lost herself in its delicate flowers, beauty for beauty's sake, a world away from the drab, depressing faded brown cottons she'd grown up in. How far she'd come these past years. Now here she was, her last day as a single woman. She could hardly believe the moment was almost here.

"That smug look on your face will be even smugger by tomorrow night," said Brenda as she arranged fabric on the shelf beside Marnie's.

"I don't know what you mean."

Marnie smiled. She knew what the shop girls said about Tom. There had been times she'd wanted to tell him, but knew it would make him uncomfortable. That was one in a long list of life's contradictions. Men could openly lust after any woman who caught their eye, but women doing the same?

A smile tugged at Marnie's lips as she thought of the comments filling the staff room when her colleagues first met Tom. She couldn't blame them. He was a very handsome man with his swarthy dark looks. A handsome man who'd be all hers by this time tomorrow.

Brenda twisted her lips together as though in the middle of a passionate kiss.

"Stop that," said Marnie. "You'll scare away the customers."

"Yes, boss. Anyway, I don't suppose you need any tips on what to do in the bedroom. You've been engaged that long, I can't believe you'd have made your Tom wait for it all this time."

"I'd mind your tongue if I were you. And besides, a lady never tells."

Brenda laughed and moved off to replenish the stock on another shelf. Marnie's fingers caressed the lace in front of her. So many times she'd sold yards of lace to women preparing for their own weddings, and finally it was her turn. Six years she'd made Tom wait. The shop girls couldn't understand it. Why risk him losing interest? What if he turned his attention elsewhere?

It was a good job Tom was a patient man. A patient man who understood it was fear which had prevented her setting a date and committing to the love of her life. Marnie pictured the life her mother Rose had led, and shuddered. She looked around the shop floor. Her empire, her domain. How would it feel to give up everything she'd worked so hard for? Loving Tom came at a high price, thought Marnie, as she turned her attention back to the lace in front of her.

"Everything all right here?" asked Mrs Sinclair, shuffling over to Marnie. Glasses sliding down her nose, her boss sounded disinterested. Marnie knew that the pride Mrs Sinclair once felt for her department was slipping. A year away from retirement, the spinster lived for her cats, her WI meetings and her crochet projects. She had long since lost enthusiasm for the women's department at Chadds.

"I just sold the rose jacket from the spring collection."

"Good, good," said Mrs Sinclair. "I'm surprised there are still women prepared to part with money for such items."

"There aren't as many as before," said Marnie, "but there are still some out there."

"The display probably helped," said Mrs Sinclair, grudgingly acknowledging the results of Marnie's free rein on the window display.

Marnie smiled. As her boss lost interest in the job, she was happy to pick up the slack. Mrs Sinclair nodded and walked away as Marnie turned back to her task.

"Of course, you'll be wanting to give up your job once you're a married woman."

Tom's mother's words haunted her. Why should she give up her job just because she was a married woman? Not that Tom's parents expected her to stop working completely. He, along with his family, saw her future role as one more fitting for a fisherman's wife; mending nets, tending the home, monitoring the family finances. Marnie thought of Rose, her fingers raw from mending nets, living below the breadline with a horde of dirty bairns around her feet. Marnie squared her shoulders. Tom wasn't marrying a Grit girl, he was marrying her. She fully intended to hold on to the job she loved for as long as she could.

Perhaps it was the butterflies in Marnie's stomach making her restless, for the hands on the clock seemed to grind, grumble and groan their way around its face. It was with a sigh of relief that she finally counted out the day's takings from the till.

"Marnie? I need you back here."

Marnie sighed again, losing count of the coins and notes in her palm. What could Brenda need her for so late in the day? Marnie prayed it wasn't another staffing issue. If there was a falling out between two of the shop girls, it always fell to her to act as referee.

"Be there in a tick," called Marnie, starting her counting once more and bagging up the takings ready to take to the bank. She crossed the shop floor to the staff room and pushed open the door. "What is it?"

"Surprise!"

Marnie's hands flew to her mouth as her eyes fell on a large cake in the middle of the table. "Oh my goodness. You didn't have to do this."

"We did," said Brenda. "We've waited long enough to see Tom make an honest woman of you."

Marnie hugged her friends and colleagues. "This is so thoughtful."

"You've not seen the best bit yet," said Brenda, pulling two dusty brown bottles from her bag.

"What is it?" Marnie eyed the bottles with suspicion.

"Dad's home-brew. He's got a shed full of it, so won't miss a couple of bottles."

Brenda uncorked the bottles and began pouring measures of brown liquid into tea cups. Marnie took a sniff and wrinkled her nose.

"Go on," said Brenda. "It won't kill you."

Marnie pinched her nose between two fingers, took a deep breath, and downed the contents of her glass in one go. The assembled women cheered. Brenda leaned over and refilled Marnie's glass before Marnie could stop her.

Three glasses of home-brew later, it was a merry gaggle of women who locked up and headed for home. Even Mrs Sinclair had sipped a half-filled glass, though Marnie caught her tutting as the conversation between the women grew louder, cruder and peppered with swear words.

"What have you got planned for your last night of freedom?" asked Brenda, linking arms with Marnie.

"Not much. I'm calling in on Kitty on my way home, then I've planned a quiet night with Jimmy."

"Are you sure you can't put in a good word for me with that brother of yours?"

Marnie gave Brenda a good-natured slap on the arm. "I've told you a thousand times, he's spoken for."

"So you say, but I've never met this mystery woman. I think it's a story you've dreamed up to keep me away from him. Worried I'll lead him astray, are you?"

"I wouldn't put it past you," said Marnie. "Anyway, you'll get to meet Clara yourself tomorrow at the wedding."

"Damn it. Right, this is me. You alright? Walking to Kitty's by yourself?"

"Of course I am. Besides, I want to stroll past the new house on my way."

"Just make sure you don't bump into that fella of yours. It's bad luck to see him before the wedding."

Chapter 2
April, 1930

After waving off Brenda, Marnie walked along the high street until she reached the grand Flint House. Her hand running along the smooth flints that gave it its name, Marnie turned right into Wilde's Score. She passed the school, its windows dark and its playground quiet since the children had gone home for tea. Red-brick walls enclosed her on either side and Marnie smiled to herself, thinking how nervous she used to be when visiting Tom at The Grit. Now it felt like home. Since her engagement, she counted as a local, even if some turned their noses up at her working in the town.

Marnie passed a row of small brick cottages, nets hanging out in their yards. An old man sat on his front step, dragging on a pipe. "If it int the bride to be," he said. "The weather looks fine for your big day tomorrow."

"You'll be coming, I hope, Fred?"

"If I can find the time." The old man grinned, exposing nicotine-stained teeth.

"Away with you, Fred. Maggie will have your guts for garters if you find yourself too busy. I'll see you at the church, one o'clock sharp."

Fred tipped his pipe in agreement and Marnie continued on her way, humming 'The Wedding March' to herself as she walked along Wapload Road. She stopped outside a two-up two-down cottage, the sound of busy family life filtering through its windows. Before Marnie had the chance to knock, the door flung open and Kitty beamed at her. Her wayward red curls lay trapped beneath a scarf, and the apron around her waist signalled she was in the middle of cooking supper. "Ah, it's the bride," she said. "Come on in and I'll make you a cuppa."

"I'd love to, but the girls at work threw a surprise party for me and I want to have a quick look at the house before I catch the train home."

"Good God, woman. Why are you rushing round the place like a headless chicken on the eve of your wedding? There's no need to see the house. Bobby says Tom has it all under control."

"I'm sure he does, but I need to see it. It will help everything feel real."

"Wait there," said Kitty. Marnie heard the cry of a baby and Kitty's cooing before her friend reappeared with a large bag. "Here," she said, laying the bag onto Marnie's outstretched arms. "Feel the weight of that?"

Marnie nodded.

"Feeling real now, I'll bet. See, there's no need to go visiting the house."

"I'll only nip up there for a quick peek."

Kitty sighed. "You're as stubborn as a mule, Marnie Watson. I'll not have you carting your dress all over The Grit. Leave it with me, and come by for it on your way back to the station."

"Thank you," said Marnie, handing the bag back to Kitty and blowing her a kiss as she ran back along Wapload Road.

Kitty was right that it was foolish to go visiting the house when she was short of time. Marnie couldn't explain it. It was something she had to do. She had to get a glimpse of Tom.

Marnie continued running, only slowing when she reached East Street. She walked along the row of humble cottages, some of which had seen better days, until she found her future home. It looked different to how she remembered. Someone had painted the front door green and given the sash windows a lick of paint.

A lamp glowed in the upstairs window. Marnie leaned against railings on the opposite side of the street. She waited, holding her breath. There he was. Her Tom. She watched as he ran a hand through his thick brown hair, then stretched his arms high above his head. Every night he'd been coming here, fixing up the house which would soon be their home.

Tom placed a vase on the windowsill, then reached down out of sight. When he straightened, he held a bunch of flowers in his hand. As he arranged the flowers, his eyes were drawn beyond the window and his mouth opened in surprise as he saw Marnie watching him. She smiled, and he smiled back, fixing her with the gaze that she still became lost in, even after so many years.

Tom drew his fingers to his lips, kissed them, then placed his hand against the window. Marnie kissed her own fingers, then held out her palm and blew the kiss in his direction. Her heart fluttered. How was it he still had this effect on her? She was like a teenager, going weak at the knees over a man she now knew better than almost anyone.

With his hand, Tom made a shooing motion. Marnie giggled, bent in an exaggerated curtsy, then turned on her heel to collect her dress and hopefully make it to the station in time. As she walked the streets of The Grit, she failed to keep the smile from her face. Only a few hours to go and she would be Tom's forever. All the doubts and concerns of the past few years left her. She was ready to embrace her future.

Chapter 3

April, 1930

"Here you go," said Jimmy, placing a cup of tea on Marnie's bedside table.

"Ta." She picked up the cup and took a sip. "This is so strange."

"Me bringing you tea?"

"No, waking up in my bed for the last time."

"Strange for you, maybe. I can't wait to reclaim this room for myself. I thought I may turn it into a library."

"Hey," said Marnie, hitting her brother with a pillow. "Won't you miss me?"

"Of course I will," said Jimmy, taking Marnie's hand. "But I couldn't be happier that you're marrying Tom. You've found yourself a good man there."

"I know," said Marnie. She pulled herself up against the headboard and looked around the room. "You remember when we first arrived here?"

"How could I forget?" asked Jimmy. "I was in so much discomfort after my accident, but this place felt like a lifeline."

"And there I was, expecting to stay in Lowestoft for only one or two weeks."

"I'll never forget the way you stuck by me, nursed me back to health."

"It's not worked out too badly for me, has it?" said Marnie, smiling. "And here you are, Mr Headmaster. We've both come a long way from our island cottage."

"And yet now you're heading back into that world by marrying a fisherman."

"I know," said Marnie. "But I'm determined it won't be like our childhood. Tom's work is his own, and my work is mine. I won't be reliant on him the way Mam was with Da."

"Tom's a very different man to our father, Marnie."

"Of course I know that. But Mam was so tied to Da, she couldn't have left even if she wanted to. I'll never fall into that trap. I intend to keep my independence. Speaking of independent women, what time is Clara arriving?"

Jimmy laughed and looked down at his watch. "All being well, she should be here within the next hour. She stayed in Norwich overnight, so doesn't have far to come this morning."

"I can't wait to see her," said Marnie. "I bet you can't either." She nudged Jimmy, and he smiled.

"Yes, I am rather looking forward to it. Do you mind if I meet her off the train alone? We've got a lot to catch up on."

Marnie giggled and winked. Jimmy blushed. "You go. I'll have a bath, so I'm presentable when she arrives."

"That sounds like a good plan. Would you like me to make you some breakfast?"

"No, ta, my stomach's doing somersaults."

"You're not having second thoughts?"

"About Tom? Of course not. I'm just nervous about starting a new chapter as a wife. I'm not sure I'm cut out for it."

"Do you love him?"

"You know I do."

"Then you'll be fine. Now get yourself washed. You've got a big day ahead of you."

*

Marnie smiled as the sound of laughter floated up to her bedroom. She never saw Jimmy as happy as when he was with Clara, and wished they weren't living so far apart. It was half a decade since Clara had returned to the island of her childhood rather than remaining in Lowestoft with Jimmy. Not that he loved her less for it, or that their love had diminished over the intervening years. And wasn't he just as stubborn? Hadn't he chosen his career in the school over being with the woman he loved? Marnie shook her head in frustration. While she understood their reasons, she couldn't help feeling that one or the other of them should compromise for the benefit of love.

Marnie held a pin between her teeth as she twisted her corkscrew blonde curls up behind her head. Pinning her hair in place, she pulled on the dress Kitty had made for her. Pale blue silk floated just above her ankles, a navy ribbon pulling the fabric in tight at the waist. A smile tugged at her lips as Marnie remembered Mrs Sinclair fussing with the till, totting up the total of the fabric and knocking it down by half. She pretended it was a mistake, but Marnie saw through the puff and bluster and knew she had given her the price out of kindness.

The veil had been a complete surprise. Another example of Jimmy's generosity, which she could never repay. He probably would have saved the surprise till today if Kitty hadn't needed to measure the length against Marnie's back. A tear sprang to her eye, and Marnie wiped it away. For so long, it had been her and Jimmy against the world. How would he manage without her? Marnie's frown melted into a smile. If the laughter from downstairs was anything to go by, he'd survive.

Marnie slipped her feet into the heeled shoes borrowed from Brenda. She fixed the clasp on the necklace that had once belonged to Tom's grandmother. After turning this way and that in front of the mirror, Marnie took a deep breath and walked downstairs, leaving her schoolhouse bedroom behind for the last time.

"Marnie, you look beautiful," said Clara, jumping from her chair and rushing forward to embrace her friend.

"Thank you so much for coming," said Marnie, pulling back and holding Clara at arm's length. "You haven't changed a bit."

"Oh, there are a few more wrinkles, I assure you. Now, tell me why I've waited so long for this day to arrive? I expected to be back in Lowestoft seeing you walk up the aisle within a year of leaving. Instead, it's been six long years of waiting."

"Sorry about that," said Marnie, laughing.

"Do you have doubts about marrying Tom?"

Marnie laughed again. "Why does everyone always think that's the reason I wanted to wait? Isn't it reason enough to be enjoying life and not wanting things to change? I saw no reason we should rush into marriage while we were happy as we were. Besides, it gave us both longer to save up for our own home. As much as I love Tom's parents, I didn't fancy starting married life under their roof."

"Fair enough," said Clara. "Do we have time for a cup of tea before we head to the church?"

"Oh aye," said Marnie. "We've got ages. I was fidgeting around in my room, so got ready early."

"I need to pop over to the school," said Jimmy. "I'll leave you two to catch up."

"Right," said Clara, when Jimmy had left the room. She pulled an apron from the kitchen door and threw it at Marnie. "Wear this. You want nothing spilling on that lovely silk."

Marnie pulled on the apron, feeling ridiculous as she sat sipping her tea. "So how are you? Do you miss Lowestoft?"

Clara paused and studied her cup. "Yes, and no. I miss Michael's family. Our marriage may have been brief, but his family treated me as their own. Susan and Joe have brought the twins up to the island to visit me. I think they'd move up there if they could. And of course I miss Jimmy. But do I miss the place? Not really. It never felt like home to me. It's strange to think that without the war, and losing Michael, I'd still have been living here."

"And things on the island are going well?"

"Aye. Things with Da have been wonderful since I've been back. And don't fall off your chair, but I'm pretty friendly with Rachel these days."

"I still can't believe my sister is your stepmother," said Marnie. "Sometimes it feels like the world is all topsy-turvy."

"Aye, I know what you mean. I said you'd call in on Da and Rachel while you're on the island. I hope that's alright?"

"Of course it is. I'm looking forward to seeing how my nephew's grown, especially after you've told me so much about him in your letters."

"And he's looking forward to seeing you. Speaking of folk we've not seen in a while, how's Kitty? I can't wait to see her again. It's strange to imagine her settled in Lowestoft, although she always kept an eye out for handsome Lowestoft fishermen. I'm so pleased the two of you have become friends."

"Firm friends," said Marnie. "I couldn't believe it when we got talking and found out we had you in common. It's hard to imagine you working beside her as a herring girl, though. Kitty will be so excited to see you. You know she's a mother now? Her house is full of boys."

"Aye, she's told me about them in her letters. I was very surprised when she got back in touch and her letter arrived with a Lowestoft postmark outside of the herring season. I assumed she'd be a Highlander for life."

"She would have been were it not for Bobby's charms."

Jimmy let himself into the room and filled a cup with tea from the pot. "Sorry to interrupt your nattering, ladies, but I'm going to nip upstairs and get myself ready. It's important I look the part when I walk my sister down the aisle."

As Jimmy headed upstairs, Marnie turned to Clara. "How do you manage being so far away from him?"

Clara shrugged. "I suppose it's all we've ever known. The letters help, and meeting halfway several times a year keeps the excitement alive."

"Well, I think you're both stubborn fools. I could never live so far from my Tom. It's bad enough when he's off on his boat."

"I thought you were all for female independence?" laughed Clara.

Marnie huffed and sipped her tea.

"I'd better get ready. Let's hope my dress complements yours."

"I'm sure it will. You can use my room to change."

"Thanks."

Alone at the table, Marnie looked down at the special outfit hidden beneath a frumpy apron. She would miss living in the schoolhouse with her brother. But today was the start of a new era, one she couldn't wait to begin.

Chapter 4

April, 1930

Marnie, Clara and Jimmy squeezed into the old Austin Jimmy's former mentor had bequeathed him and set out for the church. As the car pulled out of the village, Marnie drank in the surroundings that had been home for years. The octagonal school house, the grand hall where garden parties were held in summer, the village green, well-tended front gardens.

Life on The Grit would be in stark contrast to life in Somerleyton. In this quintessential Suffolk village, it was possible to bury one's head from the darker sides of life. If it weren't for the hungry children turning up in Jimmy's schoolroom, the depression cloaking the world would seem a distant problem.

Living on The Grit, the world's problems would be impossible to ignore. Marnie tried to think back to when it started. All she knew was that the decline had been gradual at first. The fish stocks deteriorating in tandem with the nation's wealth.

There had been no debate over where the newlyweds would set up home. Tom was a Gritster, as were generations before him. He'd been born there, in the same house where his father had come into the world. Fishing was his life, and where better to live than the place where land met sea, where folk worked together celebrating the richness of a tight-knit community despite no financial riches to speak of.

"Penny for them," said Jimmy, glancing at Marnie's reflection in the rear-view mirror.

"I'm just thinking about The Grit."

"How do you feel about moving there?" asked Clara.

"Good. It's like the island in so many ways. It may not be physically cut off from the rest of Lowestoft, but it feels like it. A town within a town they call it. Whenever I visit Tom and his parents, it feels like going home."

"That place has seen a lot of changes since I lived there," said Jimmy, tugging on his beard as he drove.

"Aye, and not for the better. I can't even imagine what it was like when the fish were plenty."

"Probably not so different in some ways, just more money to be spent in the pub. Folk still had their fair share of worries, but nothing like they have today. It was the war that scuppered things. All those exports to Germany and Russia, well, there was no way they could continue after all that happened."

"No, they couldn't. Bloody war. Why can't folk just get on? Do you miss your days as a herring girl, Clara?"

"I miss the camaraderie. It was the pursuit of silver darlings that saved me all those years ago. I don't know what I would have done without it. At least these days, I'm not in danger of losing a finger while going about my work."

As the car drove along winding country lanes, its passengers sat in silence, each lost in their own memories. When Jimmy clapped his hand down on the steering wheel, Clara and Marnie jumped.

"Right," he said. "No more maudlin talk of how times have changed. Today is a celebration. A chance to look to the future. Let the politicians of this world do their worst, for there is one thing they cannot interfere in. Love."

Clara reached a hand across and squeezed Jimmy's knee. Before long they were crossing the bridge, ships and fishing boats swaying on the tide beneath them.

"Here we are," said Jimmy, pulling the car to a stop outside Christ Church.

Marnie took a deep breath to steady the nerves reaching a crescendo in her stomach. She needed to see Tom. Once her eyes fell on him, she knew she would be alright. But first she must give herself to hundreds of eager eyes. Well-meaning folk bringing good wishes and celebrating a chance to forget the challenges of life for a day.

Jimmy climbed out of the car and opened Marnie's door, offering her an arm to hold.

"Ready?"

Marnie nodded. Clara handed her a bunch of pale pink carnations, adjusted Marnie's veil, and leaned over to kiss her cheek. "Ta," said Marnie, holding her posy in one hand and clasping Clara's fingers with the other.

"Whatever for?"

"Coming all this way to be by my side at my wedding."

"I wouldn't have missed it for the world. After all, we're family and I love you like a sister. Now get a move on, or poor Tom will have a heart attack thinking you've done a runner."

Jimmy led Marnie to the entrance of the church. Someone gave a signal to the organist who struck up 'The Wedding March'. The first thing Marnie noticed was the number of people in the building. Gritsters packed the pews, men, women, children, old and young, all in their Sunday best, beaming smiles spread on their faces. Their enthusiasm for the day was infectious, and Marnie returned their warm smiles, noticing the bunting and ribbons Kitty had used to decorate the church.

Only when she was halfway up the aisle did Marnie lift her eyes to the front. Tom stood handsome and proud, hands clasped in front of him. Beside him, his best man Bobby clapped Tom on the shoulder and muttered something in his ear. Marnie watched Tom smile, his eyes fixed on her. What was going through his mind?

As she drew level with her fiancé, a rare shyness overcame Marnie. Aware of hundreds of pairs of eyes on her, she slowly peered up from beneath her lids, catching Tom's eye.

"You look beautiful," he mouthed.

"So do you," Marnie whispered back. Tom laughed. The vicar frowned.

"Dearly beloved, we are gathered here today…"

The congregation struck up in song, their voices carrying the words of the hymn 'For the Beauty of the Earth' up into the rafters. Before she knew it, Marnie's hand was in Tom's as he made his solemn vows. A gold band slipped easily onto her finger. It felt right; it looked right. She was his, and he hers. Today was a new beginning. Whatever life threw at them, they would face it together.

The cheers came close to deafening as Marnie and Tom walked out of the church into a sea of confetti. Women rushed to hug Marnie, men came to Tom with hearty handshakes. It was as though someone had switched a light on in a dull room.

Marnie smiled as her eyes fell on two women in a tight embrace. How Clara and Kitty must be relishing their reunion. Their lives might have followed different paths since their days gutting fish on the quayside, but there was no doubt their friendship had survived distance and time.

"We'll never make it to the restaurant at this rate," shouted Tom, bending his head so Marnie could hear.

"Come on," said Marnie, pushing through the merry crowd, her hand linked firmly to Tom's. "Jimmy offered to drive us to the restaurant, but that seems silly when it's only a short walk. Besides, I'd like you to myself for a moment." Marnie pulled Tom along behind her, running up Herring Fishery Score. Halfway up, she ducked around the corner of a building, pulling Tom towards her.

"That was nice," he said, pulling back from their lengthy kiss and smiling at his wife. "I must say, you scrub up well."

"Ta," said Marnie. "You don't look so bad yourself."

"There you are." Marnie and Tom turned to see Kitty and Bobby heaving a heavy pram up the score.

"Sorry, are we interrupting?" asked Kitty, wiping a lipstick stain off Tom's cheek with her thumb.

"You know now you're married you don't have to sneak kisses in dark corners?" said Bobby, slapping Tom on the back. "Now let's hurry and get to Waller's. I'm bloody starving."

Chapter 5
April, 1930

"I t was a wonderful turnout," said Kitty as they walked.

"I know. It's really taken me aback how many well-wishers came."

"That's The Grit for you," said Kitty. "We're a tough bunch, but you won't find a tighter community. Besides, times are hard and folk are delighted to find a little cheer where they can."

"Well, I'm pleased we could give it to them. How are you doing?" asked Marnie, as Kitty stopped to catch her breath.

"Not so bad. I just feel like a walking dumpling. Mark's only just started sleeping more than an hour at a time. I don't know how I'll manage when this next one comes along."

"Where are the rest of your brood?"

"Chrissy and Stevie are with Bobby's mam. They started fighting outside the church, so she whipped them out of the way to give them a clip round the ear. No idea about Al or Simon. They'll turn up at the restaurant, no doubt."

"I don't know how you manage."

"Neither do I," said Kitty, laughing. "Just keep me in your prayers, won't you? I'm praying God gives me a girl this time."

"Here we are," said Marnie, as they arrived outside Waller's restaurant.

"It was so kind of your brother to give you a proper wedding breakfast. And what a place to choose. The cakes here are wonderful. Bobby sometimes brings me one home if he's had a successful trip on the boat."

"Such a romantic," said Marnie, smiling. "I've always thought this would be a wonderful place for a wedding breakfast, but never thought we'd be able to afford it. I told Jimmy I'd be happy to have a few folks back to our house, but he insisted."

"Well, this is more than a few folk," said Kitty, opening the door to a busy room of smiling people who cheered as the bride entered.

Marnie left Tom, Kitty and Bobby and crossed the room to greet her colleagues from the shop. Dressed in their Sunday best, they were making the most of the sherry Jimmy had laid on, eying up the other guests, trying to pick out future husbands.

Marnie walked up to Mrs Sinclair and handed her a glass of sherry. "Thank you for coming."

"It's my pleasure, dear. You're a good worker. I'll be sorry to lose you."

"Lose me? As far as I'm aware, there is no marriage bar at Chadds. It's not the civil service."

"I'm not talking about a marriage bar. I'm talking about when you start a family."

"I think you'll be stuck with me for a while yet."

"That's what they all say," said Mrs Sinclair, tutting, and wandering off to find the sherry bottle for a top-up.

"What did the old bat want?" asked Brenda, walking up as soon as their boss had moved off.

"She was offering her congratulations," said Marnie. "She's really not as bad as you think."

Brenda groaned. "Ugh. You're only saying that 'cause you're her favourite. I'm dreading when you go and it's her I'm left with."

"For goodness' sake," snapped Marnie. "Everyone's talking like I'm about to die. I'm not going anywhere. Just because I'm a married woman doesn't mean I'm disappearing off the face of the earth."

"But you won't be able to work when you have a baby."

"And who says I'm about to pop out a baby?"

"All right, all right, no need to get your knickers in a twist."

"Sorry," said Marnie, taking a sip from Brenda's glass. "All the excitement's getting me worked up."

"You'll be an enigma to those Gritsters, you know."

"Why?"

"Working up in town. Few folk from down there mix with us lot up here. I'm surprised Tom doesn't want you working in the fishing business or stuck at home."

"Tom doesn't get to decide what I can and can't do."

"Oooh, quite the little suffragette. We'll see how long that lasts now you've a ring on your finger."

"My ring has nothing to do with it, and anyway, my working has nothing to do with my rights and everything to do with what I want and what we need. We need my wage in these times."

"My God," said Brenda. "The pittance they pay us up there? You'd be better off mending nets."

Marnie tapped her fingernails against the sherry glass, fed up with Brenda's needling.

"It was a lovely service," said Brenda, lightening the mood.

"Thank you. It was short and sweet, just as we requested."

"Who's the pretty redhead fawning all over your brother?"

Marnie looked across the room and smiled. "That's Clara, my sister-in-law in all but name. Why? Are you jealous?"

"Humph," said Brenda. "I just think a fellow's best off looking for love where they live. It's a nonsense living hundreds of miles away from the woman you supposedly love."

"Each to their own," said Marnie. "Besides, it works for them."

"Looks like it," said Brenda. They glanced across to where Clara and Jimmy stood, heads nestled together, Clara's hand running up and down Jimmy's back. Jimmy turned and caught Marnie's eye.

"Best go," she said. "Grab yourself a seat. Grub will be up soon." Marnie made her way to the table where Tom sat chatting away to Bobby. "Where's Kitty?" she asked as she sat down.

"In the ladies' feeding Mark."

"I hope she's back in time to eat."

"Given how much the little fella puts away, she could be gone a while."

"Save her a plate then, won't you? Ah, Clara, there's a seat for you here."

Clara and Jimmy joined them at the table just in time for the food to come out. Waitresses laid out a spread of scones, sandwiches, cakes and pots of tea, and soon all the guests were piling food onto their plates. Marnie looked around her, feeling a wash of contentment that caused tears to spring to her eyes.

"Are you alright?" asked Tom, handing Marnie a napkin. "You're not sad on our wedding day, are you?"

"Quite the opposite. I couldn't be happier. All the people I love in one room, all the people I especially love, sat around one table. What more could a girl ask for?"

"You've made me the happiest man alive," Tom whispered in Marnie's ear, causing her eyes to well up again.

Marnie brushed away tears. It wasn't like her to be so emotional, especially not in public. Perhaps it was those missing who'd brought on her reaction. The wedding party was mostly made up of friends. Tom's brothers were conspicuous by their absence, as were all her family other than Jimmy, but for different reasons. Tom's mum, Sally, caught Marnie's eye and smiled. Beside her, Tom's dad Roy took a sip of his drink. They'd been through so much as a family, Marnie hoped her union with Tom had brought them some happiness.

"Are you sure you're alright?" asked Tom.

"Aye," said Marnie. "Thank you, Tom, for today, and for every day we've been together. I can't wait to see what our future holds."

"Me neither," he said, kissing her hand and holding it to his cheek. "Here's to married life." They picked up their glasses and made a private toast to their love and to new beginnings.

Chapter 6

April, 1930

"Good morning, wife," said Tom, carrying a tray with tea and toast into the room.

"Good morning, husband. Can I expect this level of service every morning?"

"Not likely," said Tom, climbing into bed beside Marnie. "So, what do you think of the house?"

"I love it," said Marnie, "as I must have told you a thousand times in the past twelve hours." She leaned over and kissed Tom. "You must have worked so hard on it."

"It certainly took a while. You remember how it was when we first bought it?"

Marnie nodded.

"I think the poor chap who lived here before must have had quite a few problems to let it get in such a terrible state. The amount of rats we stumbled across while clearing out his stuff..."

Marnie shivered. "I hope they've all been safely removed."

Beneath the blankets, Tom gave Marnie's leg a light tickle. She screamed, and he lay back against his pillows, laughing.

"So you're happy living here, on The Grit, with me?" asked Tom once he'd caught his breath.

"Well, it's not even been a full day yet, but so far, yes, I'm satisfied." Marnie grinned at him.

"It's a step down from your schoolhouse, though, isn't it?"

"It was never my schoolhouse, it's Jimmy's. I don't mind where I live as long as it's with you. Besides, there are far worse places than The Grit. I don't understand why it's called that, though. The Beach Village sounds far nicer. I'm surprised more people don't use that name. And isn't that what it is? A village on the beach beneath the cliffs and the town?"

"I suppose so, but The Grit's just as accurate because folk here are full of the stuff. You should hear the stories Mum and Dad tell about the old days."

"I know. Jimmy's told me what it was like, even though he wasn't here long."

"Those buggers from the council have issued a clearance notice for some houses on Anguish Street. They'll be trying to turf us all out soon if we're not careful."

"Tom," said Marnie, propping herself up on an elbow. "Today is our first day as man and wife. Do you think we could make this conversation a little more light-hearted?"

Tom laughed and pulled Marnie towards him. "No Mum and Dad pottering downstairs, no Jimmy in the next room... the whole place, our place, to ourselves. Whatever could we do?"

Marnie giggled as Tom flung sheets over their heads and blanketed her in kisses.

*

"Knock knock."

The front door opened and Marnie ran downstairs, scraping her hair up in a headscarf and rearranging the buttons on her blouse.

"Sorry," said Jimmy. "We weren't disturbing you, were we?"

"No, not at all," said Marnie, turning to hide her blush. "We've got an hour till the train leaves. Do you want to have a look around?"

"I'd love to," said Clara, slipping past Jimmy and following Marnie through the house.

"There's not much to see," said Marnie, "but it's all ours. I've been spoiled these past few years living with Jimmy, but I've not forgotten my roots. This place is a palace compared to our island cottage." She winced at the memory of the large family squashed into two rooms, cowering from the man of the house after he'd sunk too many pints in the Fisherman's Arms. "It will be strange being up on the island without you."

"I know. I wish I could be there with you, but I'm pleased to have some time with Jimmy. I've also arranged to take the twins out for a day, and Susan and Joe have invited me over for dinner one evening. You timed the wedding well, it being the start of the school holidays."

"Aye," said Marnie. "Right, so this is the kitchen, dining room, and laundry." She laughed, swishing her arms wide, proud of her humble home.

"It's very cosy," said Clara. "Is there a bathroom through there?"

"No," said Marnie, grimacing. "That door leads out to the yard. You'll find the privy and wash-house out there. That will take a bit of getting used to. It's been a while since I had to venture out at night when I need a pee. Tom says he'll move the bathroom inside as soon as we have the money."

"I'm sure Jimmy could help with that, if you're short."

Marnie frowned. "I'll not be accepting help from my brother now I'm a married woman. He's spent enough on me already, what with the reception at Waller's and the honeymoon train tickets. Both me and

Tom are working, we'll manage. That reminds me, are you sure we're alright staying at your place while you're all the way down here?"

"Marnie," said Clara, laughing, "it's a hotel. It's not like I don't have the space. My assistant Olive is a very capable girl and I've instructed her to make a proper fuss of you. Ben's in and out a lot, too. He can't wait to see you."

"Listen to you, Mrs Businesswoman. I bet your family is so proud."

"They are," said Clara, smiling. "But I'm aware my good fortune comes from luck, not business acumen."

"It's one thing inheriting money," said Marnie. "It's quite another investing it wisely. I think you do yourself down."

"Come on," said Clara. "Show me the rooms upstairs."

Chapter 7
April, 1930

"It's a cheerful little home, isn't it?" said Clara, as she and Jimmy walked along Wapload Road, a few paces behind Marnie and Tom.

"It is. This area's down on its luck, but Tom has spruced that cottage up nicely. Marnie seems very content."

"I thought so too. Unusual for her. I hope their happiness lasts."

"I share your concerns," said Jimmy, "but it seems like they've gotten off to a good start."

"What are you two blethering on about?" asked Marnie, waiting for Jimmy and Clara to catch her up.

"We were just admiring your cottage," said Clara. "You're very handy with a paintbrush from what we've seen, Tom."

"Thanks," said Tom. "Dad helped a fair bit, and quite a few local lads. With more people moving out of the area than in, I think folk were pleased to see a young couple taking on a house."

"Quite right too," said Clara. "And soon you'll have little Toms and Marnies sharing it."

"That's the plan," said Tom. He wrapped an arm around Marnie's waist, a grin covering his face.

Clara was sharp enough to catch Marnie's expression at the mention of children. Had she put her foot in it somehow?

At the harbour, Tom paused. "Have we got time to show Clara the boat?"

"If you're quick," said Marnie.

They walked towards a mass of vessels, steam trawlers and the odd sailing vessel clustered around the edge of the harbour.

"In my day, there were so many vessels you couldn't see a patch of water between them," said Jimmy.

"In your day they were probably all reliant on sail, old man." Tom winked at Jimmy, who responded with a light punch to Tom's arm. "Quite a few of the boats are down west, but Dad hasn't wanted to go the past few years. I keep trying to persuade him, but no luck so far. Now we've got steam, the journey to Padstow would be even quicker. Mind you, even steam will be a thing of the past soon. There are new diesel trawlers coming, though God knows how we'd ever be able to afford one of them. Here we are."

They stopped beside a handsome green drifter, her name, *Sally Ann*, painted proudly near her bow.

"She's a handsome girl," said Clara. "Much bigger than the ships we get on the island. How many crew do you have aboard?"

"Ten. Dad's the skipper, I'm first mate. The others are all decent, hardworking chaps. They're loyal too, sticking with us despite times being hard. Do you want to come aboard for a look?"

"I don't think there's time," said Marnie. "We can't risk missing the train."

"Another time then," said Tom.

They arrived at the station to find the train was delayed. "Why don't you men go off and find us a couple of cups of tea?" said Clara. Jimmy and Tom obliged, and Clara and Marnie found a bench to sit on. "I hope I didn't say the wrong thing back there?"

"What do you mean? You were very complimentary about Tom's boat."

"Not about the boat, before that, when I mentioned starting a family. I saw the look on your face."

"Oh."

"Aren't you keen on having children?"

"I am…"

"But?"

"I don't want to rush into it. I love my job at Chadds. I love the independence it brings. Is it wrong not to want to give that up?"

"Not at all," said Clara. "But you know the work of a fisherman's wife better than anyone. Just think back to our own mams."

"It's different now, though, isn't it? These are the days of steam, not sail. As much as I love Tom, I don't want us to be too entwined in life and work. It's fun keeping a little mystery. I know there's plenty I could do to help him, but I'd be relying on his money, not my own."

"He wouldn't be generous?"

"Oh, it's not that. He treats me like a princess. No, the problem is fishing doesn't bring in what it once did. Tom's clinging on for dear life, but my wage will make a big difference to us."

"I understand."

"I know you do. You're the only one I can talk to about such things. I look up to you, you know? Keeping your independence, even at the expense of love."

Clara laughed. "I'm not an old spinster just yet. And who said I've given up on love? There's plenty of love between me and Jimmy, I assure you. We just don't go about it in the most conventional of ways."

"But don't you want to see him every day? Wake up with him every morning?"

"Life's not always that simple. Our paths took us in such different directions, if they were to converge, it would mean an enormous sacrifice on one of our parts."

"He'd give up everything for you, if you asked him."

"And I love him too much to demand it. We're happy enough as we are. Winter is so quiet at the hotel, it's easy enough for me to get away. Even in the summer months, I've built a good team to cover me when we meet. Of course, it would be easier if he'd come to the island."

"I've tried talking to him about it, but the memories he has of that place are still too vivid. He's not ready."

"I know. And I'll wait patiently until he is."

"You don't wish you'd had children?"

"Sometimes, yes. Ah, here they come."

Marnie looked up to see Jimmy and Tom walking towards them, steam rising from the cups in their hands. As the others chattered on, Marnie sank into her thoughts. She'd always admired Clara for her independence, but she saw now that whatever choice you made in life, there was a cost attached. But she didn't need to make that choice right away. When the time was right, she'd give herself fully to Tom and their future family. But there was no rush. They had all the time in the world.

Chapter 8
April, 1930

M arnie swallowed down a lump of dread as the motor car Clara had arranged crept across flat layers of sand.

"This must wreck so many engines," said Tom, eyes wide as he gazed out at the spray coming off the wheels.

"Aye," said Geoff, the hotel chef who had been roped in as their chauffeur. "I keep telling Miss Clara these vehicles are a waste of money. She'd save herself a fair penny if she stuck with a horse."

Tom grinned at Marnie. His eyes darted this way and that, his leg jiggling, aahs and oohs escaping his lips the closer they drew to the island. "Has it changed much?"

"Not that I can see so far," said Marnie, her smile tight, her hands clasped in her lap. She wanted to get the visit to the cottage over and done with. Rose was expecting her. Marnie knew she had received the letter, even if she'd not been able to reply.

"I can't wait to see the hotel," said Tom. "All these years I've tried to picture the place that keeps Clara hostage."

"I don't think anyone or anything could hold Clara hostage," said Marnie, laughing.

"That's what Jimmy said about this island. He said it has a hold over her greater than he ever could."

"Did this conversation happen after a few beers, by any chance?"

Tom smirked and returned his gaze to beyond the window. The car met land, spewing loose sand out from its wheels as it climbed higher. Fields burned with low afternoon sun on either side of the car, birds giving them an aerial display as they hovered and swooped on invisible currents. Soon houses appeared, small stone squat cottages, and grander sturdy homes designed to withstand the weather.

"That's my cottage," said Marnie, as the car grumbled its way through the village streets.

"Very pretty," said Tom.

Marnie grimaced. "Not on the inside if my memory serves me."

"How long since you've been back?"

"A good sixteen years."

"That's a long time to go without seeing your mum."

"Is it?" said Marnie, thinking she'd have been happy with another twenty years besides.

The car turned, and they caught their first glimpse of Clara's hotel. "Flippin' heck," said Tom. "No wonder she doesn't want to stay in Lowestoft. This place is a palace."

Marnie thought palace was a stretch, but the hotel was undoubtedly grand. A large white building, it presided over sweeping gardens and unrivalled views across to the harbour and castle.

"Come on, let's check in. Clara said Olive's expecting us."

They thanked Geoff for driving them, unloaded their suitcases, and made their way to the reception desk. They were greeted by a smart young woman, who wore a pencil tucked into her hair and an air of efficiency.

"Good afternoon," said Marnie. "We're Mr and Mrs Hearn. I think we have a reservation."

"Ah yes, Clara's family. It's a pleasure to welcome you to the hotel. I'm under strict instructions to attend to your every need."

Tom gave a nervous chuckle. Marnie could tell the VIP treatment had left him agitated. He'd be wondering how an ordinary chap like him was supposed to act in such a posh place. Marnie gave him a reassuring smile and tucked her arm into his.

"We're very grateful, but we don't need any special treatment," she said. "If you could just direct us to our room, that would be wonderful. We can take care of ourselves from here."

"Clara warned me you'd say that," said Olive, smirking. "But if I don't tell you to call reception if you need anything, she'll have my guts for garters when she gets back."

"Hard taskmaster, is she?" asked Tom.

"No," said Olive, waving a hand. "I'm only joking. She's a wonderful woman to work for, not that I'd tell you any different, seeing as you're family." The smile she gave them told them all they needed to know. In front of them stood a woman proud of the establishment she worked for, keen to please a boss she admired. "Here you are," Olive said, handing them a key. "You're on the top floor. Do you want a hand with your luggage?"

"No, we'll manage," said Tom.

As they headed for the stairs, a burly young man with a thick beard walked in. Over her shoulder, Marnie watched him exchange a few words with Olive. He looked over in their direction and a wide smile broke through his hairy chin. In three steps he'd crossed the lobby to stand beside them, hand outstretched.

"Hello, I'm Ben, Clara's brother, and your nephew. Pleased to meet you."

"Likewise," said Tom. "We've heard so much about you."

"And I you."

"You've changed a bit since I last saw you," said Marnie. "You were only a baby when I left."

"Aye, I'll have grown a bit since then. Ye'll come to Da's for supper tonight?"

"Oh," said Marnie. "We don't want to be any trouble."

"Of course it's nae trouble," said Ben. "Ye kna the cottage? What am I saying? Of course ye do." He laughed and slapped Tom on the back. "I keep forgetting yer wife's a local."

"Not for a while," said Marnie. "What time would you like us to call round?"

"Six suit ye?"

"Perfect," said Tom.

They said their goodbyes and made their way to their room. Both were stunned into silence as they walked in. It wasn't just the spectacular views from the window which caught their attention. Rose petals lay strewn across the four-poster bed. On the dresser, in a bucket of ice, sat a bottle of champagne.

"Crickey," said Tom, ice cubes clinking as he lifted the bottle. "This is probably worth as much as I earn in a week."

"Then let's save it till later," said Marnie. "I know it's been a long journey, but I'd like to get our visit to Mam over and done with if that's alright?"

"Of course it is," said Tom. "Come on, no time like the present."

Chapter 9
April, 1930

M arnie stood outside the cottage she'd once called home.

"Ow," said Tom, pulling his hand from Marnie's and shaking it.

"Sorry," she said. "I didn't realise I'd been holding on so tight."

"Come here," said Tom, pulling her into a hug. "It will be fine." With Marnie still in his arms, he reached across and knocked on the door.

From inside the cottage came the sound of a chair scraping back and heavy footsteps heading towards the door. The footsteps paused, and the seconds stretched as Marnie waited for the handle to turn.

Wood creaked on its hinges, and Marnie and Tom squinted into the darkness.

"Mam?"

"Hello, Marnie."

Mother and daughter stood staring at one another, neither sure of what to say next. In the end, it was Tom who came to the rescue.

"Lovely to meet you, Mrs Watson. I'm Tom, Marnie's husband."

Rose nodded and turned her back on them. Tom pulled a face at Marnie and she shrugged. Marnie took Tom's hand and led him into the cottage. Once her eyes grew accustomed to the darkness, she struggled to believe she was in the same building she'd once shared with her family. It was clean. A rag rug lay in front of the fire, a bunch of flowers sat in a vase on the mantel. Had her mother changed that much, or was this all for show?

"I'm sorry you couldn't make it to the wedding, Mrs Watson," said Tom.

"Tea?" The question was barked, and directed at Marnie.

"Aye, ta."

"Sit yersels doon."

Rose waved a hand towards two wooden chairs, and Tom and Marnie settled themselves at the table. Marnie had heard snippets of news from Clara over the years, but Rose kept to herself, so Marnie didn't know how she'd fared since Alex's death.

Marnie and Tom sat in silence as Rose fiddled about with the kettle on the stove. The cups rattled against the saucers as she carried them to the table. Marnie wondered if Rose was nervous, but that would be so unlike the woman she'd left all those years ago, she quickly dismissed the thought.

"How've you been, Mam?" said Marnie when the three of them were finally sitting around the table.

"Nae bad, nae bad."

Tom cleared his throat. "Do your other children still live on the island?"

"Some dee, others dinnae."

"Right."

Rose lifted her eyes from the table and gave Tom a quick glance. "I suppose this is basic compared to what yer used to back home?"

"Sorry, I don't know what you mean?" said Tom, his forehead creasing.

"I mean the cottage."

Marnie's eyes widened as a blush crept up Rose's neck. Was that what all this unfriendliness was about? Both Marnie and Rose jumped as Tom laughed. Marnie's eyes widened further as he reached his hand across the table and squeezed her mother's.

"This place is wonderful," he said.

"Aye, the island's alreet."

"No, I don't mean the island, though of course it's beautiful. I mean, your home. In fact, it really isn't very different at all to the one I grew up in."

Marnie knew this wasn't true. Tom's family home had three rooms upstairs and two down, more than double those of the cottage, but she appreciated the sentiment.

Rose raised her head and looked Tom in the eye. "Yer from a fishing family?"

"Yes," said Tom. "I fish, my father fished, his before that and so on going back as long as time itself, probably."

Rose nodded, a small smile lifting her lips. "A good match then," she said, looking from Tom to Marnie.

"We think so," said Tom, smiling at his wife.

"How are the others?" asked Marnie.

"Others?"

"My siblings."

"Ah, well, Rachel's done a grand job raising that bairn. Her lad Ben's turned into a fine young man." The pride in Rose's voice brought a tear to Marnie's eye. This wasn't the harsh, brash, rough woman she remembered. "I dinna see much of Sal and Robert. He's too much like yer da fer my liking."

"Sal's your sister?" asked Tom. Marnie nodded.

"And how have things been since Da's passing?"

Marnie half expected Rose to brush the question aside, but instead her entire face lit up. "I kna I shouldn't say, but it's been better. Aye, better's the word fer it."

Marnie thought back to all those times she'd hidden in the dark, listening to a solid fist meeting soft flesh. "I can imagine."

"Are your other daughters still living on the island?"

"Na, they left with the herring years back. Some settled up in Scotland, one in Yorkshire, and one in Ireland, of all places. They were like you," said Rose, turning to Marnie. "Wanted to get away from yer da as soon as they could. Sarah would've too if the stupid mare hadn't got herself saddled with Robert. I've bin wanting t' ask..."

"Aye?"

Rose studied the table in front of her, her fingers lacing and unlacing.

"Mam? Did you want to ask about Jimmy?"

Rose nodded. Now it was Marnie's turn to smile. "Mam, he's doing so well down there. You should see him at the school, everyone loves him. He told me once the best thing you ever did for him was send him to school. That and the shillings you gave him the day he left."

Rose looked up sharply. "He told ye about that?"

"Aye."

Tears gathered around Rose's lids. "I should've done right by yer all and left that monster. It's not right, all of ye running away. It was my job to look after ye."

"You did the best you could," said Marnie, surprised to find she meant it.

Rose coughed and brushed a hand across her eyes. "I take it I'll be seeing ye at Bill and Rachel's fer supper?"

Marnie nearly fell off her chair. "You and Bill are pals?"

"Aye, no need to look so surprised. I'm his child's grandmother, after all."

"You see much of Clara?"

"Nae much. Besides, I dinnae feel that comfortable with her after what happened to Jimmy."

"Oh, Mam," said Marnie. "How many years has it been? Give Clara a chance. She's not one for holding a grudge."

"Mebbe I will," said Rose. "Right, you two had best be off. Ye'll want to get settled in."

"We'll look forward to seeing you later," said Tom.

After they'd said their goodbyes and were out in the bright sunshine, Tom turned to Marnie. "She's lovely, your mum. And nothing like you described."

"She's a different woman to the one I left," said Marnie, still trying to wrap her head around the change she'd seen in Rose. "Come on, let's see if the hotel bar's open. I could do with a drink."

Chapter 10

April, 1930

"**M**arnie!" The cottage door flung open and a bear-like man pulled Marnie into his chest. She giggled, patting his back and moving her head to find some air.

"Good to see you, Bill," she said when he finally released her. "You're looking well."

"Nae need to lie, lass. I'm looking old, that's it, old." He chuckled and pulled on his long, greying beard.

Marnie laughed and turned to the woman stood beside him. "Rachel," she said, holding out a hand.

"Oh, come here," said Rachel, pulling Marnie into a quick hug.

In contrast to Bill's softness, Rachel's arms were stiff, as though hugging did not come naturally. When she pulled away, her cheeks were flushed, and she began fussing with the cutlery on the table.

"How are you, Rachel?"

Rachel turned and held Marnie's eye as a smile lit up her plain face. "I'm well, thank you. But my, haven't we been rude? I'm assuming this gentleman here is with you?"

"Sorry, aye, this is Tom."

Tom stepped forward and held out a hand to Bill, who gripped it in a vigorous shake. "A pleasure to meet ye, Tom, lad. I hear yer another one tied to the sea?"

Clara's father led Tom to a seat at the table where they became engrossed in a conversation, comparing notes on fishing grounds.

"Is there anything I can do to help?" Marnie asked her sister.

"Nae, it's all in hand. It's good to see ye, Marnie. Ye seen Mam yet?"

"Aye."

"How did ye find her?"

"Different."

Rachel smiled. "I often wonder what kind of woman she'd have been if she never met Da."

"I know what you mean. She seems happier, now he's gone."

"Aye, she is. It was bad for a while, mind. You'd think getting sick would've made him docile. In fact, it was quite the opposite. Folk thought his death devastated her, but if ye ask me, her tears were tears of relief."

Their conversation was interrupted by a knock on the door, Rose walking in without waiting to be invited.

"Rose," greeted Bill.

"Ta fer inviting me," said Rose, sinking her large body into a rickety wooden chair.

"Those two make a funny pair," said Rachel under her breath. "I give them five minutes before they bicker, but they're very fond of one another deep down. It unsettles me sometimes, reminds me I'm a different generation to Bill when he and Mam blether about the good old days."

Marnie laughed. "I'm pleased things have worked out well for you, Rachel. I'm sorry it's taken so long for me to come home."

"I understand. It wasn't a happy place back when ye left. Ye did a good thing, rushing to Jimmy's side. He's Mam's pride and joy, ye kna.

Tells everyone about him, she does. Do ye think ye could talk to him about maybe coming up here for a visit?"

"I will," said Marnie. "Now I've seen for myself how much has changed, he may be easier to persuade."

"Good. Now let's get this stew into bowls. Ah, here's Ben. That boy can smell my cooking a mile off."

Rachel chuckled and greeted her son with a kiss. Ben pulled out a chair beside his father. Looking at the two of them was like looking into the past, Ben the spitting image of Bill in his younger days. As the meal began, Marnie stayed quiet, observing the surrounding scene. She'd been so reluctant to come back to the island of her youth, yet it was a different place from the one she'd left. Ghosts of bad times still lurked in the shadows, but there was hope, too. Unexpected friendships and fresh starts. Marnie looked forward to talking things through with Tom when they were finally alone.

*

"Thank you," said Tom, as he walked arm in arm with Marnie across the field that connected the hotel to the harbour.

"What for?"

"Coming back here. I know you were reluctant."

"I'm pleased I came. It was important you see where I came from."

"And it's been good?"

Marnie smiled up at her husband. "Better than I could've hoped. Who'd have thought my and Clara's families would've reconciled? I never thought I'd live to see Bill and Mam supping at the same table."

"Rachel seemed a good sort, too."

"Aye. I never really knew her that well before I left. She was that much older than me and so quiet. Her marrying Bill broke Clara's heart, you know. It makes me so happy to see old wounds healed."

"Now we just need to persuade that brother of yours to come up for a visit."

"Aye, good luck with that one."

Tom stopped walking and stared out towards the boats bobbing on the calm waters of the harbour. "Marnie, now you've been back, do you regret us setting up our life in Lowestoft?"

"You mean, do I wish we'd set up home here?"

Tom nodded.

"No, Tom, I don't. Your parents need us. Mam's fine up here, she's got plenty of folk around, your parents only have you. Besides, Lowestoft's home for me now."

Tom linked arms with her again, looking relieved. "We can come back and visit as often as you like."

"As often as you like, you mean," laughed Marnie. "I can see this place has gotten under your skin. This island does that to folk. There's a magic about it."

"I can't deny it's left a strong impression on me. Lucky I didn't see it before we set up home or I might have been tempted to move here myself. We'll have to come for holidays with our children, show them where their mum comes from."

Children. There it was again. Marnie brushed off Tom's comments, pointing toward the horizon and suggesting they walk to the north shore. The sun was sinking low in the sky, pooling pink light onto the calm waters of the harbour. Marnie focused on the view, determined to keep things as they were for as long as possible.

Chapter 11

August, 1934

When Marnie thought about it, she could describe her first few years of married life as blissful. It was her and Tom against the world, facing everything life could throw at them together. Between the falling fish stocks and her in-laws' deteriorating health, they'd had their fair share of worries, but tackled them as a team.

Tom had accepted Marnie's six-month moratorium on babies with his usual jovial optimism. But Marnie knew he was counting the days until they resigned the sheaths to the bin, and had taken matters into her own hands.

It had taken a while for her to identify an appropriate confidant. Kitty was no use, with her ever-growing brood bursting at the seams in her small two-up two-down. Her idea of contraception was feigning a headache and making Bobby leave her alone for a night or two. Marnie briefly considered confiding in Brenda, but her mouth was bigger than the harbour for sharing gossip and the risk of her blabbing was too great.

In the end, it was Clara who'd come to Marnie's rescue. If Jimmy knew the contents of the letters that passed between his two favourite women, he'd have been horrified. But Clara understood. Clara helped. Buying what she needed in Lowestoft was too great a risk. Clara arranged it all for Marnie, and the package she sent was easily passed off as a ball of wool, which Marnie slipped unopened into her knitting basket before Tom could quiz her further.

Thanks to Clara's intervention, Marnie remained childless and free to continue with her work. In the early days of marital bliss, Tom had been patient, caring, understanding. The change had come around their third year of marriage. That's when Marnie noticed Tom's frustrated sighs each time her monthlies rolled around. It was when conversations over Sunday lunch at her in-laws' home became focused on one topic and one alone. When would Marnie be giving them a grandchild?

It was a question which had overshadowed the last year, as if Marnie's barrenness were to blame for the falling fish stocks, or the gloom of depression that saw sunken eyes in too-thin faces shuffling their way around The Grit in search of cheap food. It was the unspoken argument that sat between Marnie and Tom when they lay in their marital bed, or hovered over them as they ate their toast each morning.

"Penny for them?" Mrs Sinclair's question was more of a command.

"Sorry, Mrs Sinclair. I got a little distracted."

"And not for the first time."

Marnie blushed at the reprimand. The one thing she could get right was her job, and now she was even failing at that. "I'm sorry."

"So you say. Wondering what to cook your husband for tea, are you? Those professions implementing the marriage bar have the right idea, if you ask me."

Did she really mean that? Marnie was sure she was still Mrs Sinclair's best worker, distractions or not. She studied the old lady's face for signs of mirth, but found none.

"Don't worry about her," said Brenda, when Mrs Sinclair finally shuffled off. "She's just peed off that she's not been able to retire yet. You must have heard her mutterings about how pounds and pennies don't stretch as far as they used to. She's probably sitting on a sum greater than us folk earn in a year, miserly cow."

Despite the truth lingering in Brenda's words, Marnie felt a tug of sympathy for the increasingly dour Mrs Sinclair. She had no man to fall back on, and how much harder must it be for a single woman to support herself, the way the world was going?

"Oh, don't do that. I see that look in your eyes. There's no need to feel sorry for that old crone."

"You're probably right," sighed Marnie, hanging a dress on a rack.

"Don't let her get under your skin."

Brenda gave Marnie a brusque pat on the back, which unsettled her more than Mrs Sinclair's words. If Brenda were showing affection, Marnie must be off her game.

On her way home that night, Marnie contemplated calling in on Kitty. But the raucous chaos of busy family life would only exacerbate the headache forming behind her eyes. Instead, she called in at Sidney Cook's butcher's shop. He greeted her as he always did, with a booming hello and exclamation that he'd missed his favourite customer. Marnie responded as she always did, that it was only three days since she'd been in and that she'd heard him say the same to at least three other women while passing his shop.

Her encounter with Sidney lifted Marnie's spirits a little and her steps were lighter as she walked along Wapload Road towards her cottage on East Street.

*

The cuts of mutton were sizzling on the stove when the door slammed shut. Marnie pulled the pan from the stove and walked through to the sitting room. Tom shouldn't be home yet. He'd said he'd be out at sea till nightfall.

Marnie folded her arms as Tom stumbled towards her. These days, his shoulders sagged as though an enormous weight sat on them. Black smudges framed his eyes, a result of the nights he lay tossing and turning, yearning for sleep but unable to still his mind. Tom lurched towards Marnie, aiming for her lips. She put a hand to his chest and held him back.

"What are you doing home?"

"No point staying out. The nets were as empty as when we first dropped them."

"So you thought you'd go to the pub and spend the money I've been earning instead?"

Tom let out a mirthless laugh. "Yes, my dear, that is precisely what I've been doing. I'm a kept man, don't you know? There I was, propping up the bar of The Rising Sun, telling all and sundry I need a woman to pay for my beer."

"Tom..."

"No, no, no, don't you worry, my dear. I know where I stand. Please accept my apologies for not being a real man."

"There's no need to be like that. Sarcasm doesn't suit you."

"Fine." Tom stomped through to the kitchen, jiggling the pan on top of the stove. "And she cooks for me, too. It's almost like I'm completely unnecessary in this marriage."

"Tom, please stop this."

Tom rounded on Marnie, his face pink, his lips moving into something of a sneer.

"This isn't you talking, it's the drink."

"It's not the drink. It's the truth. I'm useless as a man, useless as a husband. I can't catch fish, can't pay for my beer, can't keep my wife happy, can't even father a child."

"Don't talk like that," said Marnie, grabbing hold of Tom's bunched fists. "The fishing will pick up. Things will get better. And I enjoy being able to contribute my share. We're a team. Always have been, always will be."

The fight went out of Tom. Tears clustered in his eyes as his head dropped. "I'm sorry for the way I spoke to you. It's just so difficult sometimes. You're so capable, so strong. It's hard not to feel second best."

"It's not a competition."

"No, you're right. But it's frustrating, Marnie. Most of the other boats headed west after Christmas and if ours had done the same, we'd have earned enough to see us through these lean times. If only I could persuade Dad it's the right thing to do, but he won't hear of it."

"He's worried about your mam. You know her health's not what it once was."

"I know, but the fish are gone. We're left searching for scraps while the other crews have nets fit to bursting in other waters. And he used to relish our trips west. Some of my favourite memories are from the days he used to take us with him to Padstow. But now? Now he won't even consider going there, or anywhere."

"Perhaps you could try talking to him again? I'd be happy to keep an eye on Sally if you and Roy have to go away next season."

"I've told him that already, but he won't hear of it. If only he'd pass the boat and business on to me. He's more hindrance than help these days."

"You'll have a job ever getting him to retire. Fishing's his life. I can't see Roy sitting around all day with a pipe and slippers, can you?"

Tom shook his head. "No, I can't. I'm sorry I took my frustrations out on you."

Tom looked so defeated, Marnie's heart swelled with sympathy and love. She took Tom's face in her hands and lifted it until her eyes met his. Without warning, their mouths met. Despair, hurt, and love mingled within their touch. There was no warning, no time to find her sponge and slip out to the privy. Their coming together was urgent, frantic, and over almost as quickly as it began.

When they were done, Marnie sat on Tom's lap, running her fingers through his hair.

"That was unexpected."

"If that's what I get after a poor catch, I'll take more of those days," he said, grinning.

"Cheeky bugger," said Marnie, relieved the tension between them had dissipated.

"Perhaps this is the moment we'll finally conceive a child," said Tom.

Marnie smiled, while inside her, icy fingers of fear gripped her heart.

Chapter 12

November, 1934

I t felt as though the wooden walls of the privy were closing in on her. Marnie leaned against the icy wall and brushed a hanky across her mouth. Screwing it up and stuffing it in her pocket, she reached for another, scrubbing her eyes to stop the tears.

Marnie clutched her stomach as another wave of nausea threatened. She fought it, to no avail, rocking back on her haunches once it was over and submitting to tears once more. They should have had more time than this. She wasn't ready.

"Marnie?"

Marnie pulled herself to standing and gave her face one last wipe. "Aye?"

"Is everything all right? You've been out there for ages."

"Aye, everything's fine. Stick the kettle on, would you?"

"Yep."

Marnie leaned against the privy wall and took three deep breaths. With a shake of her head, and a roll of her shoulders, she plastered happiness she didn't feel onto her face. She unlocked the door and walked back across the yard towards the house. Tom was in the kitchen, filling a kettle from the tap. Marnie waited until he'd put it on the stove before asking him to come and sit down.

"What's the matter?" he asked, turning and seeing her grey face. "Are you ill? Do I need to call the doctor?"

"No, I'm fine, really. Please sit down."

Tom moved to the table and sat down without taking his eyes off his wife. Marnie sat opposite him, taking his hands in hers.

"I've news," she said. "I think I'm going to have a baby."

Tom pushed back his chair, his mouth falling into a wide O. With a clatter of wood, the chair fell to the floor and he rushed to Marnie's side, taking her face in his hands and smothering it with kisses.

"I take it from your reaction you're happy?" she asked, laughing despite the circumstances.

"Happy? I've been waiting for this moment since the first day I laid eyes on you. I want to go out there and scream it from the rooftops."

"Please don't," said Marnie. "It's early days."

"Marnie," said Tom, his eyes glistening with tears. "We're going to be parents. I'm going to be a dad."

"Yes, my love. Yes, you are." Despite herself, it was impossible not to be drawn into Tom's enthusiasm. He pulled her from her chair and began dancing her round the kitchen to music playing in his head.

"Please stop," said Marnie, covering her mouth with her hand.

"Oh dear, I'm sorry. Is the little mite making you sick?"

Marnie nodded, not trusting herself to open her mouth.

"When did it start?"

Marnie took a deep breath and a sip of water. "Ten weeks back."

Tom's hands dropped from Marnie's waist, and he took a step back. "You've known for ten weeks and not told me?"

"I didn't know, not for sure. I thought I may be sickening for something and didn't want you worrying." *Liar*, said the voice in Marnie's head. She'd known from that first morning what was happening, she'd just chosen not to admit it, to herself, or to Tom.

"My darling girl, you should have told me. I could've been looking after you. You'll have to stop work. You can't be dragging yourself up to that shop while you feel like this."

"No," said Marnie, her voice harsher than she meant. "I mean, I'm fine with working. The sickness eases by ten."

"You start at nine."

"And I put a brave face on, taking things as easy as I can. Besides, the sickness won't last much longer, all being well."

"You're stubborn as a mule," said Tom, sighing. "Crikey," he said, standing and pacing around the room. "I have to tell someone. Surely I can tell Mum and Dad? You know they'll be as excited as I am."

"I know," said Marnie, standing and taking Tom's hands to calm him, "But like I said, it's early days. I'd hate to get them all excited then for something to go wrong. Look, I'd like to speak to Kitty about this. After all, she's had plenty of experience. How about you tell Bobby? You could go for a celebratory drink? And I can pick Kitty's brains about all the gory details you won't want to hear."

"Hmm," said Tom. "Mum and Dad will be so upset if they're not the first to know."

"We'll swear Kitty and Bobby to secrecy. And besides, I haven't told Jimmy yet. We'll tell your parents before him if that makes you feel better about things?"

"How long before we can tell people?"

"Another couple of weeks. That way I'll be more confident everything's all right."

Tom dropped to his knees, wrapping his arms around Marnie's waist. "It will be alright, I know it. Our son's going to be perfect."

"Son?" said Marnie, raising an eyebrow.

Tom laughed. "Son, daughter, bloody hell, Marnie, you could be carrying a dog and I'd still be thrilled."

Marnie reached for a tea towel and whacked him with it. "I can assure you whatever it is in my belly is human. I've got a few things to do around the house today, but later on I'll head off to find Kitty and get her advice, starting with anything she can think of to relieve this godawful sickness."

Chapter 13
November, 1934

As she walked along Wapload Road towards the pickling plots, the smell of herring in the air intensified in tandem with Marnie's nausea. The lamps the herring girls used to work by threw out smoke that hung listlessly in the still air. Marnie tightened her coat around her. The air was bitter, so crisp you could almost taste the cold.

Marnie could have found the pickling plots blindfolded, for besides the smell of fish, the Scots girls' voices rang out loud and clear, as they sang through their work. Kitty was elbow deep in fish guts when Marnie found her. Jumper pulled up to her elbows, her fingers were bound in cloots, her apron glistening with the red innards of silver darlings.

"Hello, girls," said Marnie, as she walked up to the trough where Kitty's team worked.

"Marnie? What are you doing here?" asked Kitty, without raising her eyes from her work.

"I was hoping to catch you for a chat before you head home."

"Alright. Well, we're nearly done here. Why don't you beg a cuppa from Mrs Horne and sit yourself down on one of those barrels while we finish up?"

Marnie's stomach turned at the thought of sitting amongst the stench of fish and smoke, but she needed to talk to Kitty, so it was a price worth paying. Mrs Horne was clearing up for the day, but agreed to one last cuppa on the condition Marnie brought her mug back when she finished.

The girls' knitting lay strewn around, and Marnie moved a half-finished gansey to make space on a barrel. She perched on it, taking small sips of tea, welcoming the way it warmed her from the inside out. Even watching the herring girls work left Marnie feeling tired. The knives in their hands blurred as they flew through the remaining fish, working at an impressive pace. It made her work at the department store seem like leisure.

The cooper sealed the last of the barrels and Kitty walked over to Marnie, untying her cloots and wiping her hands on a cloth. "Are you alright if we walk and talk? I need to get myself cleaned up and pick the bairns up from Bobby's mam."

"Of course," said Marnie, sliding off the barrel.

"So, what's so important you had to come down to the pickling plots?"

"I needed some advice."

"Advice? From me?"

"Aye. You're the expert on the subject."

Kitty stopped walking and looked at Marnie through narrowed eyes. "You want to become a herring girl?"

Marnie laughed. "No, I'd be hopeless. I've grown too soft these past few years."

"Phew," said Kitty, walking towards her cottage. "I thought for a minute you wanted training up. I've got enough on my plate already. But, if it's not fish you want advice on, what is it?"

Now it was Marnie's turn to stop walking. "I'm pregnant."

Kitty turned slowly to her friend. "Pregnant?"

"Aye."

Kitty rushed towards Marnie, then stopped, looking down at her apron and boots. "Wait here," she said, opening the gate to her yard and disappearing behind it.

Marnie stood on the street, listening to the sound of slopping water and the scratch of a thick bristled brush. She hopped from foot to foot, trying to fight the cold biting its way through her coat.

With a yelp of excitement, Kitty rushed through the gate, grabbing Marnie and swinging her around. She pulled her close, swaying this way and that as they hugged.

"I can't breathe," laughed Marnie, trying to pull back from Kitty's arms.

"Sorry, sorry," said Kitty, taking a step back. "I need to remember there's a bairn in there. My God, Marnie, you made us all wait for this day. This is such wonderful news!"

"Is it?"

"Isn't it?"

"I'm scared, Kitty. Scared of having to give up work, scared of something going wrong with the baby, scared I won't be a good enough mam."

"Oh, nonsense," said Kitty. "You might not work at that fancy shop once the bairn arrives, but there's plenty to keep you busy around here. As for something going wrong, it might. But it might not. That's for Mother Nature to decide, and worrying won't change a thing. And motherhood? You'll be just fine. None of us knows what we're doing at the start. You just get on with it and hope for the best."

Marnie leant against the wall. "You make it sound so easy."

Kitty let out a guffaw. "Easy? Oh no, I never said that. It's the hardest thing you'll ever do."

"You're not selling motherhood very well."

"It's the hardest thing you'll ever do, but also the best. Trust me, if anyone should know it's me. Six tries I've had, and whilst it never gets easier, my heart grows with each new bairn. I never knew it was possible to love so much till I had them."

Marnie felt a wash of guilt. Here she was, worrying about one child, while Kitty juggled six, along with her work as a herring girl in the autumn and winter months. "You must think me so feeble."

"Not at all. Everyone's frightened when it's their first time. How are you feeling?"

"Sick. All the time. I told Tom it's only in the morning, but it's all day, all night sometimes."

"Why didn't you tell him the truth?"

"Because he'd want me to stop working."

"That doesn't sound the worst idea."

"I don't want to stop working until I have to. Is there anything I can do to help with the sickness?"

"Ginger biscuits. That's the only thing that helped with mine. It eases after a while. How far along are you?"

"Three months."

"Right, well, you'll feel better soon. How did Tom take the news?"

"He was beside himself. I've never known him so excited. He's taking your Bobby out for a drink tonight to celebrate. Only you and Bobby know, mind. Please don't tell anyone else until I'm further along."

Kitty made a zipping motion across her lips. "Now," she said, linking arms with Marnie, "I need to pick the bairns up, but what do you say we nip into the Rising Sun for a quick celebration first?"

Marnie grinned. "Lead the way." She smiled as they headed towards the pub. Perhaps things would turn out for the best after all.

Chapter 14

April, 1935

Mrs Sinclair tutted loudly as she squeezed past Marnie to reach the counter. From across the shop floor, Brenda caught Marnie's eye and winked. As the date of her retirement ebbed further and further away, their boss's mood darkened, a dour cloud hanging over their working days.

"You need a hand?" asked Marnie, as Mrs Sinclair stood on tiptoes trying to reach a box of ribbon.

Mrs Sinclair turned, rocking on the balls of her feet, eyeing Marnie's protruding stomach. "There's little you can help with in your *condition*. It's a scandal, working here when you're so close to time. You're not exactly an advert for the latest fashions. It's enough to put the customers off."

Marnie reached a protective hand to her belly. "You agreed to me working until a month before I'm due. I've another week to go yet."

"That week can't pass quick enough," muttered Mrs Sinclair, turning back to the cabinet that held the ribbons.

Marnie sighed and began rearranging handkerchiefs in a cabinet. It was frustrating, not being as nimble or helpful as she'd like. From the corner of her eye, she saw Mrs Sinclair, her fingertips dusting the required ribbon that remained stubbornly out of reach.

"Here," said Marnie, reaching up and pulling the box down. As she placed it on the counter, a pain tore through her belly and she bent double, leaning against the polished counter, trying to catch her breath.

"Oh dear, you're not…"

"No," said Marnie, trying to keep her voice steady. "It's not the baby. I just pulled a muscle."

Mrs Sinclair looked doubtful, but would've accepted Marnie's lie, had a puddle of water not appeared on the floor between them. "What in God's name?"

Mrs Sinclair's ashen face looked down at the floor in horror. Brenda rushed across the shop, took one look at the puddle spreading across the wooden boards, and took hold of Marnie's elbow.

"You might need to get the mop for that," Brenda told Mrs Sinclair, who was speechless with shock. "Right," said Brenda, guiding Marnie towards the staff room. "In here."

Brenda settled Marnie in a chair and filled a mug from the tap.

"I'm so ashamed," said Marnie. "That's never happened before. All I can think is it's the baby pressing against my bladder." Her face turned pink, and she shuffled in her chair.

To Marnie's surprise, Brenda laughed. "You think you peed your-self?"

"No need to laugh about it."

"Good God, girl," said Brenda, the smile falling from her face. "You really don't know what just happened?" Brenda scanned Marnie's blank expression, then crouched on the floor in front of her, taking hold of her hands. "Now, I don't want to panic you, but what just came out of you wasn't pee. It's water, the water that was holding your baby comfy all these months."

"Water? What does that mean?"

"It means the baby's coming, and we need to get you home."

Chapter 15

April, 1935

I t took Marnie and Brenda ten times as long as usual to walk down Mariner's Score. Every ten steps Marnie doubled over, her cheeks grey from the pain, damp from her tears.

"We're never going to make it to your place at this rate," said Brenda, rubbing Marnie's back while they waited for the pain to pass.

"Kitty's," Marnie whispered, pointing toward her friend's house.

"Good thinking."

After much huffing, puffing and the occasional wail, Brenda and Marnie found themselves outside Kitty's front door. Brenda knocked, keeping her fingers crossed behind her back that someone would be home. A slight young man opened the door. His eyes widened as they moved from Brenda to Marnie.

"Ma? Ma, come here, quick."

"What is it?" asked Kitty, waddling through from the parlour, a hand clasped beneath her stomach. "Oh dear," she said when she saw Marnie bent into the wall, her forehead resting against the cool pebbles. "It's Brenda, isn't it?"

"That's right."

"When did the pain start?"

"Her waters broke in the shop about an hour ago. It's taken forever to get her down here. The pain's coming every couple of minutes."

"Help me get her inside," said Kitty.

The two women positioned themselves under each of Marnie's arms. "Simon, tell the kiddies to scram. I need to get Marnie on the bed upstairs. Then, once you've done that, run down to the harbour and find out if there's any news of Tom's boat. He and Dad are due back this evening. If we're lucky, the wind will be fair, and Tom will make it home in time to greet his child into the world."

Simon ran up the stairs two at a time, reappearing with a gaggle of siblings who were so used to their mother giving birth they took no notice of Marnie, who was now on her hands and knees on their sitting room floor.

"Marnie, love, we need to get you upstairs."

"Stay... here..." said Marnie, letting a deep groan slip through her lips. She rocked back and forth, her forehead glistening despite her grey pallor.

"I'm sorry, love, but we must move you. You'll be more comfortable up there, I promise. Tell me when the pain's eased."

After a minute, Marnie nodded. Kitty and Brenda hauled Marnie to her feet, one woman under each of Marnie's arms. They were halfway up the stairs when the next contraction hit. Marnie stopped, pressing her forehead against the cool plaster, a deafening howl filling the small space as tears slipped from her eyes.

"Come on, nearly there."

Somehow, Kitty and Brenda dragged Marnie to the upstairs bedroom, easing her down onto the mattress. Kitty turned to Brenda. "Can you get me some towels from the basket beside the stove? And we'll need some water boiling. There's a bucket out in the yard beside the pump."

Brenda wrinkled her nose. She couldn't understand why folk still lived in the squalor of The Grit. Her own home had hot and cold running water in the kitchen, not some antiquated pump in the yard. With her thoughts kept to herself, Brenda left the room in search of supplies.

"I'm sorry," said Marnie, twisting on the mattress and gripping her stomach.

"Sorry for what?"

"You shouldn't have to look after me in your condition."

"My condition?" Kitty laughed. "Aren't you the one who always says pregnancy shouldn't stop you from doing things? I'll tell you what, Marnie, you've come to the right place. If anyone knows about childbirth, it's me. And don't worry, I was at the birth of my sister's five, so I've plenty of experience of it from down the business end."

Marnie managed a small smile before crying out as another wave of pain hit.

"Ma?"

Kitty turned toward the voice at the bottom of the stairs. "Simon? Is that you?"

"Yes. I've been down to the harbour, but there's no sign of Tom or Dad yet."

"Alright. Could you go out to the yard and help Brenda fetch the water? Then go back down to the harbour and wait for Tom and Dad. The last thing we want is them heading off to the pub as soon as they get in."

"Alright, Ma."

"Good lad."

An hour later, Brenda sat crouched beside Marnie, wiping her face with a damp cloth, while Kitty assessed the situation at the other end of the bed.

"Marnie, I can see the head. Only a couple more pushes, and you'll be meeting your bairn."

"I'm too tired."

"No, you're not. There's a bit of energy left in there yet."

"There isn't," whispered Marnie.

"You've not sworn at us yet, so I say there is. Right, as soon as the next pain comes, I want lots of short, sharp pushes."

"I..."

"You can."

Marnie's face creased up in pain. After five pushes, Kitty announced, "the head's out. Good. One last push is all it will take. This is going to be your hardest yet, love, but then it will be over. I want you to take a big deep breath, then push with all your might."

With an almighty roar, Marnie bore down, pushing a slippery, wrinkled creature out into the world, caught expertly by Kitty's capable hands.

"Pass me a towel," she instructed Brenda.

Towel in hand, Kitty rubbed the little body in her arms, smiling from ear to ear as an angry cry broke through the tense silence.

"How is he?" asked Marnie.

"*She* is perfect," said Kitty, handing the noisy bundle to Marnie.

Marnie pulled down a corner of the towel and stroked her daughter's cheek. "She's perfect."

"Didn't I say so?" said Kitty. "A beautiful, healthy girl."

Marnie kissed her daughter's tiny hand, deciding there and then that however hard motherhood proved to be, she would do anything to protect the little girl she'd brought into the world.

By the time Tom and Bobby arrived, Marnie had washed and was sitting in a clean nightdress in Kitty's bed, a slumbering baby in her arms. Tom took the stairs two at a time, bursting into the room, his face red and eyes wide.

"Shh," said Marnie. "We don't want to wake her."

"Her? We have a daughter?"

"Aye," said Marnie. "Are you disappointed?"

Tom came and sat on the bed beside her, taking the baby into his own arms. "Disappointed?" He looked from his daughter to his wife, his eyes glistening with tears. "How could I be disappointed? Look what you've given me."

"But you wanted a boy to help you on the boat."

"And who says a girl can't do that? Surely not you, my little suffragette?"

Marnie laughed, despite the tiredness that threatened to overwhelm her. "Let's wait and see, shall we? I want our daughter to be whatever she wants to be."

"Well, one thing we need to decide for her is a name," said Tom. "I'd only thought of boys' names."

Marnie smiled. "I'd like to name her after Clara's mother."

"Not your own?"

"No, she can take Rose as her second name, but Anna was such a beautiful, kind soul. And I think it would mean a lot to Clara, and to Jimmy, given they've no children of their own."

"So Anna it is?"

"How about Annie? It's close to Anna, but she'll be her own person."

"I love it."

"I don't know about you, but I'd like to ask Clara, Jimmy, Kitty and Bobby to be her godparents."

"I thought the same. There are no four people I'd rather have looking out for our daughter."

"Good," said Marnie. "Before long, you'll need to get me and Annie home. I can't stay in Kitty's bed all night. But perhaps I could have an hour of sleep first? Could you take the baby?"

"There's nothing I'd rather do. And there's a house full of children desperate to meet this little one."

Marnie smiled and laid her head down on the pillow. "I love you, Annie," she whispered, before sinking into a deep, deep sleep.

Chapter 16
May, 1935

Tom, Marnie and Jimmy sat around Sally and Roy's dining table wondering why they had been summoned. Usually, they only ate together on Sundays, so being invited on a Tuesday night was unusual. Beside her, Marnie rocked the pram with one hand, knowing as soon as the motion stopped, Annie would wake up.

Marnie suppressed a yawn, thinking she'd give anything for a good night's sleep. With Tom working so hard on the boat, it wasn't fair to ask him to help during the night, and besides, feeding the baby was her sole domain.

"How are you, Roy?" asked Jimmy, pointing to the walking stick behind him.

"Not too bad, just my hip giving me gyp."

"It was a nasty fall," said Jimmy. "But it's not broken?"

"A minor fracture is what the doc says. Could've been worse."

"I've been telling him for years to take things easy," said Sally, her hands shaking as she set down a bowl of mashed potatoes on the table. "But would he listen? Would he heck. Now he's gone and injured himself. I hate to say I told you so..."

"Then don't, woman," said Roy, spooning a dollop of potatoes onto his plate.

"You're probably wondering why we invited you all round for supper," said Sally, adding a bowl of carrots to the feast on the table. She'd really pushed the boat out. Marnie knew how much all this food must have cost her.

"We are a little curious," said Marnie.

"Go on, Roy. You tell them."

Roy cleared his throat. "Well, it's like this. The doc said it's going to take some time for my hip to heal, and Sally thought..."

Sally scowled at her husband.

"*We* thought..." said Roy, "it might be time for me to give up the boat. I'd like to hand the business down to you, son." Roy reached across the table and patted Tom's hand.

"Are you sure?" asked Tom. "I know how much the boat means to you."

"I'm hoping you'll still allow me on board from time to time," said Roy with a nervous chuckle.

"Of course I will," said Tom.

"And I know you've been hankering after heading west these past few years. Now you can, if you still want to. There's nothing stopping you now, son. The business is yours. I shan't be interfering."

Marnie felt the icy hand of dread gripping her stomach. These past years she'd shared Tom's frustration at being stuck in Lowestoft while the fish moved elsewhere. Now, though, was a different story. Now it wasn't just her Tom would leave. There was Annie to think about, too. How would she manage on her own?

"Marnie, if our Tom goes away, you know I'll help with Annie?"

Was Sally a mind reader? Marnie looked at Sally, clearly doing her best to hide the pain she was suffering. The arthritis would only get worse. Despite her good intentions, Marnie couldn't help feeling it would be Sally needing her help, not the other way round.

"Congratulations, Tom," said Jimmy. "And thank you for including me in this special meal." Jimmy raised his glass to Sally, Roy, and finally to Tom.

"Don't be silly, Jimmy. You're family. Of course we'd want you here to share our news. How's that lovely girl of yours?"

Marnie smiled at Sally, referring to Clara as a girl. She'd just turned forty and had left girlhood firmly in the past.

"She's very well, thank you. Keeping busy with her hotel. I'm meeting her next weekend in Nottingham."

"Ah yes, Marnie said you like to meet halfway. Right, tuck in, everyone, or this food will get cold."

*

After dinner, Roy announced that the occasion needed marking properly. "How about us chaps take our beers down to the boat?"

Tom glanced at Jimmy, then back to his father. "Are you sure you can walk that far, Dad?"

"It's only a short stroll, and besides, I'll have two strong young men to carry me home if the walk gets too much."

"Alright then, let's do it," said Jimmy, handing Roy his stick. "We'll see you ladies later."

"Don't keep him out too long," said Sally.

"We won't, Mum. See you in a little while," said Tom, bending down to kiss Marnie and Annie.

With the men out of the house, Marnie pushed the pram over to Sally. "You take over rocking Annie and I'll clear away the dinner things."

"There's no need to do that," said Sally.

"Let me look after you for a change," said Marnie.

"I'm not the one with a new-born keeping me awake at night."

Marnie yawned and laughed into her hand. "Right on cue. Anyway, how is Roy? I'm surprised how willing he seems to hand over control of the boat."

Sally gave a hollow laugh. "Don't let his calmness fool you. It's been a long, painful process coming to this decision. It's not that he doesn't trust Tom, but that he doesn't know who he is if he's not at sea. The sea has been his escape for so many years. I think he's terrified his thoughts will catch up with him now he's stuck on dry land."

Since having Annie, Marnie felt an even greater empathy for Sally and Roy, who'd lost two out of their three sons. She couldn't imagine what it must be like to live with that loss day after day.

"He'll be welcome on the boat any time," said Marnie.

"I know. Tom's a good boy. Deep down, Roy's known for a long time it's not safe for him to be on the boat anymore, but it breaks his heart."

"Jimmy can help him come to terms with it. Injury cut his own fishing career short, although I know it's not the same."

"I think Jimmy is just what Roy needs. I try to support him the best I can, but I know I only add to his worries."

"You've been through such a lot together," said Marnie. "You know both me and Tom will help you in any way we can."

Sally reached over and took Marnie's hand. "You're the daughter I never had," she said. "I've never been so happy as the day Tom married you."

In her pram, Annie cried, breaking the sentiment of the moment. "And now you've a daughter and a granddaughter," said Marnie, smiling as Sally reached into the pram and lifted Annie to her chest.

"That I do. I know this stage is hard, but I'll help all I can. And if Tom heads west, you're more than welcome to come and stay with us while he's away."

"Thank you," said Marnie. "But let's cross that bridge when we come to it."

Chapter 17
May, 1935

Despite the fading light, the two young families couldn't help but marvel at the decorations covering shops as they walked towards St Margaret's church. Red, white and blue bunting hung from shop fronts. They had put up special window displays and the town held an air of hope which had been missing for some time.

"They've made everywhere look so lovely," said Marnie, as she pushed the heavy pram along the street.

"Just wait till July," said Kitty. "Most of the celebrations are being held off till then as it will be the fiftieth anniversary of Lowestoft getting its borough status. Not everyone's happy about it. There have been grumblings that the mayor should have put all efforts into today, rather than saving up for the celebrations in July."

"It doesn't look like they've saved much up to me," said Marnie, pausing outside Tuttle & Sons to admire their window display. Ribbons, streamers, and bunting covered the outside of the premises, and even in the dull twilight, the effect was magnificent.

Outside Chadds, Marnie stopped and stared into the bunting-covered window display. Her heart twisted as though glimpsing a long-lost lover. How she missed her days working in the store, when life was about pretty dresses, not soiled nappies.

"Are you alright?" asked Kitty. She linked her arm into Marnie's and gave her hand a squeeze.

"Aye, I miss it, that's all. I know I couldn't stay there forever, but I feel on my last day I left part of me behind."

"But look at what you gained," said Kitty, gazing into the pram.

Marnie managed a small smile. She loved Annie more than she ever thought possible, but still couldn't take to motherhood with the ease Kitty seemed to.

"Come on, girls, we don't want to miss the main event," called Bobby. Marnie and Kitty rushed to catch up to their husbands and joined the hordes of locals heading towards the high ground above the church.

"Blimey," said Bobby as they reached their destination.

"I'm going to stand back here," said Marnie. "I don't want Annie too close to that fire."

As if on cue, Annie cried. "Do you mind if I go forward with the boys?" asked Tom.

"No, enjoy yourself," said Marnie. She smiled at Tom, his enthusiasm for the bonfire infectious.

Marnie stood back, observing the joyful celebrations all around her. Annie's wails were growing louder by the minute, so she reached down and pulled her daughter from the many blankets covering her.

Tom held the hands of Kitty's youngest two boys as they stood captivated by the flames pushing high in the air. It was quite the sight. Crowds over twenty deep all gathered around the beacon to celebrate the silver jubilee of George V. Marnie stood back from the flames, jiggling her baby daughter to stop the interminable squawks coming from her tiny mouth. She sighed.

"You alright?" asked Kitty, joining Marnie.

"Aye, just tired."

"Tired?" Kitty raised an eyebrow and looked down at her swollen belly. She was carrying her seventh child. Marnie didn't know how she did it.

"Sorry," said Marnie, "I know I've nothing to complain about. If Annie would just sleep for more than an hour at a time…"

"Try having boys," said Kitty. "Maybe we should do a swap for the day? Trust me, after a day with my lot, you'll be running back to that sweet girl with open arms. Did my lads tell you about the coins?"

Marnie shook her head.

"The mayor visited their school today and gave all the bairns coins to mark the jubilee; shillings for the seniors, sixpence for juniors. I wish they hadn't got an extra two days' holiday, though. It's hard to get anything done with them all home." Kitty laughed and offered out her arms to take a turn with Annie.

"Why don't I grab us some tea from the stall over there?" said Marnie.

"Why don't we get the men to look after us for a change?" said Kitty, winking at Marnie. "Bobby? Grab us a cuppa, would you, love?"

Bobby left his sons in the care of Tom and met Kitty with a kiss on the cheek. "Your wish is my command."

"Away with you," said Kitty, swatting him on the arm as he passed.

"Has Bobby told you about the boat?" asked Marnie.

"Yes, he said Roy's handed it all over to Tom. I never thought I'd see the day."

"I don't think we ever would if he'd not gone and broken his hip. It looks like he's in for a long recovery, so finally saw sense and handed the reins to Tom."

"And a fine job he'll make of it," said Kitty. "Are you going to help with the nets?"

"Yes, once this little one's settled enough to be left in a pram for over five minutes. I've said I'll help Sally with her work and we'll split the earnings. Her hands aren't too good anymore and she could do with the help."

"Good for you."

"Will you go back to the herring this season?"

"I don't think I'll be able. This little one's due around October time, slap bang in what would be our busiest time. Hopefully now Tom's in charge, we won't be so reliant on my earnings. That husband of yours has a good brain. I don't want to be rude about your father-in-law, but he's been holding them back for years."

"Roy's a fine fisherman," said Marnie, "but he loves Sally more than his work. He's been trying to juggle caring for her alongside working on the boat and hasn't managed either very well, not for lack of trying. It's best all round Tom's taking over."

"Things are looking up," said Kitty, "and about time, too."

"Have you heard Tom's planning to head west next winter? Either Padstow or Milford Haven, he says. Sally's offered for me to stay with them, but I'm not sure."

"What's to think about? I'd bite her hand off if I were you. The herring girls will have left by then, so she'll have a spare room."

"True."

"And you'll be able to help each other out. I'd move in with my mother-in-law if I didn't come with so many hangers-on." Kitty glanced across to her brood and smiled.

"Will you manage if Bobby heads west with Tom?"

"Oh yes," said Kitty, "don't worry about me. Simon and Al are old enough to help me. Even Stevie and Chrissy play their part. I wish I'd had at least one daughter, though. I'm not sure how much help they'll be with a new-born."

"I wonder what it must be like for couples whose husbands work in offices or factories?"

"Easier in some ways, I expect," said Kitty, "although I think the reason me and Bobby get on so well is he's out at sea more often than he's home."

Marnie laughed and took her daughter from Kitty's arms. "Aye," she said, "being married to a fisherman isn't all bad."

The two women laughed, and Annie, distracted from her wailing, raised a smile. The bonfire burned bright against the winter sky, and Marnie watched on, sending off silent congratulations to the King, and wondering how the world would have changed by the time the next jubilee rolled around. With Tom now in charge of the boat, at least the future of their little family was looking brighter.

Chapter 18

December, 1938

M arnie set her basket down on the ground and tied the strings of Annie's hat beneath her chin. "You need to keep this on, bairn. It's freezing today." As if to emphasize her point, a fat lump of sleet landed on the end of Annie's nose.

"I hate my hat, and I hate my mittens."

"That's as may be, but you'd hate catching a chill even more."

"What are they doing?"

Marnie looked up. All around her, people were rushing down the street toward the railway station. "I don't know. Shall we see?"

Annie nodded and Marnie held her basket in one hand and Annie's hand in the other. The closer they got to the station, the denser the crowd became.

"Excuse me," said Marnie, to a suited man walking beside them.

"Yes?" The man's tone was brusque, and he sighed as if being detained from important business.

"Why are all these people headed for the station?"

"You haven't heard?"

"Heard what?"

"About the refugees. They arrive today."

Before Marnie could ask more questions, the man marched off, disappearing among the mass of bodies. Marnie and Annie found themselves dragged along with the crowd, through the doors of the station and onto the busy platform beyond. Annie pulled on Marnie's hand and soon they found themselves near the front of the assembled group. Two women stood beside them, standing on tiptoes, hoping for a glimpse of the train due any moment.

"Excuse me." Marnie hoped she'd have more luck with the women than the man she'd stopped before.

"Yes, love."

"There are refugees arriving?"

"Yes, a trainload of children should arrive at any moment."

In front of them, a group of accordion players struck up a jolly tune, and the women clapped their hands in glee. Beside the players stood the town's mayor and mayoress, proudly wearing thick gold chains around their necks.

"Where will the children stay?" shouted Marnie over the music.

"They're being taken to Pakefield holiday park."

"The holiday park?"

The older of the two women shook her head. "Yes, dear, but not for a holiday." The woman sighed, frustrated at being distracted from the action. "They're Jews."

"Jews? But why are they in Lowestoft, and where are their parents?"

"Probably back in Austria, but they'll be running as far from it as they can if they're sensible. It's that Hitler what's done it. Got a thing about the Jews. I don't understand it myself, but as the saying goes, there's nowt as queer as folk."

A puff of smoke signalled the train's arrival. Steam filled the air as metal squealed against metal. The crowd began singing along to the accordion's tune, handkerchiefs filling the air like a flock of gulls as men and women waved them above their heads. The carriage doors opened and a sea of children flowed out. They were thin, pale and as Marnie drew closer, she could see they were frightened. Their eyes darted this way and that. Some of the younger children were crying, and older children gripped tight to the younger ones' hands. One girl clutched a teddy bear which had seen better days, and all were loaded down with canvas bags, suitcases and trunks.

"What's happening to them, Mummy?"

Marnie looked down into Annie's wide, innocent eyes. Would the mothers of these children be relieved that their offspring had escaped? Or would they be suffering from the pain of separation? Probably both, Marnie decided, pulling Annie closer.

"We're very lucky to live where we do," she whispered to Annie. "There's a wicked man who's forced those poor children from their country. They've had to leave their home and come here." Marnie turned back to the women beside her. "How long will they be staying in Pakefield?"

"Who can say? Probably long enough for homes to be found for them. Poor little mites, turning up here, miles from home in the middle of winter. The world's gone mad."

Before Marnie could react, she felt Annie slip away from her, and watched in horror as her daughter ran towards the mass of bodies exiting the train. "Annie," she cried, dropping her basket to the floor once more and racing after her daughter.

Either Annie didn't hear her mother, or she ignored her. Marnie's hand flew to her mouth as she lost sight of her daughter. She stood on tiptoes, searching desperately for a sign of her daughter.

"Isn't that her?" said the woman beside her, pointing further along the platform.

Marnie leaned against the woman, standing on one leg as she tried to scan the sea of heads. When she spotted a mop of blonde curls, she sank to her feet in relief.

"Thank you," she said, pushing forward in pursuit of Annie.

Just as she was in touching distance of Annie, Marnie stopped. What was Annie up to? Annie stood in front of a girl of around the same age. The girl had dark circles under eyes red-rimmed from tears. A thumb stuck in her mouth, the girl looked on with a blank expression as Annie untied the straps of her hat. The girl's eyes widened as Annie reached forward and gently placed her hat on the girl's head. Next, Annie repeated the action with her mittens.

Marnie stood frozen to the spot. Her chest tight, she swallowed down the emotion constricting her throat. For all her struggles with her unruly daughter, for all Annie's disobedience, Marnie had never witnessed such a pure act of kindness. Annie didn't even understand what was happening, but instinctively she'd recognised the need in a fellow human being and had done all she could to meet that need.

The moment was broken as a man carrying a notebook and pencil pushed past Marnie. He stopped in front of a girl who looked on the verge of womanhood and placed a hand on the girl's shoulder.

"Welcome," said the man. "If you don't mind, I have a couple of questions for the readers of our newspaper."

Annie turned back to her mother, a look of confusion spreading across her face. "Come here," said Marnie, taking Annie's hand. The man carried on talking, and Marnie's curiosity prevented her from moving away.

"Do you understand English?" the reporter asked the girl.

"Yes, we learned English in school."

"Good, good. So, how does it feel to have arrived in Lowestoft?"

The girl squinted at the reporter, considering his question. "We are happy to be free at last, but our fathers and mothers are in concentration camps."

The little girl wearing Annie's donated hat and mittens took the older girl's hand and looked up at the reporter. "We are glad to be away from a terrible nightmare."

Marnie placed an arm around Annie's shoulders and fought back tears. The young girl couldn't be much older than Annie, but the things she had witnessed had left her far older than her years. Her eyes were blank, devoid of the light which sparkled in Annie's. Her lips lay flat where Annie's curled in smiles or frowns.

"Come on," said Marnie. "Let's leave these children to settle in."

As they walked away, Marnie stole a glance behind them. How many children were there? Five hundred? Six? "Shall we find Daddy?" Marnie asked, feeling desperately in need of her husband's calming presence. "His boat should be in by now."

Annie's face lit up. "Yes! I can tell Daddy about my new friend."

"Come on." Marnie gripped Annie's hand tightly, afraid her daughter would go running off again. They crossed the road and made their way to the harbour. Despite the freezing weather, the harbourside was a hive of activity. Several boats had recently come in and barrels were being unloaded, ready for market.

"Look," said Marnie, pointing toward a mid-sized steamer. "There's Daddy's boat."

Mother and daughter walked along the path that skirted the harbour, avoiding the barrels, crans and boxes littering the path, stepping out of the way of men as they stored equipment or threw bags and containers onto the dock.

As Marnie and Annie approached Tom's boat, he stood up and spotted them, a smile spreading across his face. He ran towards Annie, arms spread wide, and scooped her up, spinning her around until both were dizzy.

"Be careful you don't fall in," laughed Marnie.

"This is a lovely surprise," said Tom. "What are you two doing here?"

"We were shopping in town, then saw commotion down by the station and went to look. Did you know about the children?"

"Children?"

"Aye, the ones who've just arrived by train."

"Children? Marnie, I've been at sea for the past three days. I don't know what you're talking about."

"They've just arrived in Lowestoft," said Marnie, pointing in the direction they'd just walked. "Hundreds of them. All the way from Austria, apparently."

"What are Austrian children doing in Lowestoft?" asked Tom, shaking his head in confusion.

Marnie leaned close to Tom and whispered in his ear. "They're Jews."

Tom's eyes widened. Many a night they'd sat discussing news from Europe with growing unease. It was hard to believe the reports of cruelty and discrimination. They didn't want to believe them. Life might have its hardships, but Marnie felt such a level of evil should only exist in fairy stories.

"So the reports are true?" Tom asked.

"Seems so. They've been evacuated here and taken to the Pakefield holiday park."

"Crikey, that's not a place I'd want to be in this weather. It's designed for summer holidays, little shed-like places they've got there. I hope they've found a way of heating them."

"Yes, those poor children. The things they've seen..." Tom wrapped his arms around Marnie, and Annie squirmed in between them. "We're so fortunate," said Marnie.

"Yes, we are," said Tom. "Let's hope it stays that way."

Chapter 19

December, 1938

Marnie leaned her shoulder against the door and gave it a firm shove. It opened enough to squeeze through the gap and out into the snow. Children had been busy and a large snowman stared with raisin eyes towards Marnie as she pulled her hat further down around her ears and shoved her hands into her coat pockets.

It wasn't often they got snow so close to the sea. The delighted shrieks of children cheered Marnie as she avoided the snowballs flying around. It had snowed all week, the longest she could remember. The fat, crisp flakes had turned to sleet, but there was still enough lying on the ground to make walking treacherous.

Tom had tried to persuade her to stay inside, but Marnie knew Sally's arthritis would play up in the cold weather. Even if she never asked, Marnie was sure Sally could use some help.

Roy had been out shovelling snow from the road outside the house, and Marnie let herself in through the unlocked door.

"Only me."

"Through here, love," said Sally.

Marnie found her, duster in hand, cleaning the ornaments on the living room mantel. If Sally was cleaning, Marnie knew it meant her fingers were too stiff to be mending nets. Spring couldn't come round soon enough.

"I've brought a few things round. Thought I could make you your tea?"

"You didn't have to do that, love."

"I know, but I wanted to."

Sally sighed and folded her arms across her chest. She was a proud woman, and Marnie had long since learned that the only way she'd accept help was if it were forced onto her.

"Where's my beautiful granddaughter today?"

"At home with Tom. It's rare he's home much these days, and he wanted to spend some time with her." Marnie didn't add that she'd been desperate for a break, and begged him to take over for an hour or two. "In a matter of weeks, he'll be off to Padstow and Annie will miss him terribly."

"He hasn't suggested you go with him this time?"

"Good Lord no."

"You wouldn't be the first family to join their menfolk down west. We went down there with Roy several times when the boys were little."

"I know, but Annie's still so young and there's plenty to keep me busy here." Marnie didn't add that caring for her in-laws was becoming just as time consuming as caring for her daughter. It worried her how much they'd aged in a few short years and she couldn't see how they'd cope without her nearby.

"I hope you're not staying here on our account."

"Of course not," lied Marnie. "Apart from anything, I'd feel terrible about leaving Kitty. She finds it so hard with Bobby away. Right, I'll get these bits through to the kitchen and make a start on supper."

*

"Have you heard about those poor refugees you saw arriving last week?"

"No?" Marnie turned from the pot of stew she was stirring. "What's happened to them?"

"Says here they've had to be moved from the Pakefield holiday park. Silly fools, putting them there. I could've told them it was a bad idea from the start. That place isn't suitable for winter."

"Tom said a similar thing last week. Are the children alright?"

"They will be. Do you know there was no heating at that place? No heat in this weather!" Marnie and Sally looked out of the window to the sleet slapping against the panes.

"Where are they going?"

Sally studied the newspaper in front of her. "Two hundred and fifty have been sent to the Grand Hotel, two hundred to St Felix School, fifty to Cunningham Hall, thirty to the Pier Hotel, and seventy to a convalescent home in Walton-on-the-Naze. Poor little mites won't know if they're coming or going."

"I knew there were a lot of children who arrived on that train, but I didn't realise there were that many."

"What they must have gone through doesn't bear thinking about. War is an evil bastard."

"We're not at war, though, are we?"

"Not yet, but I'm old enough to know how these things go."

Marnie turned back to the stove. This was the closest either of her in-laws had come to acknowledging the unspoken hurt that shrouded the small family. Tom hadn't always been an only child. He was the baby of the family. It was his eldest brother John who'd been due to inherit the family fishing business, but like his other brother, Alan, John had been killed in the last war. As much as Marnie struggled with motherhood, she couldn't imagine a pain worse than losing a child. To lose two? She was amazed Sally could go on at all.

"How are your hands today?"

"Oh, not too bad."

Marnie sighed inwardly. Sally was of the generation who didn't complain. Sally's face scrunched as she held her cup, a sure sign her arthritis was playing up. She'd had to give up her work at the fish house and struggled to even mend nets. Until now, they'd scraped by on Roy's fishing money and the small amount of rent paid to her by the herring girls who stayed in the spare bedrooms.

"How much longer are the girls here?" asked Marnie.

"Another week or two, then they'll be home for Christmas and we won't see them again till October. If war comes, I'll have to find a new way to earn my pennies."

"Let's hope it doesn't come to that."

A clattering in the yard outside signalled the arrival of the herring girls. Through the kitchen window, Marnie saw them remove their boots, give their aprons a hose down, and hang up their outerwear in the shed.

"Evening, Sally," they chorused, walking in from the cold. They brought with them big smiles and a lingering smell of fish. "Hello, Marnie."

"Hello, girls. Fancy a cuppa? You must be freezing after working in the snow."

"We've had worse," said a plump older woman. Marnie wondered how her family back home was faring with their mother hundreds of miles away.

"I was just talking to Marnie about the war," said Sally.

"War?" The youngest girl's face creased into a frown.

"Sally, don't panic them. There's no war. But with those poor refugees arriving, it brings home all that's happening on the Continent."

"Best leave them to it. We've no time to read the newspaper and that's no bad thing. Don't you worry, Sally. We'll pitch up at your place next winter, and the one after and the one after. There'll be no war coming to our door."

"I hope you're right, girls," said Sally. "I hope you're right."

Chapter 20

January, 1939

Marnie dropped her daughter onto the kitchen table and placed a wicker basket down beside her. While Annie picked mud from the skin of a potato, Marnie added the supplies she had bought to the pantry shelves. Her back ached from carrying Annie home after a monstrous tantrum in front of a scowling Mrs Clarke who was never keen on children in her shop. As Marnie picked up a tin of peaches, the metal scratched against her palms, raw, chapped and weeping from mending nets.

"I want bread, Mummy," said Annie, banging her potato against the table's wood.

"Come on, bairn," said Marnie, lifting Annie and placing her on the floor. "I'll make us a sandwich, then you can go play with your dolls while I see to the washing."

Annie followed her mother as Marnie retrieved bread from its bin, then butter from the cold store. Unable to face yet more fish, Marnie spooned a small pile of sugar from its jar and spread it across the bread.

"Away with you, bairn," she said. "Give your mam room to work."

Annie pouted at her mother and grabbed a fistful of Marnie's skirt. Marnie sighed. The young girl with a head full of romance and dreams felt a long way off from the reality of married life. Tom was a good man. None could say otherwise. But as the years passed, life seemed to get harder rather than easier. Whilst their finances had improved since Tom took control of his dad's boat, the increase in work meant he was away more than he was home. When he was home, he was too tired to help Marnie with the endless list of chores she never seemed to reach the bottom of.

When Tom arrived home that evening, Marnie sensed a change in him as soon as he walked through the door. Rather than taking his coat off with the usual sigh, he bounded through the house, calling her name. When he found her in the kitchen, his cheeks were pink, his face creased in a wide grin. Tom leaned against the kitchen cupboards, his legs jiggling.

Marnie narrowed her eyes and placed her hands on her hips. "Thomas Hearn, something is going on with you and I want to know what it is. Come on, spit it out."

Tom took a deep breath, then announced his plan with a flourish of hands, in a singsong voice similar to a theatre performer.

"Padstow? You've never wanted us with you before. Why now?"

Tom's shoulders sagged. Marnie felt a tug of guilt as he lost his puff and bluster, her words taking the wind from his sails. Her reaction was not what he'd been hoping for.

"I've always wanted you to come with me, but it never felt the right time to ask, what with Annie being so little and Mum and Dad being in such poor health. But Annie's getting older, and it would be an adventure. I thought you were feeling fed up these days?"

"I'm not fed up. I'm exhausted. But whether fed up or exhausted, how will things be any better in Padstow? It will be the same thing in a different place; feed Annie, jump to attention every time Annie calls, calm Annie when she's in one of her moods. Whether Lowestoft or Padstow, my life will simply be Annie, Annie, Annie."

Tom scowled. He could forgive his beautiful wife many things, but not the way she spoke of their daughter. "It's not Annie's fault life is hard. You knew you could never stay at Chadds forever."

"Maybe not, but if it weren't for her, I'd still be there."

"We always spoke of having children. You knew that when you married me. You also knew they'd never employ a mother. You made a choice."

"But I didn't expect motherhood to be so hard," Marnie cried, exhaustion removing any slice of reason left in her mind. "Tom, between Annie, caring for your mam and da, my work on the nets and keeping this home, I'm worn out. The thought of having to pack up and move, well, it's just too much."

Tom stepped forward and took Marnie's hands. "You know what they say? A change is as good as a rest?"

"Whoever said that probably didn't have to pack up a house and travel for hours with a bairn. It won't be you having to entertain our daughter on a long train ride, will it?"

"She's a lively one, I'll grant you," said Tom, adding under his breath, "I wonder where she gets that from."

"What about your mam and da? She doesn't like to show it, but Sally's arthritis is terrible, and Roy's never recovered after injuring his hip. I'm not sure you realise how much they rely on me these days."

"I know, and I'm so grateful for how much you help them. But we're not going forever. I've spoken to their neighbour, Mrs Greene, and she'd be happy to help them out with cleaning and cooking while we're away. I'll pay her, of course."

"Pay her? Are you really going to find that many more fish in Padstow than Lowestoft?"

"Yes, and also, I want you and Annie out of Lowestoft. I don't like how things are going in Europe. That Hitler has to be stopped, and it doesn't bear thinking what might happen next."

Marnie sat down, deep in thought. She'd read the newspaper. She knew things were uncertain on the Continent and what that could mean for them. "When will we go?"

"Next week. I've arranged lodgings for us. We'll all stay with Richard and Helen, who've hosted me these past few years. We can let out the house till we're back. Let's hope it's still standing by then. With all the clearances going on, I don't know how long we'll be able to stay here, anyway. Perhaps they'll offer us one of those new council houses they're planning to build, perhaps not."

Tom's eyes had taken on a faraway look, and Marnie knew he was thinking back to the days when The Grit had been a thriving hub of activity, before the clearances, before the dwindling fish stocks, before the worry that played on residents' faces. His eyes refocused. "Don't you fancy the thought of Cornwall? It's a beauty of a place. You've seen the postcards I sent last year. It's even better in real life."

Marnie sighed. It had taken long enough to feel settled in Lowestoft after her move south. Now, she would be as far as was humanly possible from the Northumbrian island of her childhood.

"What about Jimmy?"

"Jimmy? Marnie, your brother's more than capable of looking after himself. Anyway, I mentioned my plan to him and he thought it was a fantastic idea."

"You took this plan to my brother before consulting me?"

"I knew you'd worry about Jimmy. You always have, always will. I thought if he was on board with it, it would put your mind at rest. He's also agreed to look in on Mum and Dad once a week. He said it would be a pleasure."

Marnie drummed her fingers against the kitchen counter. So far, all her reasons had been artfully headed off at the pass. She tried a different tack. "But we don't know a soul in Cornwall. It's the back of beyond. I've already left one home behind. I never intended to leave another."

"There'll be lots of neighbours there. You'll feel right at home. Half the Lowestoft fishing families are heading west. Trust me, it will be a home from home. When I was last there, on my evenings off I'd go to the pub and it was easy to forget I was miles from Lowestoft, the amount of familiar faces propping up the bar." Tom crossed the room and took Marnie's hands in his own. "Things will be better down there, I promise. And Annie's getting older. Things will get easier."

Marnie sighed. "I hope you're right, Tom. That bairn's nearly five years old. She should have stopped the tantrums long ago."

"Once we're settled in Padstow, we'll find her a place at a school. That will give you more time for yourself."

"School? How long are you planning to stay there? I thought you meant we'd be gone a couple of months at most?"

"Marnie, this isn't just about fish. Those poor refugees arriving were just the start. You see that?"

"Aye."

"If, as I fear, the country's on the brink of war, I dread to think what will happen. Remember what it was like here last time?"

Marnie thought back to her arrival in Lowestoft. She'd been a hopeful teenager, grateful to leave the island to help the brother she adored. Life then had been good, full of possibilities, but even she remembered the devastation wreaked on the town by war, losing men drawn from their fishing boats into bloody battle. Marnie shivered at the thought. "I remember," she said.

"Then you'll know what I suggest is for the best. You'll be a great deal safer in Padstow than you would here. We all will be."

"You won't fight?"

"Marnie, they'll be wanting young chaps, not old codgers like me."

"Forty isn't old."

"That's not what you tell me when bemoaning your own age."

Tom's voice was teasing, but rather than lightening the mood, it grated on Marnie and she swallowed down words that could sting. "I need to check on Annie."

Annie needed no checking, for peeking around the bedroom door Marnie found her daughter dead to the world, thumb in mouth, snuffles and snores filling the air. She perched on the edge of her daughter's bed and ran her hands through the blonde curls, a carbon-copy of her own. The bairn looked angelic, but Marnie knew it would only be a few brief hours before Annie got up, squashed herself between her parents and kicked and prodded them through the night.

Perhaps, wondered Marnie, it had been a mistake to wait so long for a child. If she had had her daughter in her twenties, she'd have more energy to spare, more patience. Marnie sighed. It seemed a lifetime since she'd felt her smart Chadds uniform against her skin, and she still missed the camaraderie of colleagues and the way younger girls looked to her for advice.

But she'd done the right thing by giving Tom a child. And it wasn't always bad. Marnie remembered the way Annie had given her hat and gloves to the refugee. There was a big heart buried beneath the mischief. Tom was right, she had wanted their daughter.

Marnie laid her head down beside Annie, feeling the warmth of her breath on her cheek. Perhaps Padstow wouldn't be so bad. Perhaps it would give her a fresh start, the chance to feel like her old self. Only time would tell.

Chapter 21

January, 1939

Marnie, Tom and Annie squished themselves into Kitty's front room along with Bobby and their ever-growing brood. Her eldest were becoming men, their large bodies needing more space than they could find in the tiny cottage.

"Stevie," Bobby said to his son. "Run down to Harry Hammond's and get us a penny and a penny times ten."

"A penny of fish, a penny of chips, times ten, coming right up," said Stevie, holding out his hand for coins.

"Ah, I see, not digging into your own pocket."

"Dad, I don't earn enough at Gowings to pay for all that and the extortionate rent you charge me."

Bobby laughed. "Got to pay your way, son. Perhaps you should have joined me on the boat if you wanted more earnings?"

"I'm making ropes for the boats, that's as close as I ever want to get to the sea."

"Can you believe it, Tom? A son of mine with no sea legs. Remember the time we tried him out on the *Sally Ann*?"

"I'm still finding vomit around her hull years later."

Tom and Bobby laughed. Stevie's cheeks turned pink, and he left the house in search of supper.

"You shouldn't tease him like that," scolded Kitty. "He's a good boy and doing really well at Gowings."

"I know," said Bobby. "I was only pulling his leg."

Marnie watched her daughter playing with Sam, Kitty's youngest. With only months between them, they were as close as siblings, and Marnie knew it would be a wrench for her daughter to leave him. Would Sam end up fishing? Marnie was grateful she'd had a daughter, not a son. Even after so many years with Tom, she still worried every time he went to sea. It was all too common for boats to come home missing one of their crew. Even worse was when boats didn't come back at all. No regular job came close in danger, except the work of a soldier, and even that wasn't as bad during peace time.

"You all set for the move west?" asked Kitty, squeezing onto the settee beside Marnie.

"Aye, I think so. We're leaving all the furniture for the tenants and we don't have that many belongings. Anything we can't carry has gone into Roy's shed, ready for when we return."

"I'll miss you," said Kitty.

"And I'll miss you too. We can write to each other, can't we?"

"Of course," said Kitty, linking arms with her best friend. "Now, as we only have a few more evenings together, I suggest we pretend there's nothing happening tomorrow and enjoy the time we have."

"That sounds like an excellent idea," said Marnie.

*

Marnie held Annie's hand tight as they stood braced against the wind beside the Lowestoft dock. One of many women waiting to say goodbye, she felt the atmosphere was a strange mix of sadness and excitement. The surrounding air crackled with uncertainty. Even in their quiet corner on the edge of England, the events in Europe provoked a feeling of uncertainty. Add to that the dwindling fish stocks and financial hardship staring families in the face, and the move west felt like a last-ditch attempt at hope.

"Remember what this place was like back in the day?" Marnie said to Kitty.

"Aye, I do. I'd be over there," said Kitty, pointing behind her, "my fingers dressed in cloots, trying to keep up with herring that felt like they were falling from the skies. It's only been a year or two, but it feels a lifetime ago I stood singing songs from the homeland with the other herring girls."

"You still hanker for home?"

Kitty laughed. "This is my home now, has been for a long time."

Marnie linked arms with her friend. "Who'd have thought us northerners would become Lowestoft lasses?"

"Aye. I worry, though, about what's coming."

"What's coming? You mean Hitler?"

"And the rest. Things are changing, Marnie. The Grit isn't the place it once was. And then yes, there's this damn threat of war. If it comes, as I fear it will, my lads will be the age to be called up. The thought of that leaves me sick."

"Let's hope it doesn't come to that," said Marnie. She pulled her friend into a hug. "You're sure I can't tempt you down to Padstow with me?"

"Not this time," said Kitty. "You tell your Tom to keep my Bobby in check, though. I don't want him getting carried away with the single life while I take care of things back here."

"Tell him yourself," said Marnie, as Tom and Bobby strolled towards them.

"What's that?" asked Bobby, taking a long drag on his pipe.

"Kitty's worried the Padstow girls will turn your head."

"Stuff and nonsense," said Bobby, pulling his wife into his arms and giving her a smooch that caused Kitty to blush.

"I'll keep an eye on him," said Tom, chuckling. "Come here," he said, holding his arms out to Marnie and Annie. "I'm going to miss my girls."

"I'll miss you too, Daddy," said Annie. She stood on her tiptoes as Tom bent down, placing a kiss on his cheek and wrapping her arms around his neck.

"I'll see you soon, my beautiful girl. You enjoy your adventure, won't you? Make sure there's a hot cup of tea waiting for me when my boat arrives in Padstow."

Annie nodded solemnly.

"We'll add a dash of brandy to it for good measure," said Marnie. "You take care of yourself," she whispered, squeezing Tom's hand. "I'll need you by my side on this so-called adventure."

"When have I ever let you down?" said Tom, giving his wife a lingering kiss. "See you soon, my love."

The women watched as their husbands made their way to the *Sally Ann*. Steam and smoke filled the air, the chugging of an engine drowning out the cries of gulls. Only when the boat was a tiny pinprick on the horizon did the women turn and head for home.

Chapter 22

January, 1939

Annie dragged her feet while Marnie struggled to contain her frustration. She wished she could channel some of Tom's enthusiasm for the move. Marnie had tried her best to rally, to talk to Annie about steam trains, picnics, and adventures. As hard as she tried to muster eagerness, her attempts were in vain. Annie either didn't understand, or understood too much.

Annie stopped to watch the beaters mending nets on the Denes.

"Annie Rose Hearn. You must move yourself or we shall miss the train."

"I don't want to go on a train," said Annie, sticking her thumb into her small rosebud mouth, and clinging on to railings with her free hand.

"What about Daddy? What will he think when his boat arrives in Padstow harbour and his precious girl isn't there to greet him?"

Annie removed her thumb, looked her mother square in the eyes, and stuck out her tongue. Marnie pushed down a rush of rage. She lifted her face to the grey sky and allowed silent curses to fly up to the heavens. Packing up the house with a demanding child at her side had been no mean feat. The days had been long, the nights short, and by the time the last box of belongings had made its way to her in-laws' shed, Marnie felt like she could sleep for a week.

"Marnie, you off today?"

Marnie looked across to the nets. Old Caro Shaw was looking at her, fingers twining cord with a sixth sense that no longer required sight.

"Aye, we're off to catch the train. If I can ever get the bairn to move."

"Ah, she's a beauty. Ain't that right, Miss Annie?"

Annie gave Mrs Shaw an angelic smile. Marnie gritted her teeth. "Perhaps you could tell my daughter what an adventure it is to take a train to Cornwall?"

Mrs Shaw cackled, fixing mother and daughter with a toothless grin. "I don't know nothing about trains. Lived in The Grit all my life, wouldn't want to be anywhere else."

Annie's smile widened, as though she knew she was in the company of an ally.

"You're not scared by the threat of war?" asked Marnie.

"I'll not have Hitler turf me out of my home. If it's my time, I'll die in my bed, thank you very much. Of course, it's different for the little 'uns," added Mrs Shaw. "You've got your daughter to think of."

"Quite."

"You'll miss Lowestoft, mind. They talk funny down in Cornwall, so I'm told. My Henry went down there years back. Said they're a strange bunch."

"Right," said Marnie, feeling this interruption was not a helpful one. "We'd best catch that train, or we'll be stuck in London for God knows how long, and I don't fancy that."

"Yes, you get off. I'll see you when you get back, if Hitler's not got me by then."

Marnie hauled Annie into her arms, the sound of Mrs Shaw's cackle following them on the wind. Caro Shaw was a dying breed. Marnie couldn't shake the feeling that they stood at the dawn of a new age, where fish were scarcer than ever and women like Caro no longer had nets to mend. The Grit was losing the buzz that had held fishing families there for generations. There'd always been poverty about, but walking through the familiar streets, Marnie noticed more children in rags, more windows boarded up and shops no longer trading. What kind of place would they come home to?

The railway station was a busy, noisy place, and Marnie felt out of her depth. She had never taken Annie on previous excursions, and travelling with a child felt like a whole new challenge. Marnie checked her bag, relieved to have remembered the toys and food that she hoped would make the long journey more bearable. She wished Tom could have travelled with them by train. Even travelling with him on the boat would have been preferable to the journey she now faced.

Marnie squared her shoulders, straightened her hat, and tried to pull a breath of confidence into her lungs. If she could journey to Lowestoft alone, little more than a child, and nurse the brother she adored back to health, surely she could cope now. A flush of despair followed the brief wave of confidence. Truth be told, she relished the thought of starting again as much as her daughter did. Once in a lifetime was more than enough. If she ever left Lowestoft, she had assumed it would be for the wide skies and barren beauty of her childhood home. Not for a small fishing village at the end of the earth.

A whistle blew, and Marnie collected both her thoughts and her luggage. There was no going back. The new residents moved into her Lowestoft home the following day, and Tom would expect a family welcome when his boat docked in Padstow.

"Come on, bairn," she said, pulling Annie onto the busy platform, jostling with the crowds to find their carriage.

Annie cried. She rubbed her nose against Marnie's sleeve and whimpered as they fought through smog and noise. Marnie tried to view the scene through her daughter's eyes; the shiny traction engine appearing grotesque and angry with its spurts of steam, the chug of the engine and banging of doors piercing to young ears. A porter appeared at her side and Marnie gratefully handed over her bags, picking up Annie and holding her tight to her chest.

As the porter guided them to the carriage door, Marnie whispered soothing words into her daughter's hair. She lifted her onto the train and clasped her hand as they squeezed their way along the busy carriage to find a seat. After what felt like an age, they found a spare bench in a compartment. There were two other occupants, both women slipping past middle-age, their greying hair and wrinkled skin betraying a life of hard toil. One woman smiled at Annie, but neither seemed keen to engage Marnie in conversation, for which she was grateful.

A whistle blew, and with a jerk the train lurched forward. Annie gripped her mother's hand, her face pale as she tried to peer through the steam beyond the window.

"It's all right, bairn. We're on our way now."

"I don't like the train," said Annie, sticking her thumb in her mouth and kicking her heels against the bench.

"I'm with you on that, girl," muttered the woman opposite, her eyes fixed on the magazine she was reading.

They had only been travelling for half an hour when Annie turned green around the gills and announced her tummy hurt.

"Happened to all of mine the first time they travelled," said the woman on the opposite bench.

Marnie grabbed hold of Annie and rushed her along the corridor to the conveniences. They made it just in time. Once Annie had been cleaned up and had a sip of water, colour returned to her cheeks and she began asking for food. Marnie sighed. They were less than an hour in, and already the journey felt close to unbearable.

*

London was unlike anything Marnie had ever experienced. She was used to the noise and bustle of a busy harbour, but at least in Lowestoft, sea winds brought enough air to flush away the smells of industry. In London, stale smells hung in the air, disturbed only by the mass of bodies pressing together on the grimy streets.

Unlike Marnie, Annie was fascinated by the sights and sounds of the city. Her eyes bulged at the clothes on display, pinks, satins and crepes brightening the dull day. In the end Marnie resorted to carrying her, for Annie stopped so frequently to stare at the grand buildings, street sellers and motor cars, Marnie feared they would never reach the bus in time.

It came as a relief, having crossed London crammed into an enormous red bus, to reach Paddington station. Marnie made a mental note to write to Jimmy and thank him once more for teaching her to read. Without that skill, navigating the different platforms and noticeboards would have been near impossible.

Mother and daughter settled themselves onto the train, a little weight lifting from Marnie's shoulders as she realised there would only be one more change before they reached their destination.

With her body now used to the rocking motion, Annie's stomach settled and the fish-paste sandwich she gobbled down made no unwanted reappearance. Between London and Cornwall, mother and daughter slept a little, paced the train corridor a lot, and tried to ease boredom by playing I-spy and every other game Marnie could think of.

By the time the next change came, Marnie embraced the chance to stretch her legs. With twenty minutes before their connecting train, she and Annie paced the platform of Bodmin Parkway, stretching their clicking bones and cramped muscles.

Fatigue slipped into excitement and nervous anticipation as they boarded the train to Padstow. With coal burning fiercely in its engine room, the train sped them along through wooded valleys, the river following their progress as a constant companion. As the train slipped out from Wadebridge station, Annie's eyes widened in synchronisation with the river. Where near Bodmin the river skipped along, a narrow ribbon tripping over stones and shallow enough to paddle in, here it widened out, exposing mudflats full of birds. It was like a young boy who had hit adolescence, its shoulders broadening, its voice deepening, ready to become a man, the sea.

From the train window, Marnie spotted the sails of pleasure vessels, fishermen casting lines from the bank, and a myriad of bird life to which the river was home. Several miles from Wadebridge, the stretch of water beside them could no longer be described as a river. Now, it was an estuary, the familiar smell of home leaching through the train's open windows.

A conductor opened the door of their compartment, and Marnie produced her tickets for him to stamp. He informed them they were only a few miles from Padstow. Marnie began collecting up their belongings, while Annie's face remained pressed to the window, an opaque circle of breath forming against the glass.

Marnie's stomach fluttered, the butterfly's wings beating faster as the train slowed. This was it. Their adventure began now. There was no time for regret. Now was the time for strength. She dug deep into her reserves, and as the train pulled into Padstow station, Marnie squared her shoulders and plastered a smile on her face, ready for whatever was to come.

PART TWO
PADSTOW

Chapter 23

January, 1939

By the time the train pulled into the tiny station, both Marnie and Annie were tired, fractious, and desperate to stretch their legs. Marnie leaned out of the window and opened the carriage door. The platform was a disorientating mixture of new and familiar. Large rounded vowels slipped from strangers' mouths, the singsong lilt of Lowestoft accents easily identified among the Cornish.

Many new arrivals were dab hands, striding purposefully towards the exit with the confidence of a child returning home from school. Marnie waited for the porter to hand them their baggage and tried to ignore the impatient child tugging on her arm. Her eyes scanned the platform. Three couples stood craning their necks, any of whom could be the people she needed.

For several minutes Marnie engaged in a game of guess who, trying to decide which couple most accurately fitted the description Tom had given her. The three couples did the same, one consulting a page of writing which Marnie assumed contained a description of their charges.

"I think we'd better ask who's who," Marnie said to her daughter. She was arranging their luggage on a trolley when she saw a woman walking towards them. The woman was older than Marnie expected, and beneath her hat sat a head of greying hair. Her face was free of colour other than a natural blush, which tinted her cheeks rose.

The woman held out a hand and smiled, the crinkling skin around her eyes suggesting this was a natural expression for her face to assume. Marnie warmed to her immediately.

"Apologies if I'm wrong, but are you Marnie and Annie?"

"That's us," said Annie, giving the lady a beaming smile. "We came a long way on the train."

"So I hear," said the lady, bending down to talk to Annie at her height. "And how was the train? Did you enjoy it?"

Annie screwed up her face. "I was sick," she said. "Now I'm hungry."

The lady laughed and ruffled Annie's hair. She stood and held out her hand again. "Helen," she said. "I'm very pleased to meet you at long last."

"Marnie. It's a pleasure to meet you, too."

Helen turned and waved towards a man leaning against a railing. "It's them, Richard," she called. The man took a series of quick puffs on his pipe, then strolled over to where the small party stood.

"Pleased to meet you," he said. He was a softly spoken man and from the few seconds they had spent together, Marnie guessed his wife did most of the talking.

"Is it far to your house?" Marnie asked, eyeing the trolley of luggage beside her.

Helen laughed. "I think you need to lower your expectations. I'm afraid our home is more cottage than house. You don't need to worry about your bags. The cottage is close, and Richard will return the trolley once we've got you settled in."

"That's very kind of him. As long as the porter doesn't mind?"

Helen laughed again. "You'll get used to our ways soon enough, maid. Bertie the porter is also a fisherman and Richard's second cousin.

Everyone knows everyone here. Even the folk from elsewhere come regularly enough that we know who's who."

"That sounds like the Beach Village where we live."

"Oh, what a wonderful name for a place. Isn't that charming, Richard?"

Richard nodded, and now it was Marnie's turn to laugh. "It's also known as The Grit, and it's not as picturesque as it sounds, but it is a friendly place to live. Most of the fishing families live there. We have little to do with the rest of the town. There's no need when we have everything on our doorstep."

"Indeed. I hope you don't think me intrusive, but your accent doesn't sound like the other Lowestoft folk I've met?"

"I'm a bit of a wanderer," said Marnie, linking arms with Helen as Richard led them out of the station. "I grew up on a small island in the north of England. Lowestoft was only ever meant to be a temporary home while I nursed my sick brother, but it's a place that gets in your blood and I can't imagine leaving now."

"Except to come here."

"Except to come here," said Marnie, trying her best to smile.

They left the confines of the station and faced a scene of purpose. Men in overalls paced along a busy harbourside, lugging sacks of coal, creels, tools and baskets of fish. The noise of men's shouts and the cry of gulls reached their ears, the familiar smell of salty air mixed with rotting fish filling their nostrils.

"Not the most picturesque introduction to the town," laughed Helen. "But this is where much of the town's business happens and most of those not at sea work here."

"It's not so different from back at home," said Marnie. "When people think of seaside towns, they think of sandcastles and ice-creams. Few folk realise the amount of work conducted at the point land and sea meet."

"You're quite right there. When are you expecting Tom to arrive?" asked Helen.

"The last I heard, he should be in Padstow by the end of the week."

"That's good. You'll feel more settled once the family is all together again."

"Aye," said Marnie, wondering if that would prove to be the case.

They walked towards the town, Annie stunned into silence by the unusual scenery. "Goodness, however do the ships get in and out?" asked Marnie, staring at long islands of sand puncturing turquoise water.

"Just wait till the tide comes in," said Helen. "It's a completely different landscape then. It's much easier since we've had the new dock. It was pretty treacherous before that was built. Richard's father fished these waters in those days and his mother was forever worrying that he'd come to harm. That bank out there is called Doom Bar for a reason."

Marnie shuddered at the name, hoping Tom would stay safely away from its clutches. "Do you work the boats?" Marnie asked Richard. To her surprise, when he turned his face was creased in a smile and his eyes twinkled.

"My pa tried to get me to follow in his footsteps. I would have done too if I had sea legs. Unfortunately, I turn green around the gills the second my feet leave dry land. All involved agreed I was best off sticking to terra firma." He chuckled to himself and Marnie smiled at his candour.

"We run a shop these days," said Helen. "It'll be tricky getting supplies if war comes, but my parents managed the first time and I'm sure we'll be no different. Here we are."

Marnie looked up at the cottage perched yards from the water. It stood at the end of a higgledy-piggledy row, as though someone had tacked it on as an afterthought. At the bottom stood a shop front, wares displayed in the window and in baskets outside. The cottage was on three levels, and bigger than Marnie had been expecting, though not large enough to make her feel ill at ease.

"Is this our new home?" asked Annie.

"It is for a while," said Marnie.

Helen took Annie's hand and placed a key in her palm. "Would you like to open the door and look inside?"

Annie nodded, her blonde curls bouncing around her face.

"Follow me then, maid. We come and go through the back door so as not to disturb customers in the shop." Helen took Annie's small hand in her own and led her around the side of the building along a slate path. They stopped at a painted wooden doorway and Helen helped Annie fit the key in the lock. It turned with a click, and Helen stepped back to let Annie push the door open. A fat, fluffy cat lay sleeping on an old wooden chair. Annie rushed over, stroking her hand across its back with a care Marnie had rarely seen in her daughter.

"This way," said Helen, smoothing the cat's ruffled fur and guiding Annie to do the same. "Mr Pots likes that. Can you hear him purring?"

"Yes, I can. Why is he called Mr Pots?"

"Because he destroys all my plant pots in the garden," said Richard. "Has done ever since he was a kitten. I'd rather have complete plant pots than that darned beast, but Helen won't hear of me getting rid of him."

"Don't you pay any attention to Uncle Richard," said Helen, tutting at her husband. "He loves Mr Pots more than me. I'll often come home to find Richard snoring in an armchair with the cat curled up on his lap."

"Stuff and nonsense," said Richard, smirking as he began unloading suitcases and trunks from the trolley. "I'll take these up to your room. Do you want to follow me up and get the lay of the land?"

"Aye, I'll carry some of these up while we're at it," said Marnie, ignoring Richard's protests that he could carry all the bags, and taking one in each hand.

At the top of the stairs, Richard nodded his head to the right. "That's our room in there. The sitting room is through there. You're up another flight of stairs, I'm afraid."

Marnie followed Richard up a narrow flight of stairs. He bent frequently to avoid banging his head and Marnie thought Tom would struggle with the height when he finally arrived. Richard put down the cases and opened a wooden door.

Marnie stepped into the room that would be home for the next however long. It was a simple room with one large bed, a cot, a chest of drawers, and a wardrobe. The ceiling sloped from the middle of the room, leaving only a tiny amount of floor space where standing at full height was possible.

"I'm afraid there's not a lot of room," said Richard. "You may have to use the space beneath the bed for some of your belongings."

"It's wonderful," said Marnie, meaning it. She walked to the window and took in the harbour view.

"You'll be able to see your Tom when he gets home from sea."

"Aye, I will," said Marnie, smiling at the thought.

Marnie resolved to make up for her recent grumpiness when Tom arrived. He'd done nothing to deserve her wrath. He was only looking out for his family. Deciding that unpacking could wait, Marnie went back downstairs to find her daughter.

Annie and Helen were bending over a ball of wool, Annie fascinated by the speed and clicking of Helen's needles.

"Do you knit?" Helen asked Marnie, looking up from her work with a smile.

"No, at least not for a long time. All the women on the island knitted ganseys when I was little and Mam taught me. I've struggled to maintain the habit, or skill, since I've lived in Lowestoft."

"And how long is that?"

"Over twenty years."

"Well, you'll be rusty, but once learned, it's a skill never forgotten. Here," said Helen, holding out her needles. "Come and have a go. Your Annie will be a dab hand too by the time I'm finished with her."

Marnie sat on a chair beside Helen, watching as she showed her how to purl, seed, and cast on and off. The needles lay clunky in her hands, but Helen had been right and the training of Marnie's youth came flooding back. Focusing only on the growing line of stitches in her hands, Marnie pondered how alike these fishing communities were. Whether Lindisfarne, Lowestoft or Padstow, women would sit with needles in their hands, men out on their boats, businessmen in the fish markets, and cod, plaice, herring and hake on the plates of children. Perhaps, thought Marnie, she wasn't all that far from home after all.

Chapter 24

January, 1939

Annie's hand slipped from Marnie's and she went racing off towards the harbour.

"Annie, Annie! Come back!" Marnie stood on her tiptoes, trying to see among the crowds. The fishing boats had come in with the tide and the harbourside was awash with boxes and baskets of fish, bedraggled men longing for a bath after several days at sea, and the money men who would decide what price the fishermen got for their toil. It was organised chaos, and not the place where a headstrong, disobedient child was easy to find.

Marnie dropped her shopping bags to the ground and broke into a run. How could the bairn have disappeared so quickly? What kind of mother was she that she could lose her child a day into their so-called adventure?

Marnie glimpsed blonde among the greys and browns surrounding her. "Annie!" By the time Marnie caught another glimpse of her daughter, she was running down a seaweed-strewn slipway towards the water's edge. Time stood still as Marnie watched her daughter step into a puddle of green-brown slush. Her hand flew to her mouth as Annie's legs went from under her, her body propelled forward into the murky water.

"Help," Marnie screamed. Fishermen paused their haggling and hauling to see what the commotion was. They started pointing towards the water. The next thing Marnie knew, a man with flame-red hair was skidding his way down the slipway. Twice, he lost his balance, but righted himself. With not a moment's pause, he waded into the water of the harbour, disturbing a sheen of oil and sending its silky rainbow swirling around him.

Marnie reached the harbour wall in time to see him emerge, clothes sodden, seaweed clinging to his shirt, a trembling little girl in his arms. He marched up the slipway, men around him pointing him toward the child's mother. Marnie pushed through the gathered crowd and grabbed her daughter, her clothes growing damp as she pulled Annie tighter to her.

For a moment, Marnie thought of nothing but Annie's welfare, ignoring the stares and whispers of strangers as she kissed her daughter's sodden hair, rubbing her back to shush her cries. When Annie's sobs became tiny whimpers and ragged breaths, Marnie looked to the man who had saved her daughter. The wind tugged his unruly red hair this way and that. His green eyes stared hard back at her, his mouth downturned.

"Thank you for rescuing my daughter. I'm most grateful to you."

"Not from round here, are you?" His voice resembled a snarl, devoid of any warmth. "No local woman would leave a child this young unattended near the water. She could've drowned."

His words hit Marnie like a slap. She tried to pull a response from her mind, but her brain clouded with shame.

"How about you, princess? Are you alright?" The man's demeanour could not be more different as he reached across and tickled Annie under her chin. She looked up and gave her rescuer a small smile. He reached a hand to her waist and wiggled his fingers against her skin. Annie giggled and squirmed in her mother's arms, her trauma of moments ago forgotten.

"She ran away from me. I couldn't find her in the crowd." Marnie's defence sounded pathetic, even to her own ears. The man ignored her, giving Annie's cheek a quick stroke before turning and marching away.

"Come on, let's get you home and into some warm dry clothes."

Marnie turned her back on the harbour and its curious fishermen. Each step brought a shiver of anger. How dare that man humiliate her in front of a crowd? How dare Annie run away from her like that? By the time they reached the cottage, it was not only Annie shaking, but Marnie. If it weren't for the wet bundle in her arms, she'd march right back down to the harbour and give that arrogant, insensitive man what for.

"Whatever's happened to you?" Helen asked, opening the door and leading Marnie and Annie to the warmth of the kitchen Aga.

"Annie ran off and landed herself in the harbour. I could murder her. She scared the life out of me."

"Well, sometimes the best way to learn of danger is to experience it," said Helen. "I doubt she'll be so quick to run off near the water again."

"Hmm," said Marnie, thinking her daughter was likely to do just that. "A man pulled her from the water. He was very rude to me."

"What did he look like?"

"Red, messy hair. Tall, with a scowl on his face."

Helen laughed. "Oh, you've met Jack Tristan, have you? Don't worry, maid, he's like that with everyone. His bark's worse than his bite. I should know, he's my brother."

"Your brother? Well, I don't wish to speak ill of your family members, but he humiliated me in front of all the fishermen. I'll be embarrassed to go anywhere near that harbour again."

"Oh, don't be silly. They'll be in the pub by now drinking their earnings and will have forgotten all about you."

Marnie harrumphed, and Helen laughed. "What?" said Marnie.

"You look just like your daughter when she's in a strop. Now I know where she gets her pout from."

Marnie felt the shame and anger dissipate from her body. For all her complaining, things could be worse. "You'll be good for me," she told Helen, managing a small smile.

"How's that?"

"Your plain speaking. I admire that in people."

"Not in my brother, you don't," laughed Helen.

"That's different. He was rude. He knows nothing of me or my daughter and near enough called me a terrible mother."

"That is going a bit far, I'll grant you. I'll have a word with him about his manners. Now, how about I warm up a couple of scones for the pair of you while you find Annie some dry clothes?"

"Thank you," said Marnie.

Chapter 25

January, 1939

Upstairs in their bedroom, Marnie tugged the sodden clothes from Annie's small body. Every so often Annie shuddered, an afterthought of the earlier crying. Goose-bumps freckled her skin, and Marnie wrapped a towel around her daughter's shoulders. With a second she rubbed at Annie's hair, the gentle swirling motion soothing her daughter until her eyelids drooped.

"Oh, no you don't, bairn. Keep those eyes open. I don't want you up half the night, and besides, Helen's warming scones for us downstairs."

Annie looked up at Marnie, her lips spreading into a smile. A rush of love caused Marnie's eyes to burn with tears. Moments like this came rarely and were to be relished. It wasn't often she felt like a proper mother, able to care for her child with more love than duty. Marnie pulled Annie onto her lap and squeezed tight, breathing in the unusual scent of soap and seaweed.

"You'll need a bath tonight. You've that much sand and seaweed in your hair, folk may mistake you for a mermaid."

"I'm not a mermaid, I'm a girl. Look," said Annie, jumping from her mother's lap and lifting her towel to show a pair of small, sturdy legs.

"Very true. But don't you go falling into the sea again or you might turn into one."

Annie shivered at the mention of the sea, and Marnie smiled, confident that her headstrong daughter had learned a valuable lesson. While they were in Padstow, Marnie resolved to teach her daughter how to swim. It was the job of a father to Marnie's mind, but with Tom away at sea, she'd have to be mother and father rolled into one.

With Annie dressed in her nightshirt and dressing gown, Marnie carried her down the two flights of stairs and into the kitchen.

"This one will need a bath later, if that's all right, Helen?"

"Of course it is. Now, sit down, the pair of you."

Marnie and Annie took their seats at the small kitchen table. Helen laid out cups and saucers, a jug of milk, and a teapot with steam dancing from its spout.

"Don't go to any trouble on our account," said Marnie, embarrassed by the fuss they had caused.

"This is your first afternoon tea in Cornwall. I shall go to as much trouble as I see fit." Helen stood with her hands on her small hips, glaring at Marnie. The edge of her lip quivered and within seconds a smile had grown into a full-blown laugh. "I can see we're going to have quite an adventure with you pair of rascals," said Helen, chuckling to herself as she placed warm scones onto plates.

"I hope we don't cause you too much trouble," said Marnie, taking a bite of warm, fluffy scone. "Mmm, this is delicious."

"Thank you. And thank you for being here. I know you're paying for your lodgings, but I can honestly say it's a joy having a child in the house. Richard and I had hoped to have a family of our own, but some things aren't meant to be."

Helen smiled, but Marnie could hear the sadness in her voice. Her cheeks flushed with the prick of guilt as she considered how ungrateful she so often felt about her own experience of motherhood.

"You must have been fairly late having children, if you don't mind me saying? Did you have problems too, or was it a decision you made?"

Surprised by the bluntness of Helen's question, Marnie answered truthfully. "I had a job I loved, and I wasn't sure I wanted to be a mother. In the end, I gave in to the idea, as I knew how important having a family was to Tom."

"I've heard of women choosing not to have children, though they're few in these parts," said Helen.

"I wouldn't change my decision to have Annie for the world," said Marnie. "But I miss my working life. I suppose the grass is always greener, as they say."

"I suppose it is," said Helen, her eyes turning glassy as she watched the little girl sitting at her table. "What work did you used to do?"

"I worked in a large department store. By the time I left, I was the supervisor of my department. I loved it."

"Well, perhaps you could help us out in the shop from time to time? It's no department store, but we are often in need of another pair of hands."

"Really? That would be wonderful."

Richard joined them at the table, and it was a happy party who sat munching on scones, jam and cream, putting the world to rights. Only when Annie began yawning did they clear away their plates and run a bath. As Marnie watched Helen moving around her kitchen, she considered herself fortunate to have been placed not just with a kind couple, but with a woman whom she could imagine becoming a friend.

Chapter 26

January, 1939

M arnie rushed to the door as she heard the postman's knock. Kitty had promised to write, and with any luck she'd have news of where in the world their husbands had got to. It was three days since Tom's boat had been expected in harbour and there was still no sign of him, or his crew.

Thumbing through the letters in her hand, Marnie saw most were addressed to Helen or Richard, and she was giving up hope of news when she spotted a Lowestoft postmark. She tore open the letter and began reading before she'd even sat down.

Dear Marnie,

I hope you're settling in well down there. What are the folk like? Are your hosts kind? It's mighty quiet on The Grit with the herring girls away and half the families down west like you. Have you bumped into any familiar faces yet? I know several families have gone to Milford Haven, but there must also be some with the same idea as your Tom.

Have our men arrived in Padstow yet? I had a letter from Bobby saying they'd been delayed in Southampton as the boat needed some repairs. He asked me to pass the news on to you. Tom wasn't sure where you'd be by the time his letter arrived so sends his love via Bobby.

The boys are keeping me busy here, but the older ones have stepped up in Bobby's absence and are helping with the younger ones. Poor little Sam has been moping around like nobody's business since Annie left. The other boys have been teasing him about it, but he's that maudlin, even their teasing doesn't seem to rouse him. Hopefully, he'll get over it soon or it will be a long few months!

I went to see Sally and Roy yesterday, both send their love. Roy's still hobbling around. Sally took him to the doctor, but they've said there's nothing to be done. As for Sally, her hands are playing her up something rotten. Let's hope it warms up soon and her joints ease up with the weather. The arrangement Tom made with the neighbours seems to work well. Mrs Greene has been popping in every day and taking meals round several times a week. Sally was gushing about how helpful and kind Mrs Greene is. I had to bite my tongue, knowing how much Tom's forking out for her so-called kindness.

Anyway, I'd best get on as the bairns need their supper, but I'll write again soon. I hope it won't be too long till you're home. In the meantime, give my husband a kiss from me, and one for yours too, if you like.

Love, Kitty

Helen walked into the kitchen and gave Marnie a warm smile. "Is that a letter from your Tom?"

"No," said Marnie. "It's from my friend Kitty. Her husband's first mate on Tom's boat. Apparently, they're delayed getting some repairs done. They should be back on course now. Do you have any paper so I can write back?"

"Of course," said Helen. She moved to a drawer and pulled out writing paper and a pen. "When you're finished, I'll show you where the post office is. There's another Lowestoft family staying there, the Clements. Do you know them?"

"The name's familiar and I'm sure I'd recognise the faces. I have a feeling the youngest Clements child is the same age as my Annie."

"My friend Margaret has a Lowestoft woman and her three daughters lodging with her. Oh, what are their names?" Helen tapped her fingers against her chin. "Oh, yes, the James family. Then there's the Millar family staying at the Sea View boarding house. A family of four, they are. George Millar's been coming down here since he was a young lad and it was his father going out to sea. Now he's here with his own family. His dad's long gone, but his mother comes down for a few weeks each year when the weather warms up a bit."

"Oh, yes, I know George's wife Celia fairly well. She used to help my friend Kitty out with the gutting if they were ever short of a pair of hands. I hadn't realised the Millars would be here. The decision for us to come down with Tom was so last minute, there wasn't time to find out which other families would do the same. Do you know if any other Lowestoft families are here this year?"

"There aren't as many as there used to be. Quite a few have gone to Fleetwood this year. More money to be made up there, apparently. We still get the regulars, and of course, a lot of local women have married Lowestoft men over the years."

"That sounds like Lowestoft. There are plenty of Scots who came down either with the boats or as herring girls and married into local families. It occasionally happened on the island where I grew up, but not so much as it's a much smaller place."

"It's funny, isn't it," said Helen. "We're from all ends of the country, but there are all these invisible threads linking us to one another. It's the way of fishing, I suppose. Now, why don't you get that letter written, and we'll take it up to the post office after having a bite to eat."

Chapter 27

January, 1939

Wrapped up against the cold, Marnie, Helen and Annie set off away from the harbour. A fierce wind chased them along the street, Helen and Marnie each holding on to one of Annie's hands as angry blasts buffeted her small body. Heads down, there was little chance to take in their surroundings, the weather putting paid to any hope of dawdling.

"Here we are," said Helen, stopping outside an imposing red-brick building. They hurried inside, breathing a sigh of relief as the door shut out the weather behind them. "Morning, Mary."

"Morning, Helen. Who's this then?" The postmistress stood with her hands on her hips, a wide smile on her face and a twinkle in her eye.

"This is Marnie and Annie, they're from Lowestoft."

"Ah, you must be Tom's wife. He told me all about you when he was here last year. I thought he was exaggerating when he told me how pretty you were, but it seems he was right. Now, maid," said Mary, walking around the counter and holding out a glass jar to Annie. "Try one of these. If that's all right with your mother?"

Marnie nodded, and Annie plunged her small hand into the jar of boiled sweets. Annie popped the sweet in her mouth and began studying items in the shop, finding the sweets and stationery more enticing than the company of adults.

With Annie happily looking at a display of postcards, Marnie paid for the postage on three letters, one for Kitty, one for Jimmy, and another for Sally and Roy. "Annie, would you like me to buy you one of those postcards and you can send it to Nanny and Granddad?"

Annie picked a card from the stand and carried it to the till.

"A lovely choice," said Mary, holding up the painting of boats in the harbour. "Now, as Helen probably said, I have a family from Lowestoft staying with me. Would you like to go up and see them?"

"I wouldn't want to intrude."

"Oh, you wouldn't be. Mr Clements will be climbing the walls, desperate to get out on his boat, and poor Mrs Clements will be grateful for the distraction." Mary leaned over the counter and added in an exaggerated whisper, "Mrs Clements reckons he's like a bear with a sore head when the weather stops him going to sea. And all too fond of a drink, too. Go on, you go up and make yourselves known to them."

It was with some trepidation that Marnie and Annie climbed the stairs, leaving Helen behind to catch up on local gossip courtesy of Mary the postmistress. Marnie trusted it was early enough in the day to find Mr Clements sober and hoped they wouldn't stumble on a scene of marital disharmony.

In the event, the Clements were nothing like Mary had described. The woman who answered the door to Marnie was a petite brunette with a wide smile. Marnie introduced herself, and Mrs Clements ("call me Angela") invited them into a large sitting-room, tall windows leaving the room bright despite the dull day.

Mr Clements, or James, as he insisted Marnie call him, was sitting in an armchair, a newspaper spread across his lap. At his feet, two young boys were playing with a train set, and seemed content to let Annie join in.

"So, Mary sent you up here to check up on us, did she? She's got a big old heart, but is always sniffing around for gossip to share in the shop. I got tiddly one evening, just one, and now she's telling all and sundry I have a problem with the drink." He laughed, folding his paper and laying it on the coffee table.

Marnie smiled, noticing the cup beside James was filled with tea, and nothing stronger. "I think she thought it would be nice for two Lowestoft families to meet."

"She's not wrong. This place used to feel like an extension of Lowestoft back in the day, but there's not so many of us around now. Is this your first time in Padstow?" James asked.

"Yes, it is, although my husband Tom has been before. Do you know him? Tom Hearn."

"Ah, yes, Tom. I know him well. We went to school together many moons ago. It sounds like they've had a hard journey getting here. We saw them just before they docked in Southampton. Did they get the repairs done that they needed?"

"I'm not sure if they're back on the water yet."

"There's a weather front forecast for next week, so as long as they get here before the storms, they'll be grand. How long are you staying for?"

"I'm not sure."

"You must stay until May," said Angela, carrying a tray of tea and biscuits into the room. "Have you heard about the Padstow May Day celebrations?"

"Tom told me a little about them," said Marnie.

James let out a hearty laugh. "I'm not surprised he only told you a little. He probably didn't remember much. From what I recall, he and Bobby started drinking early morning, and only stopped when they collapsed into their beds late that night."

"James," said Angela. "Don't be speaking badly of Tom. Everyone has a skinful on May Day, even the women."

"It sounds... wonderful?" said Marnie, thinking how much of Tom's life she'd missed out on. He was right to suggest she accompany him this time, not least so she could keep an eye on him and Bobby when they reached port.

"How old is Annie?"

"Four, nearly five."

"So she'd be in Albert's class at school. Will you be sending her to the local school?"

"I hadn't really thought about it."

"Oh, you should. The teachers are wonderful and more than used to the comings and goings of fishing families. It doesn't seem like your daughter will struggle to make friends."

As they chatted about home and mutual acquaintances, Marnie felt any homesickness fade. From what Kitty said in her letter, all was well at home, and she needn't worry about Sally and Roy. Marnie resolved to make the most of the adventure she was on.

Chapter 28

January, 1939

While Marnie was grateful to Helen for the obvious joy she took in looking after Annie, and however much she enjoyed the unburdening of parental responsibilities, she wasn't used to having so much time on her hands.

"Would you mind if I pop out for a stroll?" asked Marnie. "I don't feel I've got my bearings yet and I could do with some fresh air."

"Of course not," said Helen. "Dinner won't be for another hour. Are you alright if Annie stays with me? She seems very settled with her work."

"Of course not, so long as she's no bother to you?"

Marnie watched as Annie's hands worked with increasing speed, the scarf she was knitting almost covering her knees. Despite the many dropped stitches, it was more accomplished in size than the five rows Marnie had knitted before putting her efforts down the previous evening in favour of a book.

As she stepped out of the cottage, the cold evening air bit into Marnie's skin. Storms were forecast, and the air crackled with the promise of thunder. The tide was in and the harbour's water lay ominously still, the few docked boats silent, waiting for the onslaught. *Just like the world*, thought Marnie, remembering the gloomy news from Europe which had dominated Richard's Sunday paper.

Cottages, houses and shops huddled around the harbour, surrounding Marnie and adding to the oppressive feel of the air. She followed the loop of the harbour wall, spotting a narrow path creeping upwards, almost hidden by skeleton-like bushes and a burst of yellow furze. Halfway up the slope she paused, struggling for breath. Her fingers and toes screamed with the sting of cold, but the hill had brought some warmth. The arm of her coat caught the sweat on her face, smudging it across her skin in a sticky sheen.

Marnie turned to admire the view. Turquoise water melted into green as the harbour water met with the rushing tides of the estuary. A cough startled her, and she spun around, face to face with the man who had admonished her the week before.

"It's you."

"Nice way to greet a fellow."

Marnie huffed and looked at the path in front of her. Someone would have to give way and she was damned sure it wouldn't be her.

"Perhaps if you weren't so rude to me at our first meeting, I would be more friendly at our second."

Jack Tristan's hair caught the dying sun, making it look as though it were on fire. He tilted his head, his stare adding to the heat in her face. A pipe sat between his lips, hanging languidly down and emitting occasional puffs of smoke that swirled in the freezing evening air.

"Like I said, you should be careful around the water, especially with young 'uns in tow. The sea's a dangerous place."

Marnie pushed back her shoulders and looked him square in the eye. "I'll have you know I grew up on an island surrounded by sea. I now live in Lowestoft, just a stone's throw from the water. If anyone knows about the sea and its dangers, it's me."

To Marnie's horror, Jack laughed. "Got a right mouth on you, haven't you? I wondered where that funny accent of yours was from."

"There's nothing funny about the way I speak."

Jack continued to laugh. If she could've got past him, Marnie would have happily stormed off. But the furze on either side of the path had her trapped, and she wouldn't retrace her steps because of a rude fisherman.

"A little gypsy, aren't you? What brings you here, so far from home?"

"War and fish."

"You're staying with my sister, I believe."

"Aye. Now, if you don't mind, I would like to continue that way," said Marnie, pointing to the path which he was blocking.

"Yes, ma'am," said Jack, taking a long pull on his pipe and turning his body to the side. He raised his arm with a flourish, showing that Marnie should pass.

She strode past him, keeping her eyes firmly ahead.

"Welcome to Padstow," he called to her retreating back, his body engulfed in pipe smoke.

"Grateful, I'm sure," said Marnie, pressing on up the hill quicker than she would have liked. As she walked, she heard his laughter following her.

As if moving to the other side of the country wasn't tricky enough, she had made an enemy within a week of arriving. Marnie paused on the hill's summit and stared out to sea. "Where are you, Tom? I need you here." There was no one to hear her but the gulls who swooped gracefully on invisible currents.

Across the estuary lay a huddle of houses, smoke rising from chimneys, the squat buildings protected by wide sand dunes. The light was dimming, night creeping into day, dusk setting in. The view reminded her of the sepia photographs she had seen. Soft reddish-brown tones fading to grey. The last of the sun reflected on still water, like a sequinned shawl spread out across the sands.

Marnie couldn't deny the beauty of her new home. Even through stubborn eyes, she could see Cornwall's appeal. But just because a place was beautiful, didn't mean it could become home.

When Marnie returned to the cottage, Helen was in the kitchen serving pie onto plates.

"Just in time," she said. "Did you have a pleasant walk?"

"It would have been, only I met your brother again."

Rather than being offended by Marnie's rudeness, Helen laughed. "Don't mind our Jack. Like I said, his bark's worse than his bite. What he needs is a good woman to take him in hand, but he won't even entertain the notion."

"I can't imagine any woman putting up with him."

"Ah, but you don't know him like I do. There's a big old heart buried beneath that gruffness."

"Then why doesn't he marry?"

"Our parents weren't what you'd describe as a happily married couple. Jack says living with them put him off marriage for life. That's the official line. The truth of the matter is he had his heart broken as a young man. He was engaged to a local girl, madly in love they were."

"What happened?"

"The poor maid caught tuberculosis. She was only twenty when she died. Jack closed his heart off after that. Said no woman could ever compare. He's a sworn bachelor, and seeing as he's already in his late forties, I can't see that changing. No, he's too set in his ways now. Here, can you mash up these spuds for me?"

Marnie took a pan from the stove and added butter and milk to turn the potatoes smooth. "Your parents didn't put you off marriage?"

"No. I've known Richard all my life. I told him I'd marry him when we were five years old. The poor man never had much say in the matter." Helen smiled, a far-off look in her eyes. "And you? What were your parents like?"

"No advertisement for marriage, that's for sure. Mind you, it didn't put most of my siblings off. My brother never married, though that's not to say he's lonely. He has a lady friend called Clara. They were childhood sweethearts, but various life events meant they've ended up on different sides of the country. Theirs is an unusual relationship, but it seems to work for them. I wondered if I'd ever marry myself, but then Tom walked into the department store one day and asked me if I'd go to the pictures with him. The rest, as they say, is history."

"You found yourself a good one there."

"I keep forgetting you know Tom. It must be strange having us here without him."

"Not at all. We're so used to comings and goings I take it all in my stride. I suspect it's far harder for you, being here without him."

"I miss him," said Marnie, surprising herself as she realised just how much that was true. "I'm used to him being off at sea, but coming here without him feels different. And now his boat's delayed. Goodness knows when we'll be reunited. I've not been the best wife to him and I was very grumpy about the move. Now I feel dreadful about the way I behaved."

"You? Grumpy? I can't imagine such a thing," said Helen, hiding a smirk.

Marnie laughed. "I think I get my fiery temper from my da. More's the pity. And if I'm not mistaken, I seem to have passed it down to my daughter. Perhaps you can douse the flame of temper while we're here? She's really taken to you."

"And I her." Helen's eyes drifted off somewhere far away.

"I think these potatoes are ready," said Marnie.

"Good. Richard? Annie? Supper's ready."

Richard walked through from the shop, pulling off his apron and washing his hands at the sink. The sound of scampering footsteps signalled Annie had also heard the call for food.

"A storm's on its way," said Richard, as they sat down to eat. "Best make sure everything's locked up tight before we go to bed tonight."

"I don't like storms," said Annie.

"Don't you worry. You'll be perfectly safe in here. It will be a bit of bluster then over and done with before you know it." Helen squeezed Annie's hand, but she didn't look convinced.

"Can I sleep in with you tonight?" Annie asked Marnie.

"No, your bed is right beside mine, so there's no need to invade my space. I'll not have your claws jabbing me all night long."

"I don't have claws," said Annie, pouting. The adults around the table laughed.

"Do you know what I have?" asked Richard.

"No."

"I have... tickle fingers!"

Annie screeched as Richard tickled her under the chin. Marnie caught the look in Helen's eye as she watched her husband play. There was a longing in them that made Marnie wonder if bringing a child to the house had opened a long-healed wound.

Annie gobbled down her food, thoughts of storms forgotten as she enjoyed Helen's superior cooking skills. As Marnie ate, she decided a few cookery lessons from Helen couldn't hurt. Both Tom and Annie would be grateful if she expanded her repertoire beyond the five simple dishes she'd mastered.

"Bath and bed," Marnie told her daughter.

"And story."

"Yes, of course, and story."

"I want Uncle Richard to tell me a story tonight."

"Oh, I see," said Marnie. "Are my stories not good enough for you anymore?" Her eyes twinkled as she teased her daughter.

"Your stories are good, but I've heard them all before. And Uncle Richard has a better voice for stories."

"Oh, does he now?" Marnie reached across and tickled her daughter.

"I'll tell you a bedtime story," said Richard, standing and taking a bow. "But before that, you need a good hose down. I'll leave the bath to your mother."

Later, bathed and in her pyjamas, Annie took Richard's hand and headed off to bed.

"He's wonderful with her," said Marnie, drying the dishes Helen had washed.

"He'd have made a wonderful father."

"Aye, he would. I hope Annie doesn't run rings around him," said Marnie, trying to lighten the mood.

"Ah, he'll cope. Have you thought about schooling for Annie? I know the local school has taken on several Lowestoft children these past weeks."

"Yes, Angela Clements mentioned sending Annie to school. Do you think they'd have room for her?"

"I'm certain they would. They're used to numbers fluctuating over the fishing season. I love having her around the house, but it would do her good to be with other children. You never know, she'll probably recognise a fair few from back home."

"In that case, I'll go tomorrow. She's a bright spark, and although still very young, I think school could be a wonderful challenge for her."

"I'll come with you, if you like. The headmistress is an old friend of mine. We went to the school ourselves as youngsters."

"Thank you. With Annie in school, I could help more in the shop and around the house. You know, I think I may have been too quick to doubt this move. I have a feeling Padstow could be the making of us."

Chapter 29

January, 1939

C old feet woke Marnie, pressing against her legs, a trembling body folding itself into her arms. She rubbed sleep from her eyes and pulled her daughter in close. Sounds of nature's orchestra filled her ears. The windows rattled against their frames, the rain tapping a drumbeat against them. From the fireplace, the wind sang a mournful song of storms and trouble at sea.

Marnie reached across to the bedside table and switched on the lamp. A dull orange glow turned brighter as the bulb warmed, flooding the room with light. Despite being closed, the windows' thick curtains danced a jig as blasts of air filtered through any gaps they could find.

"I don't like storms," said Annie, pulling blankets over her head.

"Don't worry, bairn. You're safe in here. The storm can't reach us through the walls or the windows." A howl redolent of an injured animal swooped down the chimney breast and Annie screamed. "It's all right, it's only the wind. She's singing to you, sending her song down from the sky."

"I don't like the wind's song. It sounds like she's crying."

Marnie bent her neck and kissed the top of Annie's head. "Hush, bairn. Listen out for the beauty held within the song."

Despite her reassurances, Marnie felt a kernel of fear growing inside her. She knew winds such as these. She knew the damage Mother

Nature could wreak when angry. As a child, she'd prayed for the wind to carry her father's boat far away, dash it against rocks, free them from the daily torment he trailed in his wake.

But the wind never proved a friend. After each storm was spent, her bedraggled father would stagger home, a little more arrogant, a little more sure he could fight nature and win. Those days after a storm were the worst. He'd drink a toast to life, turning his vengeance against the weather on the soft flesh of his family. No, the wind had never carried Alex Watson away. Marnie's prayers had remained unanswered.

As any child born to fisherfolk knows, Mother Nature is all-powerful. She does what she pleases. She can provide sunshine and sustenance, sustain life with golden fields of corn and life-giving rains. Yet she can also be a cruel mistress. In an instant, she can turn on men who search for spoils in her seas. She can upturn a boat with the smallest breath, form monstrous waves which swallow boats whole, or crush their fragile wooden bones beneath frothy white teeth.

Marnie kissed her daughter once more and climbed out of bed, pulling on her dressing gown over her shoulders. Despite Annie's protests, Marnie opened the curtains to reveal the full horror of what lay beyond. The rain was its own curtain, blurring her view of the outside world. The clock on the wall told Marnie that the sun had risen, yet outside the world lay in darkness.

With her forehead pressed against the cold glass, Marnie stared out. No clouds scudded across the sky. What lay above them was a thick wall of black. An angry, frightening sky, which stole daylight and glowered down. Marnie could just make out a plume of white, spitting angrily above the harbour walls and leaving rivulets of black water running along the village streets.

My God, thought Marnie, *Tom is out in this*. Above the noise of weather, Marnie heard snuffles and snores coming from under the blankets. It was a relief Annie could sleep through it. With Tom out at sea, no rest would come to Marnie until his safe return.

Marnie opened the bedroom door with a quiet click. She reached back for her slippers and trod silently downstairs to the kitchen. She found Richard and Helen grim-faced, cups of tea growing cold as they sat at the kitchen table.

"Morning," said Helen. When she looked up at Marnie, her face was white, the tell-tale puffy eyes telling of many tears shed.

Marnie walked over to Helen and put a hand on her shoulder. "You're worried about your brother?"

Helen nodded, and a fat tear dropped to the table beneath. It sat like a pearl against the cloth, before seeping into the fabric and leaving a dark stain.

"I told him not to go out last night. I warned him about the weather."

"But of course he went anyway. Bleddy fool," said Richard, walking over to the stove and refilling the kettle. "Tea, Marnie?"

"Thanks."

Marnie pulled out a chair and joined Helen at the table. "I'm worried Tom is out in this, too."

"Oh, you poor thing. Of course you are. I'm sorry, maid, I was so wrapped up in my own worries I didn't stop to think about you. Hopefully, they have put into harbour somewhere and are waiting for the weather to pass."

"Hopefully," said Marnie, the kernel of fear growing in size by the minute. "Why did your brother go out when he knew the weather was going to turn?"

"He's a pig-headed fool, that's why," muttered Richard.

"That's unfair," said Helen, frowning at her husband. "We've had a rough few years with the fish stocks. It's led to the fishermen around here taking risks they wouldn't have a few years back."

"I think it's the same everywhere," said Marnie. "When I first arrived in Lowestoft, the town was flush with the success of a record catch. Those days have never been replicated, but they keep trying."

"Do you have other family putting to sea, or is it just Tom?"

"I have a nephew up north still clinging on to the trade, but I don't hear from my island family much these days. My brother is a headmaster. The first in the family to make a decent living away from fish. I wish I could have seen my da's face when he found out." Marnie managed a small chuckle, despite the worry lying heavy on all their shoulders.

"Is your brother in Lowestoft?"

"Close enough. I miss him."

"I bet you do," said Helen, covering Marnie's hand with her own. "Is Annie still asleep?"

"Aye. She woke with the storm but fell back to sleep once she'd got under my warm blankets."

"That's probably for the best. A frightened child won't help us today."

"Are you opening the shop?"

"Not today," said Richard. "I don't imagine there'll be many folk about on a day such as this."

"Why don't we give the place a spring clean?" asked Helen. "It will do none of us any good sitting here worrying all day."

They agreed the day would be best served spending the time on a spring clean. Marnie was grateful for something to do. Richard had estimated Tom would be somewhere around Cape Cornwall, so even if there was news, she wouldn't hear it soon.

When Annie woke and heard of the plan, she was keen to be involved. Helen set her up with a feather duster, much to the little girl's delight, and the four of them quickly got to work. For a busy shop, it was surprisingly clean. A bit of dust here and there, but nothing too strenuous. Helen used the opportunity to reorganise the shelves, despite Richard's protests that customers liked things just as they were.

Marnie scrubbed wooden shelves, Annie sat on Richard's shoulders for the harder-to-reach spiders' webs, and Helen persisted in reordering despite Richard's frequent protests. All four ignored the banging door as the wind tried desperately to free it from its hinges. They chatted about inane matters, no one wanting to broach the fear they all carried inside.

They were considering pausing for a bite to eat when the back door slammed, making them jump. Annie screamed as a blood-soaked man stumbled into the shop, collapsing against the counter and knocking a pot of buttons to the floor.

Chapter 30

January, 1939

"Jack," said Helen, rushing to her brother. "Richard, help me."

Richard dropped Annie from his arms and raced to help his brother-in-law.

"I'll fetch a bowl of water," said Marnie, grabbing hold of Annie's hands and dragging her from the frightening scene before them.

"What's happened to the man?" Annie asked, tears in her eyes.

"It looks like he's been hurt in the storm. He could walk here, though, so I'm sure he will be all right."

"He looked scary."

"I know," said Marnie, kneeling beside her daughter and taking her hands. "He'll be back to normal once he's cleaned up, I promise. Why don't you take your knitting upstairs? I'll come and fetch you when the man's better."

Annie looked around her, weighing up whether it was less frightening to be alone upstairs, or with the bloodied man downstairs. She chose the former, and with shaking hands, grabbed her knitting from the table and ran upstairs to the bedroom.

Marnie boiled the kettle and filled a bowl. She added cold so as not to add burns to Jack's injuries and carried the water through to Helen.

"How's he doing?"

Jack was propped up in a chair, Helen stemming the bleeding on his head with a rag she'd been using for cleaning. She looked at Marnie; her face was full of concern.

"Let me see." Marnie stepped forward and examined the wound on Jack's forehead. "It hasn't gone too deep." She ran her fingers over his head, checking for any further cuts or bruises. "There's a right old egg forming on the back of his head. Do you feel dizzy, Jack?"

Jack looked up at Marnie, wincing at the movement of his head. "No. My head's banging, but not dizzy."

"Good. Helen, put that dirty old cloth away and let me see to this." Marnie rinsed a clean cloth in the water and began dabbing at the cut. The bowl's water soon turned pink, but by the time she had finished, all traces of blood were confined to the wound and Jack was looking human again. "Richard, could you fetch Jack a glass of water, please? I think he could probably do with a brandy as well."

At the mention of brandy, Jack's lips curled upwards before settling once more into a grimace as another wave of pain hit.

"Are you able to make it upstairs to the sitting room?" asked Marnie.

Jack gave a small nod. Richard appeared with two glasses, one filled with clear liquid, one brown. Marnie waited for Jack to finish them before instructing Richard to help Jack stand. Between them, they hauled Jack up the stairs to the sitting room. They laid him out on a sofa and Helen fetched a blanket to tuck him in.

"Where did you learn your nursing skills?" Helen asked Marnie once Jack was settled and snoring gently.

"My mam met with quite a few accidents at the hands of my da. It became second nature, tending to cuts and bruises."

Shock played on Helen's face. "Did he ever hurt you?"

"No. My brother took the worst of it while he was living with us. Once he left, Da's focus returned to my mam. I got out of there before he thought to have a crack at me. Anyway, on a happier subject, Jack looks to be all right. We'll need to keep an eye on that head injury, but at least the cut to his face isn't as bad as it looks."

"I'll kill him when he wakes up. If he'd only listened to me..."

"These men will do what they must do. Perhaps one day they'll learn that women always know best."

"Perhaps," said Helen, leaning over her brother and kissing his cheek. "Though I doubt most men are as stubborn as my Jack."

Chapter 31
January, 1939

J ack was to spend the night in the cottage. Whilst Marnie felt sympathy for his injuries, she had not fully forgiven him for the humiliation and disliked the thought of them spending a night under the same roof. She was careful to avoid him, feigning a headache that saw her confined to her bedroom for the evening. Annie refused to leave Jack's side, gazing adoringly at the man who had saved her life. Despite his injuries, Jack seemed content to indulge Annie's questions, and even from her attic room, Marnie could hear the girl's laughter floating up the stairs.

When Helen finally dragged Annie upstairs at eight o'clock, the child was full of praise for Jack and his funny stories. It took an age to calm her, a book proving the only thing that would soothe her excitable mind. Marnie read to Annie until the girl's eyelids drooped.

With Annie settled, Marnie picked up her knitting then threw it back down in its basket. Knitting was not for her. She was too impatient for the slow progress and frequent corrections needed each time she dropped a stitch. An idea formed in her mind. There was something she could do to occupy her fingers, something she could present Helen and Richard with as a thank-you when their time came to depart.

The wall clock told her it was ten p.m. Marnie had heard Helen and Richard heading to bed some time before, so she hoped the coast would be clear downstairs. Marnie checked Annie was fast asleep, slipped her feet into her slippers, and crept downstairs.

"I thought you'd be asleep, what with your bad head and all..."

Marnie jumped out of her skin at the sight of a dark figure hunched over the kitchen table. "You."

"I have a name, you know."

"I know. What are you still doing up? Shouldn't you be resting after your injuries?"

"I'm on the lifeboat crew and there's every chance we'll be called out on a night such as this. There seemed little point going to bed, only to be woken in the small hours. What are you doing sneaking around in the dark?"

"I'm not sneaking. I'm looking for something."

"Oh?"

"Aye. I know Helen keeps a bag of scrap fabric from the shop. I had an idea to use it to make her a present. A thank-you for her hospitality."

"Ah, so you're making my sister a present from her own bag of rubbish. How thoughtful."

Marnie bristled at Jack's rudeness. She disliked the mocking tone of his voice. "Perhaps you hadn't noticed, but fishing families aren't exactly rolling in money. At least not where I come from. Besides, a homemade gift holds more value as it comes from the heart."

Jack laughed. "I'm only teasing. What exactly are you planning to make?"

"Never you mind."

Jack laughed again. "Well, I hope you'll show me the finished product. I'm intrigued." He stood and walked towards her. As he brushed past, Marnie shuddered. Jack had an uncanny way of unsettling her, of riling her, and she didn't like it.

"Here you go," said Jack, returning with a wicker basket. "Is this what you need?"

"Aye, it is." Marnie took the basket from him, careful that their fingers didn't touch. The kitchen was in darkness, but she could tell Jack's mouth was curled in a smirk. "Thank you for finding it. Now I shall return to bed. Do try to get some sleep. You took a right knocking today and you'll recover faster with some rest."

"Thank you for your concern. I'll grab a few winks down here, don't you worry."

"Very well. Goodnight, Jack."

"Goodnight, Marnie."

Marnie climbed the stairs, wondering why she felt so ill at ease in Jack's company. It wasn't like her. She was stubborn, clearheaded, not used to feeling unsettled by men.

In her bedroom, Marnie took out scissors, needle and thread, and laid them beside the basket of scraps on her bed. Her thoughts tumbled around like the waves rolling in beyond her window. She told herself it was the storm keeping her awake, refusing to acknowledge the deep fear for Tom held in her heart.

At midnight, Marnie heard a door slam. She sat up straighter, her skin tingling, her mind alert. No other noise followed, and she put the banging down to the wind. In the watery light of an encroaching morning, Marnie finally laid her work down and gave in to sleep.

Chapter 32

January, 1939

On arriving in the kitchen for breakfast, Marnie found no Jack occupying a chair. Instead, Helen sat with her head in her hands, Richard rubbing her shoulders, his brow creased.

"What's happened?" asked Marnie.

"Jack was called out to the lifeboat last night," said Richard.

Helen's shoulders shook as silent tears flowed from her cheeks, pooling on the table below.

"What time was this?"

"Around midnight. Usually, the crew would be back by now."

"I thought I heard something," said Marnie, more to herself than anyone else. "Do you know any more about the call-out?"

Richard shook his head. "Jack left a note to say he was off on the lifeboat, but gave no further detail. I suppose we'll learn more on his return."

"If he returns," whispered Helen.

"Where's Annie?" asked Marnie. "She wasn't in her bed when I woke."

"She's fine," said Richard. "I set her up with some paper and colouring pencils in the shop. I thought it best she wasn't here to witness Helen's distress."

"I can take her out for a walk?" said Marnie.

"No need for that. The wind's dying down, thank God, but it's still very wet out there. The pair of you catching a chill won't help us."

"I'm going to the harbour to look out for them," said Helen. She stood, scraping back her chair, and reached for her coat.

"Helen, the same applies to you. You'll be no good to Jack if you catch a chill."

"Stop your fussing, Richard. You sound like an old woman."

It was the first time Marnie had heard a cross word pass between the couple. Richard stepped back as though slapped. "I'll check on Annie," he said, marching out of the room with a sideways glance towards his wife.

Helen walked to the sink and leaned her hands against it, head bowed. "Sorry," she said.

"I don't think it's me who needs an apology," said Marnie.

"You're right. I'll talk to Richard later. I know he's only looking out for me, but fussing's the last thing I need today."

"Why don't I come with you?" said Marnie. "We can huddle together for warmth if need be."

Helen smiled. "Alright then."

The two women pulled on their woollen coats and each grabbed an umbrella from the coat stand. "I'm off," called Helen. "Marnie's coming with me. We're wrapped up warm and will come back if we get too cold."

There was no reply from Richard, so Helen opened the door. Marnie shivered as a blast of cold, damp air hit them. "It's like being back in Lowestoft," she said, pulling up the collar of her coat and bracing herself.

Helen and Marnie fought their way to the harbour. The wind was picking up again and the sea in front of them looked angry, curling back its gums before charging at the harbour walls ready to bite. Women gathered along the harbour wall, clinging to each other, whether for warmth or comfort, none could tell.

Helen approached a wizened old man who stood trying to light his pipe, the wind whipping away his flame before it got anywhere near the pipe's bowl.

"Morning, Arthur. Any news?"

"None yet, maid. Tis the worst north-easterly I've seen in many a year."

"What about the boat in distress?"

"From what I heard, a steamer landed herself in trouble down St Ives way. The St Ives crew called for help and our lads obliged. More than that, I don't know. But with the wind set to calm, it shouldn't be long before our boys are safely back in harbour."

Marnie felt a chill run through her bones at the old sea-dog's words. Wasn't Tom in a steamer that should have been heading north of Cape Cornwall by now? A sinking feeling enveloped her, and she turned her attention back to Helen to distract herself.

"Helen, look. Isn't that a boat on the horizon?"

The two women watched as a tiny boat grew in size, slowly moving closer as it navigated the treacherous waters of the estuary. Shouts rang out around them, "It's them! It's them!"

As the boat neared Padstow, the onlookers could see she was in terrible shape. The hull lurched back and forth, straining against the men's best efforts to bring her back to the harbour.

"Looks like she's in trouble. Come on, lads, come on." Arthur's teeth tightened against his pipe stem as he wiped rain from his face and scrunched his eyes to view the boat better. "Come on, lads, come on," he kept muttering.

Helen's hand gripped tight to Marnie's arm, her body frozen in place as she held her breath. Marnie pulled Helen close, wrapping an arm around her waist. Their umbrellas lay unused on the ground beside them, useless against the north-easterly that, in its death throes, hit them with angry bursts.

Through the curtain of rain, the boat moved close enough that the men's faces could be seen, their teeth bared as they fought against wind, rain, and their broken vessel. Grim expressions showed from beneath hats and poked out above sou'westers. Helen counted.

"They're all there," she said, loosening her grip on Marnie's arm. "They're all there. All of them. Jack is safe and sound."

Marnie felt Helen's body soften beneath her grasp as relief washed over her. The lifeboat was now close enough for the men's safety to be confirmed. It was the result they had all hoped for, but dared not believe in.

Bodies clustered together as the lifeboat drew up against its mooring and its bedraggled crew heaved themselves up onto dry land. Helen rushed through the crowd, gripping on to her brother as though she'd never let go.

From above Helen's head, Marnie caught Jack's eye. He held her gaze, his eyes filling with sorrow, his mouth turned down in pity. Marnie froze, the noise of joyful reunions fading around her. Jack untangled himself from his sister's embrace and stepped towards her.

"No," she wanted to shout. "No." Her words lay silent on her tongue, her throat tight with fear. Jack's face told her everything she needed to know. Marnie stepped backwards, but Jack's strides were greater than hers and he reached her before she could turn and run.

"Marnie," he said, gripping her wrists and forcing her feet to still. "Marnie."

Marnie turned her head from him, not wanting to see his pity, not wanting to hear the words on his tongue.

"Marnie, I'm so sorry. It's Tom..."

Chapter 33

January, 1939

Marnie's slim body was held up by strong arms. She curled into herself, the arms that held her lowering her to the cold, damp ground. Her hands scrabbled at the stone beneath her fingers, an unearthly scream tearing through her mouth as a horror that felt close to death consumed her. Not her Tom. Not her Tom.

Seeing the commotion on the harbourside from his window, Richard had brought Annie out to welcome back the lifeboat and take part in what he assumed were celebrations. The look on his face when he saw Marnie fall to the ground was one of shock. He tried to pull Annie back, but she slipped from his grasp and ran towards her mother.

Helen looked from Marnie to her daughter, unsure who was most in need of comfort. Annie couldn't possibly understand the cause of her mother's distress, yet her bottom lip wobbled in sympathy, her limbs shaking with fear of the unknown. Helen gripped Annie's hand and tried to pull her away.

"What's happening to Mummy? Why is she on the ground? Mummy? Mummy?"

Annie tugged against Helen's hand, trying to fight her way to Marnie, but Helen held tight, knowing that any proximity to the woman flailing on the ground would only bring further distress.

"Come away, maid. Come away."

Annie put up a good fight, but Helen's hours spent hauling crates of vegetables had given her a strength not visible to the casual observer. She picked up the squirming child, pinning back the arms that threatened to hit and scratch.

"Richard, you stay with Jack and help him get Marnie home. I'm taking Annie back to the cottage."

"Are you sure you can manage?"

"Yes. This little thing's no match for me." Helen managed a smile that came out more like a grimace.

Annie tried a new tactic. She stopped her flailing and held her entire body taut until Helen was forced to sling the child over her shoulder and remove her back to the house as though carrying a heavy sack of coal.

"Right, sit down. I'm going to make you some cocoa." Helen bundled Annie into an armchair and watched as the girl's eyes turned to the door. Helen moved with speed, reaching the door and turning the key in the lock before Annie could attempt an escape. With the key pocketed, Helen crossed the room and crouched down beside Annie's sullen body.

"Listen, maid. Your mummy has had a shock. She will come to you soon, but she's unwell and you need to let me, Uncle Richard and Uncle Jack help her feel better. Once she's better, she'll explain all that's gone on."

Annie pouted, refusing to catch Helen's eye. Helen ran a hand up and down Annie's legs, feeling her muscles loosen as the stroking soothed. "I want Mummy."

"I know, I know. Look at me." Helen cupped a hand beneath Annie's chin and turned her face. "Look at me, Annie. Do I ever tell lies?"

Annie narrowed her eyes and studied Helen's face. "I don't think so."

"I can tell you for certain that I don't. I'm telling you the truth now. Hell, I'll even promise if it will make you feel better?"

Annie nodded.

"Very well. I promise that as soon as your mummy is well enough, she will come to you. She will explain what made her unwell and you will know everything. Do you understand?"

Helen felt her heart break in two as Annie's eyes filled with tears. "I want to help her."

"I know you do, but right now it's a job for the grownups, alright? You'll be able to help soon enough, I promise. But for today, I need you to take your knitting up to my bedroom. I can get you some colouring pencils too if you like?"

"Yes, please."

"Good girl. Now you go find your knitting, and I'll bring a cup of cocoa up to you."

"I'm going to knit a blanket for Mummy. That will make her feel better."

"I'm sure it will. That's a very kind thought, Annie," said Helen, ruffling the girl's hair and returning to the stove.

Helen got Annie ensconced in her bedroom and went downstairs to wait for the men's return. She wasn't waiting long before they appeared, carrying a bedraggled, tear-stained Marnie between them.

Helen rushed to them, easing Marnie into a chair. "Pour her a brandy, Richard. She's had a terrible shock."

Marnie's body rocked back and forth in her chair, water dripping from her hair and pooling on the tiles below. Helen peeled off Marnie's sodden jacket and wrapped a towel around her shoulders.

"Jack, get a bath going, would you? I need to get Marnie warmed up."

"What will I do without him?" cried Marnie, her knuckles turning white as she gripped hold of the towel. "What will I do, Helen? What will become of us?"

Helen stroked a hand against Marnie's wet hair. "There's no need to be thinking of such matters now, maid. You're welcome here as long as you need. You concentrate on your daughter, and mending that broken heart of yours. Everything else can wait."

Marnie buried her head into Helen's shoulder and dampened Helen's dress with her tears. She stayed there until Jack announced the bath was ready. Helen led Marnie to the bathroom, peeling off further layers of damp clothing.

"Would you like me to stay with you?" Helen asked. Marnie shook her head. "Alright, maid, I'll be just outside the door. I'll fetch some dry clothes for you and you shout if there's anything else you need."

Chapter 34
January, 1939

Richard laid a cup of tea in front of Helen and Jack. They sat in silence, listening to the sound of Marnie's sobs coming from the other side of the bathroom door.

"Will she return to Lowestoft?" asked Jack, breaking the silence.

"I'm not sure that's a good idea given the mood in Europe," said Richard. "If my morning newspapers are to be believed, we're heading for war. I pray to God it can be avoided, but if war reaches our shores, Lowestoft will be a dangerous place for a woman and child. They suffered badly last time around. If it were up to me, Marnie would stay put for the time being."

"I agree," said Helen. "Other than her brother and in-laws, it doesn't sound like she has any family of her own up there. I'm sure she has friends, but at this time of year, half the Lowestoft fisherfolk will be down here or over in Milford Haven. No, I think it's best she stays with us until we know she's alright and won't be in any danger if she goes back."

Conversation halted as Marnie entered the kitchen. Her face was red and puffy, her hair damp. All the fight seemed to have left her, and she moved like an old woman, shuffling across the floor to take a seat at the table.

"Tell me what happened," said Marnie, turning to Jack.

"I don't think you want to hear that."

"Tell me."

Jack sighed and took a long draw on his pipe. His hand shook as he pulled it from his mouth. "Tom's steamer sent out a rocket distress signal. The St Ives crew were the first to attend, but we and others were also called upon. I tell you, the gales whipped up waves the like of which I've rarely seen. On their way to the distressed steamer, the St Ives lifeboat struck rocks by Godrevy lighthouse." Jack paused, swallowing down emotion to steady his voice. "The crew... the crew..."

Jack's shoulders heaved violently, and Helen wrapped an arm around his shoulder. He pushed it away, jumping from his seat and turning his back on the room to stare out of the window. He drew angry puffs from his pipe, the entire kitchen disappearing beneath its smoke. Helen walked to her brother and once more wrapped an arm around him.

"What happened, Jack?" she asked, her voice little more than a whisper.

Jack bent over the sink and splashed water across his face. "All crew but one perished. We were focussed on the steamer and were some way off from them. The waves were too fierce to allow a rescue." Jack coughed, clearing his throat and rolling his shoulders. "We reached the steamer and rescued three men with the aid of rocket apparatus. Once they were in the safety of our boat, they told us of their captain who'd been washed overboard moments before we arrived. One of them gave me his name and told me I must inform his wife." Jack turned to Marnie, his eyes glassy.

"Bobby. It was Bobby who thought of me."

"Yes," said Jack.

Marnie thought of Kitty, back in Lowestoft, fearing for the war and her precious sons. How misplaced her worry had been, how close she had come to losing her husband. A shot of jealousy ran through Marnie. Why Tom? Why did it have to be him? There were ten could've been taken, yet it was him washed into the depths. She stifled a scream as the full horror sank in.

Marnie blew her nose and brushed tears from her eyes. "I need to get word to Tom's parents. And I'd like my brother to hear the news from me. Jimmy has a telephone at the school. Could one of you come with me to the public telephone box? I'm not sure I have the strength to walk there by myself."

"Of course, maid. But don't you think it's best to leave that task till tomorrow? Let the news sink in before sharing it with others?"

Marnie shook her head. "No amount of hours will change the news. It's best I send word now."

"Very well," said Helen, pushing her chair back. "I'll take you."

"Thank you. And thank you, Jack, for your honesty and your bravery. I know Bobby well. His wife is my best friend. I'll make sure she hears of how you and your crew saved her husband. But, oh, the sacrifice of those poor St Ives men. I can't bear to think of all those families suffering the same as me." Helen rubbed Marnie's back, waiting for her tears to subside.

"Marnie, I don't wish to add to your woes, but Annie was very upset when we returned. I've sent her upstairs with her knitting and colouring pencils, but I promised her you'd speak to her."

Marnie struck up her sobbing, her shoulders shaking as tears fell. "How can I tell my daughter that she'll not be seeing her father again?"

"Perhaps I could do that for you," said Jack, who until then had remained silent.

"You? But Annie barely knows you."

"True. I'm sorry, it's a bad idea, I just thought that as I was there..."

"Perhaps Jack's right. It might be better Annie hears a factual account of what has happened. She's a bright little button, and will demand to know details even if we don't tell her."

"You'll remember she's only a child?" asked Marnie, looking up at Jack.

"Of course. I shall put things in simple, factual terms. But, Marnie, the news is bound to upset her. Will you go to her once she has heard it from me?"

Marnie nodded and Jack disappeared up the stairs, ready to change Annie's world and cause her to grow up too fast.

Chapter 35

January, 1939

Helen slipped the coat over Marnie's shoulders and did up the buttons as though assisting a child. Marnie's crying had ceased, replaced by a blank face, expressionless other than the occasional frown and fluttering of lips as she held back tears.

"Are you sure you won't wait until tomorrow?" Helen knew there was no getting through to her stubborn, grief-addled friend, but felt she had to try.

"I need to speak to Jimmy."

Helen sighed. "Alright then, come on."

Helen took Marnie's arm and guided her out of the cottage. Marnie leaned against Helen, unable to support her own weight after shock had stolen her energy and grief had ravaged her limbs.

As they walked past the harbour, Marnie turned her head away. How would she ever be able to look at the sea without drowning beneath the reminders of what had happened, and all she had lost?

"This way, maid. Almost there."

Helen led Marnie through the twisting streets until they reached a red telephone box standing beside a busy pub. Despite it being just after noon, the pub was full, local men buying rounds of drinks for the weary heroes of Padstow's lifeboat. From behind steamed-up windows came the sound of laughter, and men periodically bursting into song. Helen eyed Marnie, concerned that she seemed oblivious to all that was going on around her.

When they reached the telephone box, Helen took charge. From Marnie's pocket, she pulled the notebook with the number for the school written on it, from her own pocket she pulled a handful of coins. Helen propped Marnie up against the glass wall of the telephone box and dialled through to the exchange.

The phone rang and rang before a man's voice, out of breath and holding a tone of impatience, answered with a curt "yes?"

"Oh, hello, I wonder if it's possible to speak to the headmaster?"

"This is he, but if your call is not urgent, could I please request that you call back outside of school hours? I'm supposed to be teaching a class."

"Oh, I'm very sorry, but I'm afraid it is urgent. My name's Mrs Trevorn, and I'm calling from Padstow."

"Padstow? Is this about my sister?"

The man's voice had turned from brusque to anxious and Helen took a deep breath. "Yes, I'm afraid it is. She has received some terrible news. Hold on." Helen placed her phone over the receiver and turned to Marnie. "I've got hold of your brother. Would you like to speak to him or would you rather I told him?"

Without uttering a word, Marnie took the receiver from Helen's hand. She scrunched her face in order to stop tears falling.

"Hello? Marnie? Is that you?"

Marnie tried to speak, but it came out as a sob.

"Oh my goodness, Marnie. Whatever's happened?"

Marnie tried again, with little success.

"Marnie, you're scaring me. Can you pass me back to your friend?"

Marnie handed the telephone back to Helen, leaving the shelter of the telephone box and slumping to the ground against the wall of the pub.

"Hello? Hello?"

"Hello, this is Helen, again. I'm afraid Marnie's in no fit state to talk to you."

"Please, just tell me what's happened. Is it Annie? Oh, God, I couldn't bear it if..."

"It's Tom, Marnie's husband. His boat was caught in a storm last night and he was washed overboard."

"Wh... wh... what?"

Jimmy's voice had become a whisper. Helen heard a cough down the line as he tried to gain control of his emotions.

"I can't believe it. Not Tom. And Marnie? How is she?"

"Not good," said Helen, "but we're keeping a close eye on her. She wanted to inform you of the news straight away. If you ask me, she should be at home in bed, but you know what she's like."

"Do Tom's parents know?"

"Not yet."

"Would Marnie like me to tell them?"

Helen relayed the question to Marnie, who nodded her approval. "Yes. She says yes, please."

"Very well, I shall find someone to cover my class and leave immediately."

"Thank you."

"Before I tell them, you are certain?"

"As certain as it's possible to be. Whilst a body hasn't yet been recovered, there's no way Tom could've survived the conditions. My brother was out on the lifeboat trying to rescue Tom's crew, so we've had a first-hand account of what happened."

"And the rest of the crew?"

"All but Tom survived with only a few cuts and bruises. It was Tom's friend Bobby who identified Tom as the missing crew member."

"Knowing Bobby escaped unharmed brings some comfort," said Jimmy. "But what a tragedy."

"It is that," said Helen. "I'd best see about getting Marnie home. I'll bring her back to the telephone when she's feeling stronger. She was desperate to speak to you, but it's all proved too much."

"Thank you for letting me know," said Jimmy, "and please send Marnie and Annie my love. I'll see about getting some leave to come and visit."

"I'm sure she'd appreciate that."

"Goodbye."

Helen hung up the receiver and sat on the ground beside Marnie, wrapping her arms around her and holding her until she was ready to stand and make the short walk home.

Chapter 36
January, 1939

As Marnie and Annie clung to each other for comfort in Padstow, Jimmy stepped off the train at Lowestoft station, dreading the task he was about to perform. The day was bright and crisp, the harbourside quieter than usual due to so many boats having gone in search of fishing grounds further afield. The Grit, however, was humming with life, children heading home for their lunch after a busy morning at school, women making the most of the cloudless day to hang washing on lines.

Jimmy kept his head down as he walked. There were few who'd remember him these days, but the last thing he wanted was to be drawn into conversation. Instead of heading straight for Sally and Roy's cottage, Jimmy took a slight detour and found himself outside Kitty's door.

Kitty answered the door with surprise, her hair caught up in a scarf, the apron around her neck suggesting it was washing day. "Jimmy? Whatever are you doing here?"

"Can I come in?"

"Of course." Kitty stepped aside so Jimmy could enter the small sitting room. She pushed aside the laundry she had been sorting, and Jimmy took a seat in an armchair.

"I'm afraid I've come with bad news, but before I go on, I want to reassure you that Bobby is fine."

"Bobby? Jimmy, what's happened?"

"Tom's boat was caught in a storm shortly after they'd passed Cape Cornwall."

"Oh, no." Kitty's eyes squeezed tight in disbelief.

"Several lifeboat crews went to assist them and they rescued all the crew, all except for Tom." Jimmy's voice broke and he pulled a handkerchief from his pocket.

"Oh, no," said Kitty again, her hand flying to her mouth. "Not Tom."

"He was washed overboard," said Jimmy. "Bobby made sure the Padstow lifeboat crew knew his identity and told them to inform Marnie."

"Poor Marnie, have you spoken to her?"

"I tried, but she was so distraught she couldn't speak. Her friend Helen telephoned and told me what had happened. I said I'd pass the dreadful news on to Sally and Roy and I was wondering..."

"You'd like me to come with you?"

"Would you mind? I know it's not a task to be relished, but I thought a female presence may help Sally."

"Of course I don't mind. I can't imagine what this will do to them. With all the loss they suffered in the war, this could break them."

"I know. They're going to need a lot of support."

"Will Marnie return to Lowestoft?"

"I'm not sure. I know they have let her house for six months. It's best she takes some time to weigh up her options. I'm going to visit her as soon as I'm able."

"Come on," said Kitty, gathering up her coat. "Let's get this awful moment over with."

*

Kitty and Jimmy stood outside Sally's home, neither wanting to knock. In the end, with a deep sigh, Jimmy stepped forward. When Sally opened the door, she beamed at the pair of them.

"What a wonderful surprise," she said. "I wasn't expecting either of you today. Come in."

Kitty glanced at Jimmy as Sally turned on her heel and walked towards the kitchen. Jimmy shrugged and showed they should follow. In the kitchen, Sally filled a kettle and placed it on the stove.

"Sally," said Jimmy, his voice quiet. "I'm afraid this isn't a social call. Is Roy at home?"

"No, he went out for a walk. He's trying to loosen up his hip."

"Come and sit down," said Jimmy. Something about his tone caused Sally's face to crease in a frown. She left the kettle and pulled out a chair.

"Jimmy? You're scaring me."

"I'm so sorry, Sally. There's no right way to say this..."

"Tell me," said Sally, her voice hard, her hands clasped tight in front of her.

"Tom's boat was caught in a storm. I'm afraid he didn't survive."

The scream which tore from Sally's mouth bounced off the walls and travelled to streets beyond. Kitty jumped from her chair and wrapped her arms around Sally, pulling the older woman tightly into her and stroking her hair.

From beneath Kitty's embrace came shrieks of, "No, no, no."

The back door opened, and Roy stepped into the kitchen. He took one look at his wife and staggered, supporting his weight against the kitchen counter. "Tom?" he whispered, eyes on Jimmy, voice hoarse.

Jimmy nodded, and Roy staggered again. Jimmy leaped up to support his friend, but Roy waved him away, taking deep breaths as he struggled to stay on his feet. Sally tore herself from Kitty and rushed to her husband. He held her to him, their tears mingling as the horror of Jimmy's news sank in. Jimmy and Kitty watched on, helpless to relieve any of the devastation the news had brought.

It was half an hour before Sally and Roy, wrung out from tears, flopped into chairs around the kitchen table. By now, Roy's face was impassive. His eyes had dried, yet held an emptiness that concerned Jimmy more than any amount of tears.

With quiet authority, Jimmy ran through all the information he had. Neither Sally nor Roy could look him in the eye, and guilt washed through him as he tore down their world with his words.

"What about Marnie and Annie?" asked Roy when Jimmy had finished.

"I don't know. Marnie was too distressed to speak to me earlier. I'm going to catch the next train down there and I'll find out what she plans to do. You know, Kitty and I are here for you, whatever you need. We can't take away your pain, but if there's anything at all we can do for you, you only have to ask."

Sally reached across the table and took Jimmy's hand, looking up at him for the first time. "Thank you," she said. "Thank you for being straightforward with us, and telling us the truth."

"How about a cup of tea?" asked Kitty. Sally nodded, and Kitty moved to the stove.

"Would you like us to stay with you for a while?" asked Jimmy. "I can spend the night here if it helps?"

"You're a good man, Jimmy," said Roy, his voice gruff, "but I think it might be best if the two of you make your way home. Me and Sal could do with some time to get our heads around all that has happened."

"Of course," said Jimmy. "We'll head off now, but I'll call on you tomorrow and don't think about stopping me. You're as good as family, and while I'll respect your need for privacy, I won't have you going through this alone."

To Jimmy's surprise, Roy pushed back his chair, walked around the table, and took Jimmy in his arms. So unusual was this display of affection, it left Jimmy breathless. Once over his shock, he put his arms around Roy, rubbing his back and telling him everything would be alright, even though they both knew this to be a lie. As quickly as the hug started, it stopped, Roy dropping his arms and moving to stare out of the window.

Jimmy and Kitty said their goodbyes, closing the door on a couple whose world had just been shattered.

Chapter 37

February, 1939

I n the week since Tom's death, Marnie had barely left her room. Her throat was raw, the skin around her eyes and nose dry and itchy from wiping so many tears away. Her sewing project provided some distraction, but not enough to prevent the frequent bouts of crying or the mounting feeling of guilt that she hadn't been the wife Tom deserved.

Marnie crossed the room and stared out of the window. Force of habit kept her returning to the view, looking out for the distinctive green hull of the *Sally Ann* edging her way into harbour. Among the trawlers, drifters and pleasure boats, there would never be the one vessel she longed to see.

The future of the *Sally Ann* would need to be discussed, eventually. It was a relief to know she was down in Hayle waiting on repairs. It delayed the moment they must decide. If it were down to Marnie, she'd pass ownership of the boat over to Bobby. He had more than proved his loyalty, and it wasn't as if she could go to sea herself. But it was only right to leave the final decision to Roy.

"Knock knock."

Marnie jumped and turned away from the window. "Who's there?" For the first time in a week, a smile tugged at the corner of her lips. The greeting was so familiar, despite it being many years since she'd heard it used.

The door swung open and a tall, handsome man with a shock of blond curls stepped into the room.

"Jimmy!" Marnie cried, crossing the room and flinging herself into the arms of her brother. More tears broke free from her eyes and she found herself unsure if they were from happiness, sadness, or both. "When did you get here?"

"Ten minutes ago. Richard met me at the station."

"I can't believe you came all this way."

"Of course I came, Marnie. I'm so sorry for what has happened to you. Tom was such a good man, he didn't deserve this, neither of you did."

"Thank you for coming. Yours was just the face I needed to see."

Jimmy sat down on the bed. "You were there for me in my hour of need. It was only right I returned the favour. It's been hell waiting for the school to find a temporary replacement for me. I wanted to rush to you as soon as I received the news."

"Well, you're here now."

"How are you, really?"

Marnie's eyes filled with tears. "Not so good," she sniffed. "This was Tom's adventure, but it's over before it began. And I keep thinking back on my years with him. I wasn't good enough, Jimmy. I should've been a better wife."

Jimmy wiped away Marnie's tears with his thumb. "That man adored you, Marnie. Never have I seen a man so in love with his wife. He knew you were fiery when he married you. You brought him so much happiness."

"But all those years making him wait for a child. Then, when we had her, I resented my loss of freedom and made sure he was aware of it. He was a loving husband. I was a nagging, irritable wife."

"That's not true," said Jimmy. "All marriages have their bad times, but yours had no more than most. As for motherhood, you've a beautiful little girl who is adored by all who meet her. Tom's gone too soon, but the life he lived with you was all he wanted. Mourn his loss, yes, but don't diminish the life you had together. That would be a disservice to his memory and all the two of you had."

"I've missed your wisdom," said Marnie, wiping away tears with her sleeve.

"I know it's hard so soon after Tom's death, but have you thought of what you might do next? Will you be returning to Lowestoft?"

"I've been thinking of nothing else," said Marnie. "The family renting our house has it for six months."

"You could stay with me?"

"I wouldn't want to impose on you."

"You wouldn't be, and I have space."

"It isn't just about space, though. You'd be supporting us financially, too."

"Which also wouldn't be a problem."

"Jimmy, I don't want to be reliant on your kindness, however freely it's given. I've been speaking to Helen and Richard. Tom paid for our room and board up front, and they're happy for me to stay. Richard has offered me work in his shop so I could have an income. With everything so uncertain in Europe, it seems wise to bide my time here. I can reassess my situation in the summer when the tenants move out of our house."

"And you're sure you won't feel too alone if you stay here?"

"Jimmy, there are plenty of Lowestoft families here chasing fish. Helen adores Annie and enjoys helping me with her."

"Have you spoken to Sally and Roy yet?"

"They responded to my letter. Thank you for breaking the news to them. I know how terrible that moment must have been. As you know, they're shattered by Tom's death. I don't know how they'll bear the loss. I thought they'd want us on the first train back to Lowestoft and moving into their house, but Roy has told us to stay put, citing much the same reasons I've come to myself. Part of me wants to rush up there and be by their side, but I'm not sure I could bear the weight of their grief on top of my own. I know that's horribly selfish, but I honestly believe my being there would only make things worse. They need time to grieve for Tom. Our being there would only give them more to worry about."

"You don't think going back would help them as well as you? A child always brings light into a home."

"Possibly, but I'm not sure it would be the best thing for Annie. Tom planned for people to help his parents while we're away. At the end of that period, I'll reassess."

"I understand. I've promised I'll call on them as often as I can. My time's limited during the week, but I can spend all my weekends with them if that's what they need."

"Oh, Jimmy, you're such a kind man. You know they see you as part of their family. But are you sure it wouldn't be too much bother?"

"Bother? Marnie, I love your in-laws almost as much as you do. It's about time I returned the kindness they've shown me." Jimmy became quiet, pulling on his beard. He cleared his throat and looked at Marnie. "This is a difficult topic to raise, but is there any news about a funeral?"

"They still haven't found Tom's body," said Marnie, silent tears snaking down her cheeks. "The storm was that bad, there is no knowing if they ever will. Oh, Jimmy. It's too awful." Jimmy held his sister tight as she emptied herself of tears.

"That's decided it. I'm staying as long as you need me to help get you back on your feet."

"But what about your work?"

"They can manage without me for a week or two."

"Thank you," said Marnie, nuzzling into her brother's neck as she had done as a child.

"How has Annie been coping with the news?"

"She's been a little tearful, but with Tom away at sea so often, not much has changed in her day-to-day life. She adores Helen and Richard and they've done a marvellous job of distracting her from grief she's not yet old enough to understand. Speaking of Annie, shall we find her?"

"Yes, let's. I could do with a cup of tea."

"I thought Helen would've forced one down your neck the moment you were through the door."

Jimmy smiled. "She tried, but I wanted to come and see you first."

Jimmy took his sister's hand and helped her off the bed. They found Helen and Annie at the kitchen table drawing pictures. As soon as Helen saw Jimmy and Marnie, she jumped up to put the kettle on the stove. Annie climbed down from her chair and wrapped her arms around Jimmy's legs.

"It was good of you to come all this way," said Helen.

"It's no bother," said Jimmy. "Marnie's done so much for me in the past, I couldn't leave her to deal with this alone."

"Are you staying forever?" asked Annie.

"No," said Jimmy, lifting her into his arms. "I'll be staying for a week or two, though, so we'll have plenty of time together. Perhaps I could take one of those lovely pictures you've drawn with me and give it to Nanny and Granddad Hearn?"

"I want you to stay forever," said Annie, pouting.

Jimmy laughed. "Yes, but if I did that, Nanny would never get to see your beautiful drawing. And I have lots of little girls and boys who need me."

"Then I want to go back to Lowestoft with you. Aunt Helen and Uncle Richard can come too."

"No, maid," said Helen, setting a pot of tea down on the table. "We have to stay here and open the shop. Your Uncle Jimmy is welcome to stay with us anytime."

"Thank you," Jimmy said. "But on this occasion, I've booked a room at a local hotel."

"Are you sure?" said Helen. "As long as you don't mind a makeshift bed in the sitting room, you're welcome to stay here."

"That's a very kind offer, Helen, but the room isn't just for me."

Marnie looked up at her brother, her eyes full of questions.

"Clara's coming too. As soon as I told her your news, she insisted on coming. I hope that's alright? I think she feels that she's experienced a similar loss in her life, and that it might help you to have someone around who understands something of what you're going through."

"Of course, I'd love to see her," said Marnie. "But to come such a long way? Jimmy, there really wasn't any need. I don't want to be a burden to anyone."

"You're not a burden," said Helen and Jimmy in unison.

Marnie managed a small smile. "When does Clara arrive?"

"Tomorrow."

"As long as you know you're both welcome here any time," said Helen. "Now, how about some cake? I've got one fresh from the oven."

The thought of cake lifted Annie's spirits, and she went back to her colouring, content.

"Why don't you show your picture to Uncle Richard?" asked Helen.

Annie jumped from her chair and ran through to the shop. When Helen was sure the child was out of earshot, she turned to Jimmy. "Marnie's told you her plan to stay with us for the time being?"

"Yes," said Jimmy. "It sounds sensible. Annie seems to have settled well here, and it would seem foolish to uproot her again."

Helen turned to Marnie. "I've been thinking about the funeral. Why don't we have a brief ceremony for Tom ourselves? There are plenty of folk in the village who knew him and many more from Lowestoft he counted as friends."

"That sounds wonderful," said Marnie. "I think it would also help Annie understand what's going on."

"I'm sure the vicar would be happy to lead some prayers," said Helen.

"Perhaps we could do it by the harbour rather than in the church?" said Marnie. "The sea was part of Tom's life. Fishing was his world, so saying goodbye beside the harbour seems a fitting tribute."

"I'll speak to the vicar in the morning," said Helen.

Chapter 38

February, 1939

With Marnie resting and Annie back at school, Jimmy let himself out of his hotel and walked the short distance to the station. When Clara stepped off the train, he rushed towards her as quickly as his limp would allow.

"My darling," said Clara, dropping her bags and pulling him into her arms.

"It's so good of you to come," said Jimmy. He squeezed her tight, breathing in the scent of her skin, which had become so familiar to him over the years.

Clara pulled back and held Jimmy at arm's length. "How is Marnie?"

"Not good," said Jimmy. "She's still very tearful, and I don't think she's sleeping at night."

"Does she know I'm coming?"

"Yes, she was pleased when I told her."

Clara frowned. "I hope she doesn't feel I'm intruding on her grief."

"Not at all. I, like you, agree you're the person best placed for her to talk to. You've experienced the loss of a spouse, not to mention losing your mother."

"I'd rather not be an expert in grief," said Clara, "but I'm pleased it has some uses."

Jimmy managed a small smile and stroked Clara's cheek.

"I've booked us into a hotel near the harbour, under the name Mr and Mrs Watson, of course."

"Of course," said Clara, smiling. "We wouldn't want to raise any eyebrows with our unconventional relationship on top of everything else that's going on."

Jimmy picked up Clara's bags, and she followed him out of the station.

*

Helen opened the door to Jimmy and a striking redhead, not batting an eyelid as the unmarried couple walked in holding hands.

"Good morning, Helen. This is my friend, Clara."

"Lovely to meet you, Clara. I hear you've travelled even further than Jimmy to be here."

Clara smiled. "Two days by train."

"Well, Marnie's lucky to have such caring folk around her. She'll need all the help she can get if she's to get through the next weeks and months."

"Aye," said Clara. "Unfortunately, I'm all too experienced in loss. First with my mother, then I lost my husband during the war. Everyone's keen to say time heals all wounds, but I'm not sure grief is as simple as that."

"Yes," said Helen, "I suspect you're right. I also suspect you're exactly what Marnie needs right now."

Right on cue, Marnie appeared at the bottom of the stairs. Whilst pale and tired-looking, she had washed and dressed in fresh clothes and run a brush through her unruly hair. "Clara," she said, rushing across the kitchen to embrace her friend. "You really didn't have to come all this way."

"Of course I did," said Clara. "I wanted to be by your side as soon as Jimmy told me what happened. Now, I believe there's a member of the family I'm yet to meet?"

Marnie frowned in confusion.

"Your daughter?"

"Oh, goodness, yes, Annie. I forgot you've not met her. It's been an age since you were last in Lowestoft." Marnie turned to Helen. "Jimmy and Clara usually meet in Lincolnshire or Nottingham, so neither has to travel too great a distance."

Helen raised an eyebrow but kept her thoughts on how strange some couples were to herself.

"I feel terrible that I've not been able to meet Annie, but my assistant Olive has taken a few years off work to care for her sick mother, and finding a replacement has proved impossible. It turns out few people want to live and work on an isolated island. I've only been able to snatch the occasional weekend off, and that hasn't allowed time to travel all the way to Lowestoft."

"And we haven't brought Annie up to the island," said Marnie. "We always intended to, but since Tom took over the boat..." Marnie sniffed and accepted a hanky Helen passed her. She took a deep breath. "After Tom took over the boat from his dad, he was working all hours and it was never the right time. I wish I could've taken him back there. He adored the island when we went for our honeymoon. I think that's the hardest thing, thinking of all the plans we'd made, all the time we've lost." Marnie dabbed the handkerchief against her eyes.

"I'll fetch Annie for you," said Helen. "I think she's in the shop with Richard."

While Helen went to fetch Annie, Clara pulled Marnie into her, soothing some of the pain of loss. Marnie let herself relax into Clara's warmth, only breaking away when the sound of scampering footsteps hurtled towards the room.

Annie ran to Marnie, hiding herself behind her skirt. "Who's that, Mummy?" she whispered.

Marnie bent down and whispered in Annie's ear, "That's Clara, Uncle Jimmy's friend. Remember the photographs he showed you?"

Annie smiled and looked up at Clara. "I like your hair."

"Thank you," said Clara with a laugh. "I like your hair, too."

"Mine gets tangled sometimes," said Annie, "and it hurts when Mummy brushes it."

"It's a small price to pay for such beautiful curls," said Clara, smiling and bending down to Annie's height. "I've wanted to meet you for such a long time. I bought you a present when you were born, but it's taken me five years to give it to you. You're probably too grown up for it now."

"What is it?" asked Annie, her eyes wide.

Clara pulled a beautifully crafted rag doll from her bag and handed it to Annie. Annie clutched it to her, grinning from ear to ear. "Thank you."

"You're welcome. Are you sure it's not too babyish? I can take it back if you like?"

"No!" said Annie. "I want to keep her. Her name is Clara."

"I'm honoured to have her named after me," said Clara.

"Mummy, can I take Clara dolly up to my room and make a special bed for her?"

"Of course you can," said Marnie. "Thank you," she said to Clara as Annie left the room.

"Why don't I spend some time with my niece while you two catch up?" said Jimmy.

"We could go for a walk?" said Marnie. "I don't feel very strong at the moment, but I'm sure I could make it around the harbour."

Behind her, Helen smiled, relieved Marnie was ready to leave the house at last.

"That sounds wonderful," said Clara. "I'd love to see a little more of the place."

Arm in arm, Marnie and Clara walked around the harbour, through the winding village streets and back down to the station. "How are you feeling?" asked Clara. "Would you like to go home and rest?"

"No," said Marnie, "I've been stuck inside for a week. I'd forgotten what fresh air on my face feels like. Shall we walk along the coast a little way?"

"If you're up to it."

"I am," said Marnie.

They strolled back to the harbour and took a path beyond it, climbing steeply until views across the estuary spread out before them. "What a beautiful place," said Clara. "I can see why you want to stay."

"Do you think I'm doing the right thing?" asked Marnie. "I wonder if I'm being too selfish and should go back to Sally and Roy?"

They turned from the view and walked on further before Clara answered. "The honest answer is, I don't know. In these situations, you rarely know what's right or wrong until you look back with the benefit of hindsight. I don't doubt it would help Tom's parents having you and Annie around. But Jimmy said Annie's settled into school here?"

Marnie nodded. "She only started there two weeks ago, but loves it already."

"Then you have to do what's in her best interests. I continued living with Michael's parents after he died, but my situation was different. I'm not sure if it helped them to have me around. Nothing and nobody can lessen the pain of such a loss. You can support someone, but you can't take that pain away."

"How did you get over the losses you've had in your life?"

Clara smiled, but her eyes were sad. "I'm not sure you ever do. Michael's death was tragic, but I think it was the death of my mother that affected me in ways I'm only just coming to terms with."

"Like what?"

"Not wanting children would be the most obvious. I was there when Mam died, giving birth. The memory of that night haunted my dreams for years. It still does sometimes. I wonder if she'd lived, or if I hadn't witnessed her death, whether Jimmy and I would have a different sort of relationship. Perhaps we might have had a family of our own? But there's no point in what-ifs. All we can do is focus on the here and now, and learn to live with the choices we've made." Clara stopped walking and turned to Marnie, taking her hands in her own. "These things change us, Marnie, but that doesn't mean we have to stop living. Live with the pain as best you can, for the sake of your daughter. And if one day you wake up and Tom isn't the first thing you think of, that's all right too. There's no right or wrong with grief. Everyone has to muddle through in their own way, at their own pace."

"Thank you," said Marnie, "for coming here, for understanding."

Clara pulled Marnie into a hug. "You know I've got a telephone at the hotel. You can call me anytime you need to talk to someone. Now, how about we head back to the cottage and I can get to know my niece?"

*

Clara appeared at the bottom of the stairs and smiled at Marnie. "Annie was out like a light before I'd finished her bedtime story."

"She's really taken to you."

"And I her."

"Sit down, maid," said Helen. "Let me get you a drink."

"Thank you," said Clara, pulling out a chair and sitting beside Jimmy. Marnie noticed them take each other's hands beneath the table and felt a pang of sadness that she no longer had a hand to hold.

"Marnie, I've been thinking about Sally and Roy," said Jimmy.

"You think I should go back to Lowestoft?"

"No, I'm not talking about where you live. But you mentioned a memorial service for Tom. I think it's only right that they're given the option to attend."

"Are you sure? I was only thinking of a short, low-key event, nothing very formal. And I'm not sure how they'd cope with such a long journey."

"They wouldn't have to do anything other than sit on a train. I could organise a taxi to take them across London so there's even less time on their feet, and I could borrow a car and pick them up in Bodmin so they only have to change trains once."

"I think Jimmy's right," said Helen. "It's important they're given the choice to come, and if you're set on staying here until your house is available again, then at least it would give them a chance to see you, and of course Annie. Saying goodbye when someone you love has died is an important part of the grieving process."

"I'll send them a telegram in the morning," said Marnie.

Chapter 39

February, 1939

Annie kicked her feet against the wall in impatience. Marnie sighed and pressed a hand to her daughter's knees. "There's no need for that. They'll be here soon."

Annie ignored Marnie, her legs swinging out further, her feet kicking harder. From the far side of the harbour came the unmistakable shape of Richard's van. Marnie lifted Annie off the wall and held tight to her hand. Annie jumped up and down, desperate for a glimpse of her much-loved grandparents.

The van pulled to a stop outside the shop and Richard and Jimmy climbed out, opening the doors for Marnie's in-laws. Their clothes crumpled from the journey, Roy and Sally looked far older than Marnie remembered, despite less than two months passing since she'd seen them last.

Annie broke free from Marnie's grip and flung herself at Roy, almost knocking him off his feet. He picked his granddaughter up and held her tight. Marnie noticed his shoulders shudder in a sob and he buried his face in Annie's hair. When he looked up, he'd gained control of his emotions and gave Annie a small smile.

Sally stood clinging to the van door, her eyes darting around in confusion as though she didn't know where she was or how she'd got there. Marnie stepped forward, took Sally's arm and guided her towards the cottage.

The clanking of metal stopped Marnie in her tracks. "Richard, what's that noise coming from your van?"

"Ah," he said. "We have a stowaway."

"A what?"

Richard opened the back door of his van, Marnie's mouth dropping open as a familiar figure emerged.

"Kitty?"

Kitty blinked as her eyes adjusted from the dark van to bright sunlight. She smoothed out her dress and shook herself like a dog coming in from the rain. "I thought you'd forgotten about me. That van's got to be worse than the cattle class trains we used to take during herring season."

"Kitty? What are you doing here?"

"Come to see you, of course." Kitty stepped forward and took hold of Marnie's hands, holding her at arm's length and studying her from top to toe. "You've not been sleeping. Or eating much, by the looks of you."

"What about the boys?"

"Bobby's mam's looking after them. I've promised I'll only be gone a few days. Sam was very cross he couldn't come with me, but I came to help Sally and Roy. I'll bring Sam with me on another visit."

Helen leaned out of the door of the cottage. "What are you all doing out there in the cold? Richard, Jimmy, show our visitors up to the sitting room. I'll put the kettle on."

Annie pulled Roy towards the cottage, Kitty following close behind to make sure he didn't fall. Marnie waited outside with Sally until the others had gone inside.

"If you'd rather go straight to the hotel, Helen will understand."

"No, I wouldn't want to be rude." Sally's voice came out in a monotone, her thick Lowestoft accent buried beneath the weight of grief.

"Sally, I really think..."

Sally shuffled along the path and Marnie wondered if she'd even heard her. As she stepped over the threshold, Sally looked around the small kitchen.

"Here you go, maid," said Helen, rushing over with a cup of tea. "The others have gone upstairs to the sitting room, but would you like a minute by yourself down here before going up?"

Sally nodded. The teacup shook in her hands, liquid spilling over its edges. Helen took the cup from Sally and guided her towards a chair. She placed the cup on the table and helped Sally sit down. Without a word, Helen crossed the kitchen, reached into a cupboard, and pulled out a jar of sugar. She spooned three heaped measures into Sally's cup and stirred it around.

"Come on, maid, have a sip of this. It will help."

Sally took the cup and lifted it to her lips. Her eyes were glazed, as though amid a dream. She could have been mistaken for a sleep-walker, were it not for the rustle of her clothes as her limbs shook beneath them.

"Marnie, you sit here with Sally. I'm just popping upstairs to speak to Jimmy."

Marnie nodded, the concern in Helen's eyes mirroring her own. The cup hovered in front of Sally's face, the rim not meeting her lips. Marnie wrapped a hand around Sally's and helped move the cup closer, until, as if waking from a dream, Sally's eyes focussed and she took a sip of sweet tea.

"That's it," said Marnie. "And another." Marnie waited until half the tea was drunk before resting the cup back on the table. Helen appeared at the bottom of the stairs and cocked her head at Marnie. "I'll be back in a tick, Sally," said Marnie.

"I think we need to get Sally to the hotel," said Helen, muttering under her breath despite Sally showing little interest in anything going on around her. "Are you alright to go with Jimmy?"

"Aye, of course."

Jimmy found the two women lurking on the stairs, and explained under his breath how, according to Roy, Sally had been like this since hearing the news. They agreed the best thing for her was a lie down at the hotel until she felt strong enough for company.

"How did she make the journey in that state?" whispered Marnie.

"With Kitty's help. When she heard they were coming down here, she offered to come with them. She's been a godsend. Apart from anything, it took a lot of worry from Roy's shoulders."

"Where are they staying?"

"The Metropole. The least they deserve is a little comfort while they're here."

"That's very generous."

Jimmy waved away the compliment and pulled on his coat. "Are you sure you're up to this?"

"Of course," said Marnie. "It's the least I can do after they've travelled all this way. Is Roy staying here?"

"Yes, I don't think I could prise him away from Annie. She's got him smiling again, which, frankly, is a miracle. We'll borrow Richard's van to get to the hotel. Come on."

The van sputtered its way through the town, reaching the hotel in a matter of minutes. Marnie waited in the van with Sally as Jimmy went and sorted out the booking. He appeared, holding a key aloft. "All set, Sally."

Sally gave a tiny nod of her head and climbed out of the van. As they walked through the grand hotel lobby, she seemed unaware of her surroundings. Marnie held on tight to Sally's arm, feeling small among the opulence of polished wood and marble counter tops that greeted them.

Jimmy took charge. "Your room is on the fourth floor. But there's a lift, so Roy won't need to worry about his hip on any stairs."

Sally gave a tiny nod of her head to show she understood, and Jimmy helped her into the wooden-panelled compartment that would take them to the fourth floor. The lift cage had mirrors on the back of its doors, and on glimpsing her reflection, Marnie was shocked. Grief was painted across her face in the blacks and purples surrounding her puffy eyes, and her collarbone was protruding from the skin above her blouse.

A bell rang out and the lift doors opened onto a corridor of thick carpet and portrait-adorned walls. "Here's your room," said Jimmy, opening the door to a palatial room dominated by an enormous bed and floor-to-ceiling windows framing a view of the sea.

Even the grandeur of the room couldn't muster a reaction from Sally. She shuffled to the bed, perching herself on the edge, her hands folded neatly in her lap.

"Would you like something to drink?" asked Marnie.

Sally shook her head, leaning back until her head met the soft goose-down pillows.

"Right," said Marnie. "You get some rest." She peeled off Sally's shoes and pulled a blanket up around her. "Would you like us to stay with you?"

Sally shook her head again, and Marnie looked to Jimmy for guidance.

"I'll tell you what, Sally. We'll leave you to get some rest, but we'll be back in an hour to check on you. If you need anything in the meantime, use the telephone beside the bed to call down to the reception desk. Ask for whatever you like. It's all included in the price, so you don't need to worry about cost."

Sally turned on her side and pulled her knees up to her chest. Marnie and Jimmy left the room, closing the door behind them.

"Will she be all right on her own?" asked Marnie.

"I think so. She's still in shock by the looks of things. Why don't you get back to the cottage, and I'll wait here in case I'm needed."

"Thank you, Jimmy. For everything."

Jimmy pulled Marnie into a hug, and despite the grief and desperation surrounding her, in her brother's arms Marnie felt at peace for the first time in weeks. Between them all, they would muddle through somehow. Things would never be the same for any of them, but they would face their new reality together.

Chapter 40

February, 1939

Marnie's legs swung against the harbour wall as she stared out to sea, delaying the moment she'd need to go back to the cottage. A blustery wind forced her to tighten the shawl she'd worn over her coat. The weather was like a mirror to how the family felt. A dreary grey sky met grey water that lapped against the grey concrete wall.

"There you are."

Marnie turned to see Roy hobbling towards her.

"Sorry, Roy, I'm coming back now."

Roy dismissed her apology with a wave of his hand. Leaning against a bollard, he lowered himself down with some difficulty until he sat beside Marnie. "Is Sally all right?"

"She's asleep, or at least I hope she is. We saw her to her room, and Jimmy's waiting downstairs in the hotel in case she wakes and needs anything."

"He's a good lad, is Jimmy."

"I agree," said Marnie, raising a small smile. "How are you, Roy, if that's not a silly question?"

"I've been better." Roy reached across and squeezed Marnie's hand. He kept his eyes focussed on a steam trawler, bobbing lazily in the harbour. "Anyway, it doesn't matter how I feel. Sally needs me to keep my head together."

"It's awful seeing her like this," said Marnie.

"It's frightening," said Roy. "Apart from the day we heard the news, she's not shed a tear. It's like she's buried under a mound of blankets and I can't find her beneath them."

"Perhaps it was the wrong thing coming down here? We could have had a memorial in Lowestoft, then at least she'd have been spared the journey."

"No, it was right to come. I think it's better to have some separation between what happened and home."

"Annie and me could come back with you if you need us to?"

"No, as we said in our letter, it's best you stay put. I'm not sure Sally could cope with having guests in the house. She needs time to feel however she wants to feel without being hampered by politeness."

"All right, if you're sure that's for the best."

"It is. Dear God, I miss my boy." Roy let out a long sigh and sniffed. Marnie wrapped an arm around his shoulder. "I've been wondering if we're cursed. I know plenty of others lost sons to the war, but to have this happen a few short years later... No parent should ever have to outlive their children. With them all gone, there's not much to keep going for."

"There's Annie, Roy. She's your blood and more like Tom every day. She'll need her grandparents more than ever now Tom's gone."

"Oh, I know. I'm just being a silly old fool. Take nothing I say to heart. I'm not myself at the moment."

"None of us are. Look, Roy, I know this may not be the time, but I've been wondering what will happen to the *Sally Ann*?"

"I thought that would have been obvious?"

Roy looked at Marnie, but she shook her head. "I know what I think's best, but she's your boat. What are you thinking?"

"She'll go to Bobby, of course. He's always been like a brother to Tom. It's right the boat passes to him. I never want to set foot on her again, not after what's happened. Bobby's welcome to her. Right," said Roy, pulling himself to his feet. "I'd better go check on that wife of mine."

"Would you like me to help you walk up there?"

"No, love. You get back to your daughter. I could do with a spot of fresh air and some time to myself."

"Alright."

Marnie watched Roy limp away, leaning heavily on his stick. His back was hunched, his grey hair toyed with by gusts of wind. Tears flowed down Marnie's cheeks as her heart broke all over again. This time, rather than for Tom, the tears shed were for those he'd left behind.

*

The following day, the family gathered in the lobby of the Metropole. Dressed in black, they were given solemn nods by the few other hotel guests as they passed. Annie clutched a piece of paper to her chest, a family portrait she'd drawn as a parting gift to her father.

"It's time," said Jimmy, glancing at his watch.

Jimmy and Roy positioned themselves on either side of Sally, offering their bent arms in support. She clung on tight, letting them half carry her out of the hotel. Kitty took Marnie's hand, and Annie slipped hers into Clara's. The greyness of the previous day had given way to a weak winter sun, colouring the area around them as though it were a watercolour painting.

The area around the harbourside was filled with brown, grey and black figures wrapped up against the cold. Children fidgeted to keep warm, and adults spoke in hushed tones, keeping heads and voices low as a mark of respect. As the family drew near, heads bowed and gloved hands stilled. Marnie caught the eye of Mrs Clements, who gave a sympathetic half-smile. Her boys were drawn close to her, holding caps to their chests. Beside the Clements stood other Lowestoft families, the women dabbing tissues to their eyes, the men grim-faced as they recognised the memorial could just as easily have been for them.

It appeared, whether from Lowestoft or Padstow, every household had come out to pay their respects in a show of solidarity typical of a community tied to the sea. Tom was one of their own, and Marnie took comfort in how many folk had turned out to mourn his loss.

After the family took up position at the front of the crowd, the vicar cleared his throat, and welcomed them all to the sombre occasion. In contrast to the day Tom died, the sea was like a sheet of glass, the occasional cry of a gull the only sound competing with the vicar's gentle tones. He led the assembled mourners in prayers before everyone joined their voices in the hymn 'Eternal Father, Strong to Save'.

There was not a dry eye among the mourners as the last notes of the hymn rang out. "And now," said the vicar, "Tom's brother-in-law will say a few words."

Jimmy stepped forward, his page of handwritten notes shaking as he clutched them tight. "Tom's father Roy, his mother Sally, and his wife, Marnie, have asked that I say a few words about Tom." Jimmy took a deep breath. "When Marnie first brought Tom home to meet me... I... I..." Jimmy scrubbed his eyes with his sleeve and tried several times to continue. Clara stepped forward. She handed Jimmy a handkerchief, then took his hand in hers. With Clara by his side, Jimmy squared his shoulders and took a deep breath. "When Marnie first brought Tom home to meet me, I knew straight away that he was the man for her. Kind, funny, hardworking, Tom was everything you could want in a brother-in-law, and I know he was a fine husband to my sister. When

Tom became a father, all his good qualities intensified, and his daughter, Annie, could not have wanted for a better daddy. Not only was Tom a loving husband and father, he was also a much-loved son and brother. He brought joy to all those who knew him and will be deeply missed. Tom came from a long line of fishermen. The sea was his life, and, you could say, his first love…"

A murmuring spread through the crowd. Jimmy paused his eulogy to look in the direction others were pointing. On the horizon, a plume of smoke trailed behind a handsome green steamer. As she drew closer, her bow sliced through clear water, sending a ripple of waves across the calm sea.

"Bobby," said Kitty, dropping Marnie's hand and rushing to the harbourside.

Kitty shielded her eyes with her hand, the other clutched to her chest as the *Sally Ann* manoeuvred its way into the harbour. Marnie moved to Roy and Sally, wrapping an arm around each of them as the *Sally Ann* moored up. The crew had got themselves black suits from somewhere and one by one climbed onto dry land, their heads bowed.

After a quick embrace with Kitty, Bobby walked to where Jimmy stood, whispering something in his ear. Jimmy nodded, moving aside for Bobby to take his place.

"Hello, everyone." Bobby cleared his throat. "I hope you don't mind me interrupting, but we, the crew, wanted to pay our respects to the finest gentleman we've had the pleasure of knowing. We should have been arriving in Padstow under happier circumstances. Ten men, not nine. The night we lost Tom, we lost the best skipper any of us have worked under. Tom was a family man, a best friend, and to those of us who worked with him, our beloved brother. Tom, we shall miss you, lad."

After the formal ceremony, Richard opened the shop to allow for a small wake. No one stayed long, but they greeted Marnie with a long line of sympathetic faces, sharing tales of Tom from when he was a boy to when he was a man. It was a relief when the doors closed on the last well-wisher and they left the family alone to their grief. The *Sally Ann* would leave at first light, and Kitty with them. Sally and Roy were due to stay for two more days, and Jimmy and Clara three. Marnie dreaded the moment she had to say goodbye, for it would mean facing a future that had never been less certain.

Chapter 41
May, 1939

"Well," said Richard. "That's us ready for tomorrow."

"It's a half-day opening, isn't it?" asked Marnie, stretching out her aching back.

"Oh, yes. We don't want to be missing out on all the fun. Are you sure you don't mind working?"

"No, not at all. As long as Helen doesn't mind watching Annie while I do."

"Of course not. Besides, there'll be plenty to keep her occupied."

Marnie stifled a yawn. Since Tom's death, she'd kept dark thoughts at bay by staying as busy as she could. On the days Annie was at school, she threw herself into work at the shop, putting on her best smile and proving a hit with customers. When Annie was home, Marnie did her best to be mother and father rolled into one. Annie was developing into quite the reader, and their swimming lessons could begin now the weather was warming up. Motherhood still didn't come easy, but if the cheerful little girl who bounded around the house was anything to go by, Marnie was giving it an excellent shot.

*

"The Old Obby Oss came to visit us at school today," said Annie as Marnie tucked her in for the night. "Aunt Helen said there'll be singing and dancing all day tomorrow."

"You'd better make sure you get plenty of rest then," said Marnie, leaning over and kissing her daughter's forehead. "Goodnight, my beautiful girl. Sweet dreams."

Annie snuggled down beneath her blankets, her eyelids fluttering, thoughts of the imminent celebrations whirring through her mind. Marnie picked up a pile of letters and made her way to the sitting room, where she found Helen knitting and Richard reading the paper.

"Did she settle?"

"Her eyes are closed," said Marnie, "but she's so excited, I think it will be a while before she's asleep."

"I know how she feels," said Helen, a twinkle in her eye. "You just wait, you'll have seen nothing like it. Are those from Lowestoft?" Helen pointed to the collection of letters in Marnie's hand.

"Aye, some. I brought them down as I need to reply. It's hard keeping up. Everyone writes so often since Tom's death."

"How are Sally and Roy?"

"As good as can be expected. They've both started volunteering for the Fishermen's Mission, so at least they aren't at home brooding every day. I think Sally's still struggling, and although they put a brave face on things, Kitty told me their health has declined these past months."

"It's no wonder," said Helen. "How's Bobby getting on with the *Sally Ann*?"

"Good, I think. Kitty doesn't say much about it, probably because she thinks it will upset me, but from what I gather, Tom taught Bobby well and he's making a good go of things. The other letters are from Jimmy and Clara. They're much the same as ever. I think they'd hoped to come and visit for May Day, but neither could find anyone to cover for them at work, and it's such a long way. Anyway, I'll write my replies, then I should get an early night. It sounds as though I'll need plenty of energy tomorrow."

"That you will, maid, that you will."

"Well, you maids may head to bed soon, but I'm going to the Golden Lion to enjoy the preparations."

"Preparations?"

Richard grinned at Marnie. "Drinking, dancing, singing. The lads who'll be inside the Osses tomorrow will practise their dances. And mind, if you're planning on getting to bed early, you may be in for a rude awakening."

"Why?"

"You'll find out, maid. You'll find out."

Richard folded his paper and headed out into the night. Helen and Marnie spent a quiet few hours, each engrossed in their own activity. Marnie finished her last letter, folding it into an envelope and stretching in a loud yawn. "I'm off to bed," she said.

"Goodnight, maid. I hope you get some sleep."

Marnie climbed the stairs and tucked herself into bed beside Annie, who had snuck out of her cot and now lay in the double bed, hogging most of the blankets. Although Marnie drifted off to sleep with ease, an hour later she woke to raucous noise flooding through her open window. She climbed out of bed and peered out, but could see nothing other than the dark outline of the harbour.

Marnie pulled on her dressing gown and crept out of the room. She found Helen on the stairs, pulling on her coat. "Helen, wherever are you going?"

"If you can't beat them, join them, I say," she said with a smile.

"Join who?"

"Come on, maid, I'll show you."

"I can't leave Annie."

"It's only a couple of streets away. Come and have a quick look, then return straight home. Annie won't miss you if you're gone five minutes."

"All right, but only five minutes."

Despite the darkness of the streets, as they stepped out of the house their direction was clear, the sound of singing intensifying as they walked away from the harbour.

"Oh my goodness," said Marnie as the Golden Lion came into view. "The whole town's out here."

"Waiting for the bell to chime midnight," said Helen.

"It's an impressive sight," said Marnie. "But I really must get back to Annie."

"Just a minute more," said Helen. "They're about to sing the 'Night Song'."

The pub door opened and men appeared, their accordions, drums and voices bouncing off the walls around them and spreading excitement through the gathered townsfolk. A bell rang out. The instrumentalists ceased their playing. The assembled crowd cheered, before bursting into song.

Unite and unite and let us all unite, For summer is acome unto day, And whither we are going we will all unite, In the merry morning of May.

I warn you young men everyone, For summer is acome unto day, To go to the green-wood and fetch your May home, In the merry morning of May.

Marnie clung to Helen's arm, overwhelmed by what she was witnessing. Lights went on in the surrounding houses, women and children leaning out of windows to join the celebration from the comfort of their bedrooms.

Arise up Mr. Peneer and joy you betide, For summer is acome unto day, And bright is your bride that lies by your side, In the merry morning of May.

Arise up Mrs. Coots and gold be your ring, For summer is acome unto day, And give to us a cup of ale the merrier we shall sing, In the merry morning of May.

The crowd swelled around Helen and Marnie like a wave lapping the shore.

"Where are they going?" asked Marnie.

"All around the town."

"I'd better get back before Annie wakes."

But Marnie found she couldn't move, trapped by bodies caught up in their song. A group of men surrounded her. Rather than feeling intimidated, she found their joyful song was infectious, and they delighted Marnie by naming her in their song.

Arise up Miss Marnie, all in your gown of green, For summer is acome unto day, You are as fine a lady as wait upon the Queen, In the merry morning of May.

Now fare you well, and we bid you all good cheer, For summer is acome unto day, We call once more unto your house before another year, In the merry morning of May.

The crowd surged forward, and Helen and Marnie disentangled themselves from the mass of bodies. "You're a proper local now," said Helen. "Being named in the 'Night Song' is an honour. Now, let's get home before Annie wakes up and wonders what's happened to us."

"Will Richard be coming home soon?"

Helen laughed. "Not for a while. You may find yourself alone in the shop in the morning. Come on, we're going to need our sleep."

Chapter 42

May, 1939

Marnie yawned and took a sip of her tea. Whilst she was pleased to have seen the spectacle outside the Golden Lion, her late night combined with Annie's early start had left her exhausted before the celebrations had even begun.

A hammering on the door made Marnie jump. She opened it to find a gaggle of young children holding tins and small drums. One had his masked head poking out of a circular black contraption. "Can Annie come out with us? We're waking up the town for May Day."

"Oh, I don't know... What's that you've got there?"

"It's the colt."

Marnie looked at the boy, bemused.

"The junior 'oss," he explained, his voice slow as though talking to an idiot.

Annie rushed into the kitchen. "Please, Mum, please can I go with them?"

"Oh, all right then. But you stay close to your friends. Albert Clements, I'm putting you in charge of Annie. Don't let her out of your sight."

The young boy tipped his cap at Marnie. "I'll guard her with my life, Mrs Hearn."

"Good lad."

The children ran off laughing, Annie skipping along beside them, delighted to be included in their gang. As they turned a corner, Marnie could hear their singing ring out, which, added to the drums, would have the townsfolk up and out of their beds regardless of what time they'd arrived home the night before.

"Richard's changed his mind about opening the shop," said Helen, walking into the kitchen carrying a vase of spring flowers.

"Really? I don't mind working."

"We had a talk about it last night. This could be the only Padstow May Day you'll get to witness, and if you're tied up in the shop, you'll miss half of it. Why don't we go for a wander and see the preparations?"

"Aye," said Marnie, "and it will give me a chance to check up on Annie while we're at it. She went off with a gaggle of bairns, waking up the town apparently."

"It was good of you to let her go. You know she's been up in the meadows every day after school with them collecting wildflowers?"

"Oh, so that's why she's been late every day."

"Come on, I'll show you what they're doing with her spoils."

Helen led Marnie through streets that were already becoming busy with locals and visitors alike. Streams of colourful flags hung across the streets, and they passed a group of men tying branches of sycamore and ash onto telegraph poles.

"Someone's been busy overnight," said Marnie.

"Yes, not much sleep happens around May Day," said Helen.

"Oh my goodness," said Marnie, as they turned a corner and came across a maypole stretching into the sky. A man stood at the top of a ladder hanging garlands of primroses, cowslips and bluebells. What yesterday had been an ordinary street was now a burst of colour, the scent of spring flowers filling the surrounding air. "No wonder the Lowestoft families stay for May Day. I understand the draw of it now."

"You've seen nothing yet," said Helen. She called a greeting to the man hanging garlands, wishing him a happy May Day.

Annie and her friends ran past in a frenzy of song and laughter, Annie waving at Marnie as she passed. "It's wonderful to see her so happy," said Marnie.

"It must feel bittersweet."

"It does. Not only do I wish Tom was here, if he was, we'd be thinking about heading back to Lowestoft in a matter of weeks. Now everything feels so uncertain."

"Let's put all thoughts of uncertainty to the back of our minds, just for today."

Marnie smiled. "Aye, you're right."

"Now, let's get ourselves some breakfast before the proper celebrations begin."

*

At ten o'clock Padstonians, their Lowestoft counterparts, and visitors to the town gathered outside the Golden Lion. The whole town fizzed with anticipation. The locals, who had been darting around in a frenzy of preparation, now eagerly awaited the beginning of proceedings.

"Hello, Marnie."

"Mrs Clements, lovely to see you."

"It's Angela, I've already told you. Is your Annie out with the other children?"

"Aye. I asked your Arthur to keep an eye out for her. I hope they're all right."

"Oh yes, they'll be fine. This is Arthur's fourth May Day, so he knows the ropes."

"How long until you head back to Lowestoft?"

"A few weeks, give or take. This is our last hurrah. Will you be returning soon?"

"I don't know."

Any further difficult conversation was halted by the arrival of the children, red-faced and worn out from their careering around the town.

"Come on, Arthur," said Angela, "let's find Dad. See you later, Marnie."

The Clements family disappeared into the crowd and a man stepped onto a podium. "Let's give three hearty cheers for the Old Oss! Oss, Oss!"

"Wee Oss!" replied the crowd.

"Oss, Oss!"

"Wee Oss!"

"Oss, Oss!"

"Wee Oss!"

The accordions and drums struck up along with the crowd. As they sang the 'Day Song', the Old Oss appeared. Annie moved closer to Marnie, gripping tight to her leg, frightened by the painted mask that made up part of the Oss costume.

"Watch out," said Helen, as the circular frame danced towards them. "If the Oss catches you beneath its skirt, legend goes, you'll be pregnant before the year's out."

"God forbid," said Marnie, moving back deeper into the crowd. "What happens now?"

"The Old Oss will make its way through the town, prodded along by the Teaser. Shortly, the Peace Oss will make its way from the top of town. They'll meet later by the maypole."

"There's two of them?"

"Yes. Depending on where you live in town, you follow a different Oss. It used to just be one, but the Methodists introduced a temperance Oss to discourage drinking."

"That doesn't seem to have worked," said Marnie as a half-cut man lurched towards them.

Helen laughed. "It changed to the Armistice or Peace Oss after the war. We could do with some peace if Richard's papers are to be believed."

"Do you want to find your friends, Annie?"

Annie shook her head, her hand gripping tight to Marnie's as the Oss lurched back and forth among the crowd.

"It's all right," said Marnie. "There's an ordinary chap beneath the costume. Why don't we follow it from a distance?"

Annie screwed up her face.

"You stick with us, maid," said Helen. "We'll keep you safe."

"Where's Uncle Richard?"

"Goodness knows," said Helen. "Somewhere in that crowd with a pint in his hand, I should think. If last year's anything to go by, he and Jack will egg each other on and we'll see hide nor hair of them until their hangovers have calmed down in a couple of days' time. Come on, let's follow that Oss."

The day passed in a blur of colour, dance and song. By the time they gathered beneath the maypole to watch the Osses meet, the sun was setting and Marnie's legs were leaden with tiredness. Annie cuddled into Marnie as she held her, the excitement of the day proving too much as the little girl slipped her thumb into her mouth.

"Don't fall asleep yet, maid," said Helen. "The two Osses will do one last dance, then they'll be sent back to their stables until next year."

By the time the Osses had departed, Annie's eyelids were drooping, her head bumping against Marnie's shoulder as she fought sleep. The revellers showed no sign of slowing down, accordions, drums and voices ringing out as loud as ever, despite the words of the songs being now more slurred.

"I need to get Annie to bed," said Marnie. "Thank you for today, Helen. It's been wonderful."

"It's been a pleasure to share it with you," said Helen. "Do you mind if I stay on for a while? I need to keep an eye on my husband and brother, or goodness knows what they'll get up to."

"Of course," said Marnie. "I'll see you in the morning."

As Marnie carried Annie towards the cottage, she thought back over the day and wished Tom had been there to share it. Only once had she been caught beneath the Old Oss's skirts, but with Annie lying heavy in her arms, Marnie considered it fortunate she didn't believe in old wives' tales, as one child was more than enough for her.

Chapter 43

June, 1939

*D*ear Jimmy,

   Last week I received word from our tenants asking if they could extend their lease for a further two months. For several reasons, this seems like a sensible plan. It will allow Annie to finish the school year here and have a proper ending to our time in Padstow. I think to remove her with only a few weeks of term to go would be too unsettling. It also gives me more time to build up my finances by working in the shop. I know there are still nets to mend back in Lowestoft, but between the generous wage and low rent Helen and Richard provide, I'm able to save for my and Annie's future.

   My only concern in staying on longer is Sally and Roy. They tell me they're managing fine in their letters, but I'd be grateful if you could reassure me this is the case. If Mrs Greene is still happy to continue her work with them, that will put my mind at rest, although I also worry too much of the burden is falling on you and Kitty.

   I'll wait to hear from you before giving the tenants a final decision. Send my love to Clara. I miss you both, Marnie.

   Dear Marnie,

   I think you should agree to your tenants' extension of their lease for all the reasons you gave. Mrs Greene is doing a splendid job helping Sally with practical household matters, and their volunteering work keeps both

Sally and Roy in as best spirits as can be expected. They haven't and won't ever come to terms with the loss of Tom, but at least they are trying their best to muddle through day by day. Of course, it will disappoint them not to be seeing you as soon as expected, but another few weeks can't hurt. If you're going to be staying in Padstow until the end of August, I'll come down for a visit in July once the summer holidays have started. It's been too long since I last saw that niece of mine! I'd better go as the children are about to arrive, but I'll write again soon with firm plans for a visit, Jimmy.

"Jimmy says I should agree to the tenants' request," said Marnie as Helen walked into the sitting room.

"I agree. It's much better for Annie to see the term out here, and Richard loves working with you in the shop."

"And you don't mind us being under your feet for a couple more months?"

"I'd keep you here forever, if I could." Helen smiled at Marnie. "What time are you meeting the others?"

Marnie looked at the clock. "In an hour. I'd best get the letter sent off to the tenants and get Annie ready to leave."

"You sort out your letter. I'll see to Annie."

"Thank you."

When Marnie returned from posting her letter, she found Annie waiting beside a large bag. "What's all this?"

"Annie's bathing suit and towel, and a picnic."

"You didn't have to do all that."

"I wanted to."

"Are you sure you won't come with us?"

"No, you two enjoy yourselves."

Marnie reached over and hugged Helen. Annie yanked her hand, pulling her towards the door. "We'll see you in a few hours."

"No rush."

Annie chatted all the way to the beach. She hadn't thought further than a day out, failing to comprehend that this was also a goodbye. Marnie hoped the local friends Annie had made would be enough compensation for losing her Lowestoft pals.

As a band of sweeping sand came into sight, Annie sprinted off ahead, her arm flying through the air as she greeted her friends. Marnie followed, removing her shoes as her toes met warm sand and following the trail of footprints to where a small party had gathered.

The group was made up solely of women and children, their men busy in the harbour making last-minute preparations. Not all the Lowestoft families would leave that day, but with all due to leave within the space of two weeks, it was a last opportunity to gather before they dispersed for another year.

"Are you all set for the journey home?" Marnie asked Angela as she spread a blanket across the sand.

"Yes, though I'm dreading it. None of my boys are good travellers and it's such a long way. How are your own plans shaping up?"

"I'm staying a while longer to let Annie finish the school year."

"She'll be pleased about that."

"Aye, although I don't think she's realised your boys are leaving. She may feel differently once half her friends have upped and gone."

"She'll see them soon. What will you do when you get back?"

"I suspect I'll have to sell up and move in with my in-laws. I shan't be able to earn enough to keep on top of household expenses."

As the surrounding women discussed travel plans and shared their excitement about returning home, Marnie sat on the sidelines, feeling more alone than ever. The request from her tenants had come as a relief, a reprieve from having to make hard decisions about the future. She dreaded the thought of returning to the home she'd shared with Tom. But moving into his childhood home would be little better. There would be reminders of him everywhere.

The children frolicked at the sea's edge, sending crystal-clear water spraying up around them. They shrieked as cold water hit their skin, collapsing in heaps of giggles and splashes on the shoreline. Annie practised a few strokes, staying near the edge of the water. Marnie had drummed in the sea's dangers, although given what had happened to her father, Annie needed little reminder to take care.

After two hours of the children playing and the women talking, they packed up the remains of their picnic, ready to say their goodbyes. The tide was almost at full height, the enormous expanse of sand now a thin sliver. The women and children made their way along the cliff top. As they reached the harbour, Marnie hugged each woman, wishing them well on their forthcoming journeys. The Clements boys held out their hands for Annie to shake. She surprised them by standing on her tiptoes and kissing each boy's cheek.

"You'll have to watch that one," said Angela, laughing. "Will you come and say goodbye to James?"

Marnie glanced to where a cluster of trawlers lay side by side in the harbour. "If it's all the same, could you pass on my best wishes? I'm afraid being near the boats…"

"I understand," said Angela. She waved as Marnie and Annie walked hand in hand back towards the cottage.

At the door, Marnie turned and looked back towards the harbour. Playing out in front of her was a version of her life she hadn't got to live. She should be there with the other women, kissing Tom and watching him set sail back towards the east. They should have been celebrating after a successful six months, where fish were plentiful and the future was bright.

Marnie shrugged off the hopelessness that cloaked her. She had another couple of months before reality would need to be faced. Until then, she would carry on as she had been, pretending Tom was away at sea and that nothing had changed.

PART THREE

WAR

Chapter 44

September, 1939

M arnie, Helen, Richard and Annie sat around a table empty other than for Richard's small radio. For once, Annie was still, aware that this was an important moment and not a time for mischief. Richard turned a dial, and the radio crackled into life.

Helen gripped her husband's hand as a slow, calm voice, not without a hint of sadness, flooded into the kitchen.

"I am speaking to you from the cabinet room of Number 10 Downing Street..."

Annie climbed up onto Marnie's lap. Something about the slow, methodical way Mr Chamberlain spoke spooked her. Annie might not understand the gravity of his words, but she understood his tone. Marnie wrapped her arms around Annie, breathing in the scent of her hair, resolving she would do all she could to protect her daughter's innocence for as long as possible.

"This morning, the British ambassador in Berlin handed the German government a final note, stating that unless we heard from them by eleven o'clock, that they were prepared to withdraw their troops from Poland, a state of war would exist between us. I have to tell you now that no such undertaking has been received, and that, consequently, this country is at war with Germany."

"What does the man mean, Mummy?"

Marnie stroked a hand across her daughter's hair. "It means there's a nasty man in Germany doing terrible things. You remember those poor children we saw at the railway station last year?"

Annie nodded.

"The nasty man had made them leave their home. Now he's doing it to other people too, so we've got to stop him."

"We have?"

Marnie managed a smile. "Not us, but our soldiers, although we'll need to play our part, too."

"How?"

"We'll see how we go," said Helen, reaching forward and patting Annie's hand. "Mr Chamberlain will tell us what needs to be done, but for now, in this house, nothing has changed. We'll go on with our lives as usual until we're told different."

That evening, Marnie sat down and wrote letters to Kitty, Jimmy and Sally, informing each of them she and Annie were safe, and asking for news of Lowestoft. As she sealed the envelopes, her heart ached to be with those she loved. She'd landed on her feet with Helen and Richard, but longed to take a walk along the promenade with Jimmy, sit in the chaos of Kitty's house nursing a cup of tea, or stand by the stove cooking for the in-laws she loved.

A week later, an envelope arrived containing three letters. Marnie pulled out the first, recognising her friend's small, neat handwriting.

Dear Marnie,

I'm sorry it's been so long since my last letter, but things have been changing so fast here, my head's been in too much of a spin to put any thoughts down on paper. I wish I was writing to you with happier news, but things here have not been good. Everyone is terrified by the prospect of war coming to our shores. Folks say that given we're the closest British town to Germany, and a twenty-minute flight from Holland, our town will be first in the firing line.

Of course, you'll remember what it was like before. I was away at home for most of it, but Bobby told me stories. I wish things had worked out differently, and he was down in Padstow with you, and your lovely Tom. Here, there'll be no avoiding his duty and I fear that duty will be minesweeping.

The Sparrow's Nest is now known as HMS Europa. Those in power must have known what was coming, as it was back in August it changed from a place of entertainment to a place of war. They've drafted in 300 fishing vessels, 3,000 seamen and I'm heartbroken to say my Bobby's one of them. Folk talk of a phoney war, I've seen it in the papers. Let me tell you, there's nothing phoney about what's going on here. It's all happening at sea. The waters that once sustained us are fast becoming a place of horror, to be filled with mines and U-boats instead of fish.

Dear God, here I am, bemoaning things here when you have your own challenges to face there. How are you managing since Tom's passing? Your decision not to return has proved a sound one, but it must be so difficult making choices about Annie's safety and future alone. My Bobby hasn't been the same since Tom's death. He and Tom were like brothers and I don't think he'll ever get over losing him. But, there I go again, bemoaning my life. Sorry, Marnie.

Me and Jimmy have been keeping a close eye on Sally and Roy. Both saw an improvement in health during the warm summer months and Roy is now walking without his stick. Every time I go round, Sally shows me the drawing Annie did for her. If you could send her another, I know it would bring her much happiness. They hide their feelings well, those two, but they seem so much older since losing Tom. I just hope this winter's milder than the last as it will help their health no end.

Did Jimmy write and tell you of the paddle steamers full of evacuees? It was quite a sight, and I saw it happen with my own eyes. After news of the war broke, I took a walk with Sam to clear my head. You wouldn't believe it, but as we reached the beach, we saw an entire fleet of paddle steamers packed to the rafters with what we now know to be evacuee children, their teachers, and women in the family way. They'd come up from the Thames Estuary, Dagenham, someone said. There must have been thousands of evacuees as many had already landed in Felixstowe. Some were bound for Yarmouth, but one pulled right up to the Claremont pier. You should have seen them when they all disembarked. Poor little mites carrying bags and suitcases, gas masks slung around their necks. Sam's school is staying shut with extended school holidays, so the poor mites from the boat can stay there for a few days. They've put straw down on the floor, and we've all been donating blankets and any food we can spare to make them as comfortable as possible. They should only be there for a few days before moving off to nearby villages, but my, what a sight it was. Sam was full of questions, but I found it hard to explain what was happening. I just pray that our own children won't need to be evacuated. If bairns are being sent here, my hope is the folks in power think we're safe, at least for the time being.

Bobby's just got back in, so I'd better go. I'll keep you updated on how things are here, but keep us in your prayers, Marnie. You don't know how much comfort it brings knowing you and your darling girl are away from Lowestoft during these dark days. I've put letters from Jimmy and Sally in this envelope to ensure they reach you.

All my love, Kitty.

Marnie folded Kitty's letter, her head full of news and fear for her friend. Bobby minesweeping? The thought sent a chill through her, remembering how Clara's brother-in-law Joe was blinded while on his boat in the previous war. Marnie prayed to God Bobby would remain unharmed. She pulled the next letter from the envelope. This one was shorter, the spidery writing filling less than half a page.

Dear Marnie,

Thank you for your last letter. It brings such comfort to know that you and Annie are safe with Richard and Helen. Tom spoke so fondly of Helen and Richard when he returned from Padstow last year, and although not in my right mind when I met them, I could tell they were kind, decent folk. It speaks of the man Tom was that his last act was to see you safely installed in their home.

I know you miss us up here, and we you, but you're better off away from here for the time being. My prayer is that this war will be a flash in the pan and we can return to normal life, with you here, before the year is out.

Roy has recovered well from his fall, and the weather has been kind to my joints. I'm still waiting to hear whether the herring girls will return this year, but I think it unlikely given the activities up at Sparrows Nest.

Take care of yourself, Marnie, and write soon. Keep that granddaughter of mine safe. The pair of you are all we have left, and we'd rather the pain of separation than have you closer and in harm's way. Sally.

Whilst Marnie admired Sally's stiff upper lip, she feared for her mother-in-law should the winter bite as hard as the last. And how could she carry the grief of losing her sons? Sally was a stronger woman than she, Marnie decided, for losing Tom was bad enough, but to have lost three children? It didn't bear thinking about.

Marnie pulled the last letter from the envelope, a smile flooding her face as she recognised her brother's handwriting.

Dear Marnie,

Just a quick note this time, as things are frantic here. The village has welcomed refugees from London and the school numbers have swelled significantly. Thankfully, the children arrived with a teacher, and the extra pair of hands makes all the difference. Your old room is now being used to accommodate a rather fierce spinster by the name of Mrs Crawshaw. She's not much of a conversationalist but is an excellent teacher and the children are fond of her. So much for using the room as a library!

I'll write a longer letter once the new children have settled in and I have more time. Give my niece a big cuddle from me.

Jimmy

P.S. Clara sends her love. Our letters are still reaching each other with their usual frequency and she is safe and well, for now, at least.

Marnie brushed away a tear as homesickness and fear for those she loved threatened to overwhelm her.

"Is everything alright?" asked Helen, coming into the sitting room.

"Aye," said Marnie, "just letters from home making me miss everyone. Oh, Helen, things are frightening up there. I feel both fortunate and guilty to be so far from Lowestoft."

"You have nothing to feel guilty about," said Helen. "You're in the right place and both you and Annie are safe. That's all that matters."

"You're right," said Marnie, folding the letters back into the envelope and slipping it into her pocket.

Chapter 45

September, 1939

Marnie sat on the edge of the harbour, her legs dangling above the glinting water below. Seaweed swirled on the tide, mirroring the thoughts going around her head. In her hand, she held the letter from Kitty. Marnie longed to take her friend's hand in her own and offer words of comfort, but she was as far as she could get from Lowestoft, and a letter would have to suffice.

News of the war had left everyone unsettled, and Sunday 3rd of September 1939 would be a day forever etched in her memory. For days after Mr Chamberlain's announcement, it was as though they were in a trance, his words too horrific to absorb. The country was now at war. Again. Hadn't these politicians learned anything from last time?

"Whatever should we do, Tom? Richard says we're safer here than at home, and we were right not to go back, but it's hard to feel safe anywhere." Marnie sighed. Talking to Tom had become a habit since his death, a way to salve the loss and sadness that still haunted her nights, despite her days being too busy with Annie and the shop to dwell on past hurt.

Marnie couldn't believe over six months had passed since she'd left Lowestoft. In some ways, it felt like only yesterday she had stepped off the train. In other ways, it seemed like a lifetime. At some point they would need to return home, but with the war hanging over them, everything felt up in the air. Marnie knew how much it would help Sally and Roy to have Annie around, but with Lowestoft so vulnerable to attack, reuniting granddaughter and grandparents would be foolish.

"Penny for them?"

Marnie looked up to see Jack blocking the sun. "I was thinking about Tom, and the war."

"Nothing serious then," said Jack, laughing and sitting down beside Marnie. "Shop not busy today?"

"Fairly busy. I left early to collect Annie from school and couldn't resist spending a few moments with this view."

"Helen said trade's up since you've been working in the shop."

Marnie gave Jack a begrudging smile. Over the past few months, her feelings towards him had thawed, but not so far that she'd call him a friend. "I'd better go. Don't want to be late to collect Annie."

"Isn't she able to walk home by herself?"

"I enjoy meeting her. It gives us a chance to talk about her day."

"You won't want me tagging along, then?"

"You want to?"

"I wouldn't mind catching up with little Annie. I've missed her while I've been away at sea."

"Come on, then." As they headed up the hill towards the school, Marnie's thoughts turned once more to war. "Will you still be able to fish with the war on?"

"I should think so. The navy has requisitioned some of the fishing boats, but an old man like me should be able to carry on fishing. After all, folk still need to eat."

"True."

The noise of merry children hung in the air as they approached the school. Marnie greeted the other mothers at the gates.

"Just the woman I wanted to see," said an eager young mother. Marnie smiled politely while groaning inwardly. The woman was the type of parent she tried to avoid; overenthusiastic, utterly absorbed in the life of her child, constantly boasting about her offspring, and unwilling to accept her daughter was anything short of perfection.

"What can I do for you?"

"We haven't seen you at any of the whist drives." The young woman linked her arm with Marnie's, pulling her away from Jack. "You know they're in aid of the Red Cross?"

"I do. Unfortunately, I don't know how to play whist, and even if I did, Helen and Richard like to attend those events and I can hardly leave Annie at home alone."

"I understand," said the young woman. "And I don't suppose you'd want *him* babysitting." She cocked her head towards Jack and pulled her mouth into a grimace.

"I'm not sure what you mean?"

"Well, he's a little odd, don't you think? Choosing to live alone all these years, letting that sharp tongue of his loose on anyone he takes against."

"I think you're being unkind," said Marnie, as shocked that she was defending Jack as the other woman was.

"I suppose you know him better than the rest of us..."

"What's that supposed to mean?"

"Just that he's your landlady's brother. That said... I'm not sure having him accompany you to the school gates is the best idea. Not with you being a widow and he a bachelor. Folk may take things the wrong way and you know what village gossips can be like."

"I certainly do," said Marnie, narrowing her eyes at the woman in front of her. "Thank you for your advice. I'm sure it was kindly meant."

The woman beamed, missing the sarcasm dripping from Marnie's words. "Good. Us mothers have to stick together. Now, I understand about the whist drives, but we have a dance planned for two weeks' time and your help would be much appreciated on the organising committee."

The school bell rang, and a sea of excitable children flooded from its doors. The woman unlinked her arm from Marnie's and began waving frantically at a little girl with pigtails. "I'll see you at the next meeting. Three p.m. tomorrow, meet at the British Legion."

Before Marnie could protest that she'd be at work tomorrow afternoon, the woman had drifted off into the crowd.

"What was all that about?" asked Jack.

Annie interrupted Marnie's answer by hurling herself towards them. "Jack!" she cried. "You're back."

"I am, and I brought plenty of fish home with me."

Marnie smiled at the pair of them, but couldn't shake the suspicion that Annie's feelings towards Jack were misplaced. As with Richard, Annie seemed to be looking to fill the void left by Tom. Neither Jack nor Richard was a good long-term prospect for a father figure, and Marnie worried about her daughter's growing attachment.

"Come on, Annie. Let's get you home."

"I want to see Jack's house."

"No, maid, you wouldn't like it."

"But I want to *seeeeee*."

"Annie, stop being rude."

Annie looked up at Jack. "You've never shown us inside your house. Don't you like us?" Annie stared up at him with her big blue eyes. To Marnie's horror, her daughter even squeezed out a tear.

"Very well," said Jack, submitting to Annie's manipulations. "But I can't promise you'll like it. It's a man's house, remember?"

Annie grinned and took Jack's hand. Marnie wondered what the other mothers would think if they saw her going into Jack's cottage. *Let their tongues wag*, she decided. There was not and never would be more than friendship between her and Jack Tristan. Both had lost the love of their life and both understood that another could never replace them. Added to which, whilst Marnie had settled into Padstow life, she had no intention of making it a permanent home.

"Here we go," said Jack, stopping outside a tiny cottage and opening the door.

Marnie and Annie followed him inside. The room they walked into was small and sparse. The stone walls were whitewashed, the floor slate-flagged with a couple of rugs thrown across it as an afterthought. There was one armchair beside a fire, a small table and two chairs beside the stove at the far end of the room. "As you can see," he said. "I'm not used to entertaining."

"Is this the only room?" asked Annie.

"No, I have a bedroom upstairs and a toilet out in the garden."

"That sounds like our house in Lowestoft. I hate going outside for a wee. It's cold and there are spiders."

Jack ruffled Annie's hair. "You're a funny one," he said. "I'll make us a pot of tea."

While Jack busied himself with the stove, Marnie looked around the room. The walls were bare, not a painting or mirror in sight. On a small table sat a photograph of Helen and Richard on their wedding day.

"Do you have any other family?" Marnie asked, picking up the photo.

"I'm probably related to half of Padstow," said Jack. "But Helen and Richard are the only ones I'm close to. They're all the family I need."

"Don't you want a child of your own?"

"Annie, that's a very rude question."

Jack smiled and shook his head. "No, Annie, I don't. I'm happy being an uncle to you, if you'll let me, but I've never fancied a family of my own. I'm happy by myself."

"But being by yourself gets lonely."

"Not for me, it doesn't."

Annie frowned, and Jack laughed again. Marnie felt flustered by her daughter's candid questioning. She shifted uncomfortably in the hard-backed wooden chair.

"Can I look upstairs?" asked Annie.

"Fill your boots," said Jack.

Annie ran up the wooden staircase and Marnie studied Jack. He was different in his own home, softer, less brittle. "You really don't get lonely?" she asked, as curious as her daughter.

"Really. I enjoy living alone. I'm set in my ways and no one can tell me my ways are right or wrong. I have company when I'm out on the boat, or visiting my sister, but I enjoy coming back to my cottage for a bit of peace. Does that surprise you?"

"After the way you spoke to me the first time we met? Not really. I didn't have you down as a people person." The corners of Marnie's lips twitched.

"So kind," said Jack.

Marnie smiled. "I understand, probably more than you think. Clearly, our choices are different. I married and had a family, but I understand the need for independence."

"Do you think you'll remarry one day?" asked Jack, quiet enough so that Annie couldn't hear.

"Honestly? No. Despite the way I sometimes treated him, Tom was the love of my life. I'd never want to replace him."

"I know that feeling well," said Jack, pouring out three cups of tea. He and Marnie shared a sad smile.

"I'd give anything to have Tom back," said Marnie, "but I have to move forward, and there is an independence as a single woman that you lose when you marry. I intend to get my old job back, for starters."

"Don't all wives of fisherman work?"

"I suppose they do. Before I married, I tried to escape the fishing life. The signs of its future don't look good. Sorry," said Marnie.

"Nothing to be sorry about. What you say is true. The fishing will always be there, but I've witnessed the decline you speak of in all corners of the country. Yes, the fishing will continue, but will it be able to sustain entire communities as it once did? I fear not."

"Let's hope we're both wrong," said Marnie.

"Do you worry about loneliness?"

"No, I don't. Here I'm surrounded by wonderful people, your sister being one of them. Back home, I have my brother, Tom's parents, and several close friends. And my daughter, of course," said Marnie, as Annie's thundering footsteps hurtled down the stairs. "Come on, bairn, come and drink your tea. We'd best not be too long or Aunt Helen will think you've fallen in the harbour again."

Jack looked up from his cup and grinned. Marnie smiled back, finally comfortable in his presence now she understood him a little better.

Chapter 46

October, 1939

Whilst news of the war hung in the back of everyone's mind, life moved on. Nature, unperturbed by human folly, showed its force with an impressive high tide.

"Forecasts aren't good," said Richard, as Marnie pulled on an apron ready for her day's work after dropping Annie at school.

"Forecasts for what?"

"The tide. We're due a spring tide this evening."

"And that's bad?"

"It could be. We'll open the shop as usual this morning, then close at lunchtime and board up the front."

"But surely the sea won't reach us here?"

Richard laughed. "The sea will do as it pleases, Marnie, and neither you nor I will stop it."

"You should see the island tides. The sea comes in with such speed and stealth, it often catches folk by surprise, even those who've trod its sands for years."

"Thankfully, the sea doesn't reach us here often, but when it does, you'll know about it. We need to monitor the wind direction. If it blows a south-westerly we're done for and no amount of boards out front will stop it."

"Let's hope the wind is in our favour," said Marnie, unlocking the front door. By now she needed no instruction from Richard, having got the morning routine down to a T. After unlocking the door, Marnie began carrying wooden crates filled with fruit and vegetables onto the pavement, finishing with a blackboard and winding out the canopy.

First through the doors was Mrs Keswell, carrying with her a basket and an air of efficiency. "I suppose you've heard about the tide?" she asked, filling her basket with dried goods and a few vegetables.

"Aye," said Marnie. "Richard's just told me. We're closing at lunchtime."

"Wise," said Mrs Keswell, "and lucky I popped in early. Now, I hope I can rely on you to support the dance we're holding next week in the Legion hut?"

Marnie looked at Richard. "I'll have to check with Helen," he said.

"It's in aid of the Red Cross, and I'm sure you'll all want to support the cause. We have to do our bit to help the war effort. Mrs Hearn, I haven't seen you at any of the whist drives we've held. I thought you'd be keen to help with our fundraising efforts?"

"It's a little tricky with the bairn at home," said Marnie. "She's not old enough for me to leave her."

"Hmm, I see. Bring her to the dance though, won't you? All her classmates will attend and the children love these events so."

"Alright," said Marnie, adding up the contents of Mrs Keswell's basket and ringing it through the till.

The shop proved busier than usual, everyone trying to stock up before the tide came and cut them off. Marnie and Richard had no time to catch their breath or drink their tea, and by ten Helen was working alongside them, trying to meet the demand.

At midday, they locked the door and sat down to a bowl of soup.

"Did you get the wood?" asked Helen.

"Yes, don't worry. We'll do everything we can to stop the water in its tracks. There's an easterly wind, so it shouldn't be too bad this time."

"Has it been bad in previous years?"

"Oh yes," said Helen. "Three years ago we had a terrible time of it. The water came into the shop and reached five feet at its highest. Of course, the kitchen behind flooded too. We had an awful job trying to clean the place up. So much of our stock was ruined. It took weeks to get back on our feet again."

"The joys of living by the seaside," said Marnie with a wry smile.

*

The easterly wind might have its benefits, but it reached them in fierce, squally gusts, tugging at their jumpers and sending Marnie rushing inside to add another layer. They'd almost finished nailing boards to the shopfront when Jack appeared.

"You're a bit late if you're here to lend a hand," said Richard, cursing as he hit his thumb with the hammer.

"Just came in on the boat," said Jack, "or I would've helped."

"Good catch?"

"Yes, not bad. Weather's picking up now."

"You're telling me," said Marnie, her hair blowing in her face, hampering her work.

"I never had you down as someone handy with a hammer," said Jack.

"When you grow up in a fishing community, you learn to turn your hand to all sorts, as you well know."

"Right, well, if I'm not needed here, I'll head home, wash, then hunker down for the night. Give me a shout if the water breaches your defences and you need help."

"Thanks, Jack," said Richard, straightening up and surveying their work. "That should do it," he said. "Now all that's left for us to do is pray."

*

At five o'clock, the household wrapped up against the weather and ventured outside. Marnie kept a tight grip on Annie's hand, afraid one of the powerful gusts might blow her off her feet. The streets were quiet, other than a few locals clustered around the harbourside.

"Oh good Lord," said Helen.

Marnie identified the cause of her distress. Boats which should be several feet below the wall were now level with their feet.

"Are the boats going to come into our house?" asked Annie, wide-eyed as Jack's trawler loomed large.

"No," said Marnie. "They're tied and anchored. They'll not move from their spots."

"But look at the water."

All four of them gazed at the wind-buffeted scoops of water. Annie squealed as a wave broke, rushing onto the stone and turning her feet into small islands.

"Back you come," said Marnie, pulling her daughter beyond the water's reach.

"There's an hour yet till high tide," said Helen, clinging to Richard's arm.

"Hmm," he said, lost in thought as another wave crested above the harbour wall. "I think we need to get back and move some of the stock."

"Even with an easterly wind?"

"Even an easterly can't hold back a tide this high," he said, turning back towards the cottage. "Helen, do you think you could run and get Jack? We could do with another pair of hands."

Helen turned and disappeared down a lane in search of her brother. Richard led Marnie and Annie back to the cottage, trying his best to answer the many questions about the sea and tides that poured from Annie's lips.

Without stopping to remove their coats, they made their way into the shop. "Annie, can you help move some of these baskets onto the counter?"

Annie nodded, her face serious, glad of the responsibility.

"I thought this was what you were doing earlier," said a bleary-eyed Jack as he followed Helen into the shop.

"We should've done, only with the wind direction I thought we'd be alright. It was only when we went down to the harbour and saw the tide that I had second thoughts."

"Right. Where do you need me?"

"Could you carry some of the dried good sacks up to the living room? If they even get a whiff of dampness, they'll spoil."

"Yes, sir," said Jack, bending down and heaving a heavy sack of grain onto his shoulder.

The shop was soon a hive of activity, everyone moving supplies to any spare shelves they could find above ground level. Just as they were finishing up, Marnie turned around to see Annie crouched down, staring at the bottom of the door.

"What are you doing down there, bairn?"

Annie turned, white-faced, a small finger pointing to the gap behind the front door.

"Oh no," said Marnie, rushing to Annie and scooping her up in her arms. "Richard, look."

They all looked on in horror as water slicked like oil beneath the front door.

"There's no stopping it," said Richard, "and nothing more we can do. Jack, you'd better head off home while you still can."

"I'll be over in the morning to help with the clear-up," he said.

Two minutes after leaving, Jack was back. "There's no way I'm getting home," he said, "not without getting a boot full. The water's covering the marketplace."

"Lucky I made extra sandwiches just in case then, isn't it?" said Helen. "Come on, let's head upstairs while we can still walk, not swim."

Marnie carried Annie upstairs, the little girl shivering and shaking. It was no surprise she feared the sea's power after what had happened to Tom, and no amount of soothing words from Marnie could ease the fear held in Annie's eyes.

"Annie," said Jack, offering arms that she climbed into. "Ever since I was as young as you, I've seen a spring tide every year. A spring tide is like a naughty little boy. Do you have any of those at school?"

Annie gave a solemn nod of her head.

"Ah," said Jack, "then you understand what naughty boys are like. Good. Well, here's what our naughty spring tide does. Sometimes he floods the marketplace, sometimes he doesn't. Sometimes he comes up to a man's knees, sometimes his ankles. Sometimes he stays within the harbour walls and behaves himself. Sometimes he's in the mood for mischief and comes into town exploring. But each time he comes, do you know what?"

"What?" asked Annie, her eyes wide.

"Each time he's come, he's done little more than make mischief for shopkeepers and homeowners. He likes to have a bit of fun, popping the odd crab into people's cupboards, covering carpets with sand. But he's never, ever, hurt anyone. He's not *bad*, just a little naughty. A mischief-maker."

"The spring tide's like John Moore?"

"What does John Moore get up to?"

"Last week, he brought a dead crab into school and chased the girls around the playground with it."

"Ah, he sounds just like our spring tide. And has John Moore ever hurt anyone?"

"Not badly. But he pinched Katy Truman once because she wouldn't kiss him on the lips."

Jack laughed, breaking any remaining tension in the room. "The only thing our spring tide wants to kiss is the tips of your toes. You've nothing to fear, child, nothing to fear."

Annie snuggled into Jack's neck, sticking a thumb firmly into her mouth. For once Marnie didn't take it out. Let her daughter find comfort any way she could.

After a round of sandwiches and mugs of tepid tea, Marnie announced it was Annie's bedtime. Instead of putting up the fight Marnie expected, Annie meekly agreed to go to bed, so long as Jack took her and told her stories while she went to sleep.

"That's fine by me," said Jack, looking at Marnie for approval. "It will help pass the time."

"If you're sure?"

Jack nodded, then slung a giggling Annie over his shoulder in a fireman's carry. With the sound of Jack's footsteps retreating up the stairs, Helen pulled out a pack of cards and began laying them out on the table.

"It's such a shame that man never had a family of his own," she said, "or nieces and nephews."

Marnie squeezed her friend's shoulder. "You're right," she said, "he's wonderful with children."

"Yes," said Richard, "but it's easier to be fun and patient when they're not your own. Jack's more than happy with his lot, I assure you. He can be fun and playful one minute, then retreat to his cottage when the real work of raising a child gets too much."

"Hmm," said Helen, in a way that was impossible to tell whether or not she agreed with her husband.

Chapter 47

November, 1939

*D*ear Kitty,

Thank you for your last letter. I'm so sorry to hear about Simon, Al and Stevie joining up. What a worry that must be for you.

While war lingers in everyone's mind, we've had the threat of nature to deal with this week. Being a spring tide, the sea breached the harbour walls two days ago, flooding the area around Helen and Richard's shop and causing damage to many properties nearby. Thankfully, because of the wind direction, the water only came up two feet, but even that caused enough damage that it's taken us a full two days to clean up.

I helped Richard build defences outside the shop, but I don't think my skills lie in carpentry, for they proved no match for a spring tide. Annie was very frightened by the water, understandable given what happened to her da, but Helen's brother Jack calmed her. You'll remember me writing to you about an encounter with a rude, nasty man. You'll be surprised to learn that this is the same Jack. It will surprise you even more to hear I may have been wrong about him (aye, I'm admitting to being wrong sometimes). I think he's a decent enough chap disguised in a grumpy old fool's clothing. Anyway, between us all we got through the flood, and have repaired the damage, so things could have been far worse.

How is everything in Lowestoft? Have you heard from your boys yet? Have the navy requisitioned the Sally Ann for the war effort as you *feared? I hate not being able to help you in these difficult times and feel so guilty that here, at least, the threat of war has changed little. I know it's different there, and must be such a constant source of worry.*

I hope Sally is alright. She hasn't written yet this month, but her hands are that stiff these days I expect holding a pen is too much for her. How she and Roy must be suffering after Tom's death. At least I have to keep going, for Annie's sake. I'm so grateful to you and Jimmy for checking in on them.

The war makes the prospect of coming home ever more distant. My plans to return before the end of the year are in tatters. Although the tenants in our old house stayed beyond their six months, they wrote last week to say they're moving out and away to somewhere safer. It means our home is now standing empty and likely to fall into disrepair, but I can't bring Annie back yet, not until we know how long this war will drag on for.

You, the family, Jimmy, Sally and Roy are always in my thoughts, especially those sons of yours. I miss you all so much. All my love, Marnie.

*

Dear Marnie,

Thank you for your letter. You were right about Sally's hands. The arthritis is back with a vengeance, and she's needing more help than ever. Between me, Jimmy and Mrs Greene, we're keeping them going and have a rota system set up for meals. Roy's hip has never fully recovered and now he's having problems with his knee. It never rains, but pours for those two. Sally asked me to pass on her thanks for your frequent letters and Annie's drawings. She has them tacked up all around the house. I've promised I'll take some writing paper with me next time I visit so she can dictate a letter to you. I know their ongoing health concerns will worry you, but you're right to stay where you are and neither Sally nor Roy would want either of you in harm's way.

I received letters from my boys last week. They're due to be sent out to France within the month. I try not to think of what they'll face when they get there. As for Bobby, he's out on the Sally Ann *minesweeping. He's glad to be playing his part, but I'm finding all the worry hard to bear. If it weren't for the younger bairns, I'd struggle to get out of bed each morning.*

I'll write again soon, but for now I'd better see to the boys. Love, Kitty.

Chapter 48

December, 1939

Annie bounded around the room, unable to settle at anything.

"Annie, you'll ruin your pretty hair if you don't stop that," said Marnie, as her daughter hopped up and down on the spot.

"But I want to go!"

"There's an hour yet till we leave," said Helen. "Why don't you settle yourself down with a puzzle and give your mummy a chance to get herself ready. Besides, she's right about your hair. You don't want those pretty pigtails falling out, do you?"

Annie stood on tiptoes to look in a mirror. She frowned, turned her head to the side, then with a sigh grabbed the box containing a jigsaw and walked upstairs to the living room.

"Go on," said Helen, "she won't be distracted for long, so you'd best use the time wisely. And don't give me that frown, you know it's in aid of a good cause."

"Aye, you're right," said Marnie. "I just can't bear the thought of endless competitive talk about children."

"Don't you worry about that. I'll stay by your side, and most are sensitive enough not to mention children around me. Besides, if you join in the dancing, there won't be much time left for any chat."

"It's been that long since I went dancing, I'm not sure I remember how."

"It will come back to you as soon as you hear the music," said Helen. "Now scram upstairs and I don't want to see you again until you're in your glad rags."

Marnie smiled and made her way to her bedroom. Once in the privacy of her attic room, she closed the door and leaned against it. She remembered so well the last time she went dancing, that the thought of replacing the memory with a new one stole her breath and caused her heart to ache. It had been during one of the tougher moments of her marriage, when Annie was a baby and not sleeping. Both she and Tom had been sleep deprived and snappy with each other.

When Sally suggested they needed a night on the town, both had tried to protest. What they longed for was sleep. But Sally had insisted, offered her babysitting services and packed them off in their finery the following Friday.

Sally had been right. It was just what they needed. A lightness came over them as they left the house, feeling like a couple again rather than sleep-deprived parents. It was raining, and they huddled beneath Tom's jacket, giggling as they raced towards the hall where the dance was being held. They drank a little too much, laughed until their stomachs hurt and remembered everything they loved about each other before their feelings were buried beneath a sleep-deprived haze. The strongest memory of that night was Tom spinning Marnie round and round in his arms until they collapsed, giggling and out of breath at the side of the dance floor.

The memory faded and Marnie brushed away the tears clustering on her eyelids. It felt so wrong to be going to a dance without Tom. Everyone expected her to have moved on from his death, and most days, she almost felt normal. Sometimes hours passed without her thinking about him. But then something mundane would cause a memory to hurtle into her mind and she had to fight to stop her smile slipping, for Annie's sake if nothing else.

Marnie pulled herself together, and by the time she'd changed into her Sunday best and dragged a lick of rouge across her lips, Helen, Richard and Annie were waiting for her in the kitchen.

"Pretty Mummy," said Annie.

"Annie's right, you look lovely," said Helen.

Marnie looked down at the blue tea dress peppered with forget-me-nots. "Ah, it's only the dress I wear to church each week. You all scrub up well too. And you," said Marnie, picking Annie up and kissing her nose, "look like a princess."

They called at Jack's house on the way to the dance, Helen determined to persuade him to come despite the many refusals already given.

"Come on," she pleaded once he'd opened his door. "Annie wants you to come."

Jack scowled at Helen, then bent down to speak to Annie. "I'm sorry, Annie, but I've been out on the boat all day and my legs are too tired for dancing."

"That's alright, Uncle Jack. You should probably go to bed with a cup of cocoa if you're tired."

"I couldn't have put it better myself," said Jack, standing and giving Helen a smug grin.

"Very well, but do as Annie says and get your rest."

"Will do," said Jack, closing the door.

As they walked back past the harbour, Helen took Richard's arm. "I wish Jack would come to some of these functions. The villagers already have him down as an odd bod. It wouldn't hurt for him to show his face from time to time and prove he's an ordinary chap and nothing to fear."

"It's only the women that think that," said Richard. "He spends enough time with their husbands in the pub for them to put in a good word. He's shy, that's all. Besides, there's no harm in wanting a little privacy. To be honest, I envy him. What I'd give for a peaceful evening with no women fussing around me." He grinned at his wife, who slapped his arm.

The noise of the band spilled out onto the street as they made their way towards the Legion hall. Union Jack bunting hung from the hall's porch, and candles burned in the windows.

At the front door, Mrs Keswell stood shaking a collecting tin. As she saw Richard, Helen and Marnie, she smiled, and did a little dance with her tin, shaking the coins inside as though she were auditioning to join the band on stage.

Richard dug into his pocket and pulled out a few coins. Marnie did the same, having insisted she pay for Annie and herself.

"Thank you *sooo* much," gushed Mrs Keswell. "Your hard-earned coins will be so appreciated and will help with the sterling work the Red Cross is undertaking."

"We're happy to support the cause," said Richard.

"Well, in you go," said Mrs Keswell. "Enjoy the dancing and don't forget to purchase some raffle tickets."

Richard nodded and led his household through the doors. The heat of bodies hit them, the noise making it hard to think, let alone speak.

"Folk seem pleased to let off a bit of steam," shouted Marnie, close to Helen's ear.

"And who can blame them?" Helen shouted back. "Quite a few have sons who've joined up. They'll be needing something to take their minds off things."

Richard jerked his head, and they followed him towards the refreshment stand. As soon as Annie had a cup of squash and an iced bun in her hand, she disappeared off to find her friends.

"Don't you worry about her, maid," said Helen, noticing the concern on Marnie's face. "With Mrs Keswell on the door, she'll not get further than the hall. That woman's a force of nature. It's a shame the army won't let women join up. I reckon Mrs Keswell would have bossed Hitler into a corner in minutes."

Marnie laughed. With Richard deep in conversation with a neighbour, Helen and Marnie found their seats at the edge of the hall. They weren't sitting down for long before two old farmers persuaded them to dance.

Two hours later, Marnie flopped down into her seat, rubbing at the blisters forming on her heels. Helen soon followed, wiping her brow with her sleeve and blowing air up onto her forehead.

"I haven't danced that much in years," she said, her eyes sparkling.

"Me neither. You were right to drag us here," said Marnie.

"Blame Mrs Keswell, not me," said Helen. "She's the one who twisted my arm."

"I might take a minute to get some fresh air," said Marnie.

"You want company?" asked Helen.

Marnie saw the way Helen's eyes flitted longingly back to the dancefloor. "No, you're alright. You get back to the dancing. I'll only be a minute."

Marnie walked down to the harbour. The evening was still, the air crisp with an autumn chill. She stood staring at the array of masts just visible against the night sky.

"I went dancing, Tom. I went dancing without you and oh, how I wish you were here with us. How I miss you." Marnie wrapped her arms around herself. From out of nowhere, a gentle breeze reached her cheek. It was warmer than she expected, caressing her skin like a light kiss. "I know you're out there," she said. "You can hear me, can't you?" Marnie waited for the breeze to return, but the surrounding air stayed stubbornly still. With a sigh, Marnie tightened her coat around her and headed back towards the hall.

Chapter 49
May, 1940

*D*ear Marnie,

    I hope this letter finds you and Annie well. How are things feeling down there? Events have been moving at lightning speed here. With enemy troops now occupying Holland, parts of Belgium and France, all areas within ten miles of the Suffolk, Essex, Kent and Norfolk coasts have been declared evacuation areas. As my useless leg prevents me from joining the fight, I am to join those of my pupils who evacuate. It seems they shall send us to Derbyshire, although I've not received the exact location.

    I feel for those children already evacuated who now have to move again. How disruptive for them and how terrible for their parents. I have had many mothers and fathers appearing at my door seeking advice whether they should send their children away. What a painful choice to make! In all cases, I advised they should comply with the order, for while the separation will be terrible, staying could prove far worse. Our duty is to protect the next generation as best we can.

    There have been times over the years I've regretted missing the opportunity to become a father. Now, I feel nothing but relief. I see the destruction of happy families around me and it breaks my heart. How glad I am that you are far away from all this. Had you stayed, you would have been sending Annie off on a coach to God knows where. I'm so relieved you've been spared that heartbreak.

My leaving will place more responsibility on Kitty's shoulders, where Sally and Roy are concerned. I'm sure she will write to you herself to tell you, but Sam, Peter, Mark and Chrissy are among the children leaving the area. I'm sure Kitty would appreciate a letter from you, as it will break her heart to say goodbye to those boys.

Preparations have begun for us to leave, so I shall pause my letter here. I'll write again once I'm settled and give you my new address. The one silver lining I can see among the horror is that, for a time, at least, I shall be closer to my beloved Clara.

All for now, Jimmy

Marnie smoothed out the letter and passed it to Helen.

"Good Lord, maid," she said once she had finished reading. "They're having a right old time of it up there. What a relief, though, to know your brother will be out of harm's way."

"Aye," said Marnie. "As much as I feel for those poor families, I'm happy to know Jimmy is safe, and those children couldn't be in better hands. That must bring their parents some reassurance."

Both women looked up as the back door opened.

"What's the latest news, then?" asked Helen, as Richard arrived home from his visit to the post office.

"News?"

"Oh, come on, Richard. I know you'll have picked up many titbits down there."

"I don't know what you mean..."

"Stop teasing."

Richard smiled. "Fine. Well, yet again, your presence has been requested at the knitting group." Richard addressed this first piece of information to Marnie, who sighed dramatically, dug her hand into a basket and pulled out a holey sock.

"Take this with you when you go this week, Helen. Perhaps if they see my skill, or lack of it, they'll stop trying to rope me in?"

"Practice makes perfect," said Richard. Marnie threw the poor attempt at a sock at him.

"I'll help with the war effort any way I can. Just not by knitting. If Annie weren't at school on Wednesday mornings, you could take her. She's much more accomplished with a ball of wool than I am."

"Knitting aside, what else did you hear?"

"There's an appeal for anyone with a car to help collect servicemen from the railway station."

"Have you signed up?"

"Of course. The old van isn't the most comfortable way to travel, but I offered my services to Major Martin."

"So there are more arriving?" asked Marnie.

"Yes, a lot more. There's a strong feeling Hitler will try to invade after his success in Europe, and we're very vulnerable here, what with our harbour. They're bringing in reinforcements all along the coast."

Marnie shivered. "I thought we'd be safe, tucked away down here."

"I don't think anyone's truly safe, not until this blasted war is over," said Richard.

"We must make the servicemen welcome when they arrive," said Helen. "If we're feeling scared, imagine how much worse it must be for them. They'll most likely be homesick, some of them still boys. We'll do all we can to make their time here the best it can be."

"Aye," said Marnie. "When I hear of servicemen, I picture Kitty's lads. They're still boys in my eyes, but now they're out there somewhere, facing untold horrors. I sometimes think it was for the best Tom didn't live to see this. It would've broken his heart after what happened to his brothers in the last war."

"We just have to be strong," said Helen, "pull together and do all we can."

"Like knitting socks?" asked Marnie, eyebrow raised.

"Practice makes perfect," quipped Helen.

Later that day, after collecting Annie from school, Marnie walked with her daughter beside the harbour. The navy had been busy, and the harbourside was a hive of activity.

"Do they live on their boats?" Annie asked.

"Sometimes," said Marnie, "but while they're here, most are camping up on the hill behind the town."

"I'd rather sleep in a boat than a tent," said Annie.

Marnie smiled, thinking how happy those words would've made Tom.

"There's Jack," said Annie, tugging on Marnie's hand.

"Hello," said Jack, waving.

"Hello," said Marnie. "Are you just in, or on your way out?"

"I'm just heading out. Need to make the most of this fine weather we've been having." A navy officer walked past and gave Jack a friendly wave.

"You've been making friends, I see," said Marnie.

"Yes, they're a good bunch. We'll be in safe hands should..." Jack paused and looked down at Annie. "Should anything happen."

"Do their boats have guns, Uncle Jack?"

"They do, and from what I hear, they're setting a few traps for the Germans below the sea, too."

"Traps? What traps?"

Jack tapped the side of his nose. "That's top secret, little Annie. All I know is no German boat will get anywhere near this harbour while our navy friends are around."

"But what if they mistake your boat for a German one?"

Jack laughed and ruffled Annie's hair. "That won't happen. Those chaps know me and my boat. Besides," said Jack, pointing up at the mast, "I doubt the Germans have a Union Jack flapping about in the wind."

"Come on," said Marnie. "Let's leave Uncle Jack to his work."

"Can I come out on the boat with you one day?" asked Annie.

"Of course you can. But let's wait until this silly war is over and done with, shall we?"

Annie gave a solemn nod, and they said their goodbyes. As Annie chattered beside her, Marnie fought back tears. It was kind of Jack to offer Annie a trip on his boat, but how she wished it could be Tom introducing Annie to the sea.

Chapter 50

July, 1940

*D*ear Kitty,

It's been a while since I heard from you, so I hope all is well with you and the family. The war has reached us, with the navy strolling around like they've always been here. Last week, Richard helped transport some newly arrived soldiers from the railway station to their camp, just outside of the town. He said it was an impressive set-up, and very well organised. It's a relief to have protection, but also frightening that we need it at all. Folk fear an invasion by the Germans, with Padstow a likely target. It's hard to believe this little backwater could form part of Hitler's masterplan, but given what we've seen of him so far, I wouldn't put anything past that evil man. Both the army and navy are hard at work, adding defences to Cornwall's coastline. The hum of aeroplanes overhead has become all too familiar. Helen has already invited one of the newly arrived servicemen to join us for Sunday lunch, so we'll get a first-hand account of all that's going on.

In other news, Annie continues to thrive at school. She's made plenty of friends, and skips out of the house each morning. How are your boys coping away from home?

Last week, I had a letter from Sally. She didn't say much, which worried me. How are they, really? I worry so much about them and feel torn between my need to protect Annie, and their need to have me close by.

As ever, I'm thinking of you all up there. Lots of love, Marnie

Dear Marnie,

Thank you for your last letter. I'm pleased to hear Annie is doing well at school. It will be the making of her, you'll see. Bobby had a rare day off last week and we went out to Waller's for lunch with Sally and Roy. Roy insisted on paying, despite nearly getting into a punch-up with Bobby over it! We were missing you and Tom as we reminisced about your wedding day. I think it's good for Sally and Roy to talk about Tom and remember him fondly.

I expect you heard from Jimmy that Roy is still struggling after his latest fall. Sally does her best with him, but the neighbours on either side have left to live with family in the countryside. I've been trying to get over there more often to give Sally some help. It's been harder since Jimmy was evacuated. He did so much for Sally and Roy and has left an enormous gap by his absence, although we're relieved he's out of harm's way. He probably played down his role in his letters to you. You know what he's like. I don't know how they'd have managed without him. He used to go round every Saturday morning with a bag of food and would stay with them until Sunday night. Roy's eyes are getting worse, so Jimmy would read him the paper and spend hours debating the latest news from Europe and putting the world to rights. He became a surrogate son to them, and his absence has hit them both hard. The only positive to my boys being evacuated is that I have more time on my hands to pick up the slack now Jimmy's gone. I try to call round once a day, sometimes more. Jimmy has been sending money for supplies, so I take shopping round and cook for them when I can. We all have to muddle through the best we can during times like these.

You'll be pleased to know Chadds is still standing. It's a miracle given the battering the town has taken. Last week seventeen bombs fell on the town centre. Four poor souls lost their lives with another twenty-seven injured. It's a wonder more weren't hurt.

Everyone who's able has been ordered to leave Lowestoft. They've evacuated my youngest four to Derbyshire. Although they're not in the same town as Jimmy, he's promised to look out for them and visit them when he can. Sam and Peter are lodging with an elderly couple, and Mark and Chrissy are being put to work on a farm somewhere. Poor Sam and Peter were so confused when I took them to the railway station, but I held back my tears till I was alone. I didn't want them upset. I'd hoped they would keep the four of them together, but I realise asking anyone to take in four growing lads was a lot to ask. Please add your prayers to mine that the folks they're housed with will treat them with kindness.

Our house is too quiet without the lads in it. The town is even worse. Gone are the cries and laughter of bairns. Everyone is tense, like coiled springs waiting for the latest onslaught from the Germans. Blackouts are in place. I've fitted new curtains to the windows and we're to head to the brewery's cellar should there be a raid. Sometimes it feels like I spend more time down in that damned cellar than I do in my home.

I had a few letters from my older lads when they first joined up, but they're over in France now and it's several months since I heard any news. I shan't sleep a wink till I get them home safe and sound.

I know you worry about us all up here, but please stay where you are for now. It would be a job getting back even if you wanted to as they're not letting folk travel here easily. It's like we're cut off from the rest of the world. There have been some new residents arriving, naval men from Canada and Australia. You'd think the town would be used to new faces, what with the herring season, but these new arrivals have really put the local girls in a spin. You should see them swooning every time they hear an exotic accent!

Stay safe, Marnie. I long for the day I see you and little Annie again, but for now, your letters keep me going. You can't imagine the cheer they bring, and the relief at knowing at least two of the people I love are safe. Lots of love, Kitty

Chapter 51
July, 1940

"How's your friend?" asked Helen, as Marnie folded Kitty's latest letter and placed it on the table.

"Putting a brave face on things. I worry about her. Her three oldest boys have joined up, and the others have been evacuated. Kitty's whole adult life's been about looking after those boys. She'll be lost without them all home."

"Any news from your brother or your in-laws?"

"Yes, I heard from Jimmy yesterday. He's up in Derbyshire with the evacuees from his school. My in-laws' health isn't too good. With Jimmy leaving Lowestoft, it's falling on Kitty to help them. I wish there was somewhere Roy and Sally could go, but they won't leave the town. It's such a worry. Part of me wishes I'd gone back when I'd planned, but even if I had, Annie would have been evacuated by now. They've been trying to get all women and children out of the town." Marnie put her head in her hands and sighed.

"It's hard not to worry, but it won't help anything. You're in the best place for you and your girl. How about we see what those soldiers are up to? I heard they're working on the gun battery and beaches today."

Marnie shuddered. "It might make war feel too close to home."

"Or it could remove some of the worry, to know we're protected should the worst happen? Besides, it's a beautiful day, and we could all do with some fresh air."

"Alright then," said Marnie. "Annie's at her friend Sandra's house. It might be best to leave her there. So far, the war hasn't touched her, but seeing preparations for a German invasion could give her nightmares."

"Wise," said Helen with a nod.

There was no need for cardigans or coats. As they stepped outside, the heat hit them as though they'd stepped into an oven. Marnie fanned her face with her hands, praying there would be a sea breeze closer to the water. As they walked, their cotton dresses clung to their skin.

"We should have brought our bathing suits," said Helen.

"With all those soldiers gawping? No thank you," said Marnie.

The harbour lay still as a millpond, its water glinting, golden shapes shifting slowly as the lazy water reflected the sun above. Gulls bobbed on the water, lethargic in the heat. An old fisherman sat on a stool beside his boat, mending a creel perched on his lap.

"They'll be up by Gun Point," said Helen, turning away from the harbour and gazing out at the estuary beyond.

"I'll never get used to these hills," said Marnie, as they panted their way up a path hugging the cliff.

They reached the top and caught their breath. The tide was in, and water in a thousand shades of blue stretched out as far as they could see. On a beach in the distance, tiny figures moved like ants across the sand. As they drew closer, Helen and Marnie saw men carrying armfuls of something shiny, their loads catching the sun and sending sparks of light toward Marnie and Helen.

"Do you know what they're doing?" Marnie asked Helen.

"Yes, Richard told me they're putting barbed wire along the beaches."

"I wondered if they'd be putting mines down."

"According to Richard, there was some discussion of it, but they decided it held too many risks and barbed wire would be a better option."

"Let's hope a bit of spiky wire is enough deterrent," said Marnie, frowning.

"I think its purpose is more for buying time. If the Germans do land here, the wire will delay them enough that the troops can mobilise."

"You know your stuff," said Marnie. "I'm impressed."

"There's a reason I'm happy for Richard to go to the pub in an evening. He gets all the news while he's there."

Marnie laughed. Deciding the soldiers wouldn't welcome the interference of two curious women, they headed higher up the hill, until they had a view directly onto the beach below.

"Oh my goodness," said Marnie, a hand flying to her mouth. "Look."

Marnie pointed down to the beach, and both women stared at the sight before them. Their eyes widened as the soldiers stripped off and ran towards the sea. Whoops and cheers filled the air as heads ducked down, emerging with sprays of water, disturbing the otherwise calm estuary.

As quickly as they went in, the men left the sea, dressed, and returned to their work.

"I suppose it is hot work down there," said Helen.

Marnie giggled. "We had a better view than I thought we would."

The moment softened some of the unease at seeing long stretches of barbed wire rolling out across the sand. Up on Gun Point, a separate group of men armed with shovels and buckets were working on the old gun battery.

"They'll have quite the view from in there," said Helen, "and be well placed to spot any unwanted visitors."

The two women shielded their eyes and watched the men at their work.

"I wish I could do more to help," said Marnie.

"You want to turn your hand to building, do you?" teased Helen.

"You know what I mean," said Marnie, nudging her friend. "It's all very well knitting socks, but other women up and down the country are driving ambulances, working as nurses, running businesses their menfolk have left behind."

"You help in the shop."

"And I'm happy not to be idle, but it's not essential work, is it? You and Richard managed just fine before I arrived. If I could, I'd pick up a gun and head off to France."

"Don't be ridiculous," said Helen. "That's no job for a woman. Besides, raising your daughter is the most important job you can do. We need the next generation to be wiser than ours. All this damn fighting, all this war, and for what? To appease a madman's ego?"

Marnie sighed. "You're right. I suppose part of me feels guilty. I read Kitty's letters and feel like they're going through so much while we're here in relative safety. It will have broken her heart saying goodbye to her bairns, while my child keeps her normal life and stays with me."

"True, but be careful what you wish for. We don't know what will happen here. Yes, it's terrible the danger your friends and family are suffering in Lowestoft, but how much worse would it be for them if they were worrying about you, too?" Helen pointed to the soldiers working on their defences. "This isn't some training exercise, Marnie. The threat here is real. Let's just enjoy our relative peace while it lasts."

Marnie placed an arm around Helen's shoulder. "Thank you," she said. "For all you've done for us since we arrived. I'm pleased we're here with you, truly I am. I just sometimes feel so torn."

"I understand," said Helen. "Now, all this talk of being useful makes me wonder if we should get back to help Richard in the shop? And besides, those socks won't knit themselves."

With a smile, Marnie stood, holding out a hand and pulling Helen off the ground. "All right," said Marnie. "If picking up a pair of knitting needles is the only way I can help with the war effort, I suppose I'd better get practising."

Chapter 52

September, 1940

T he pews of the chapel were full, only the town's young men conspicuous by their absence. Strangers filled the spaces left by sons, brothers and husbands as soldiers and naval officers stationed in Padstow sought solace within the chapel's walls. The community welcomed these visitors with open arms, aware that if German troops descended, these men would be on the frontline of the town's defence.

Prayer provided an outlet for feelings of helplessness as families waited for news of the men they loved. The previous week had brought the news the town had been dreading. Several families had lost men, their brave fight ending as they made the ultimate sacrifice for King and country. Reports of bravery did nothing to salve the feelings of loss, and the congregation waited in mournful silence for the service to begin.

It was a sombre service. Even the heartiest singers of hymns produced little more than a mumble. Heads bowed, hands gripped together as they said fervent prayers for those still fighting and the souls of those who weren't. Marnie prayed for Kitty's boys fighting somewhere on the Continent. She prayed they would return home in one piece, both in body and in mind.

As the service drew to a close, folk scurried off, reluctant to linger despite the promise of Mrs Keswell's fruit cake for those who did. Marnie, Annie, and Helen walked out of the church to find Richard talking to a young soldier. He was a slip of a thing, lanky, with a boyish face. He couldn't have been older than twenty. His mother must be relieved he'd ended up in Padstow, not on some far-flung battlefield, thought Marnie.

"Helen, this is Private Jones. I've invited him for lunch," said Richard.

"If that's alright with you?" asked the young man.

"Of course it is," said Helen, "the more the merrier."

Despite the ongoing rationing, Helen pulled together something of a feast. She'd got hold of a ham from a local farm, which was accompanied by carrots, potatoes and swede that Richard had been growing in the garden. Richard had taken Chamberlain's plea to dig for victory to heart, and Annie proved herself green-fingered after taking on the role of his apprentice.

Jack arrived just as Helen was serving food onto plates, and Annie was delighted to have three men to talk to.

"Are these veg from your garden, Richard?" asked Jack.

"Yes, they are." Richard's chest puffed out as Helen served up misshapen carrots.

"I've been meaning to ask if you'd like more growing space? I've that little parcel of land behind my cottage that gets left to weeds while I'm at sea."

"What do you say, Annie? Think we can expand our fruit and veg operation?"

"Yes," said Annie, insisting Private Jones follow her out into the garden to see what they'd squeezed into the small space.

Private Jones came back five minutes later carrying an armful of leeks. "I hope you don't mind, Richard. Annie said I can take these to the cook in the mess hall."

"Of course not," said Richard.

"I'm afraid we won't all fit around the table in here," said Helen. "Richard and Jack, show Private Jones up to the sitting room. I'll bring your plates up once you're settled."

Annie surprised Private Jones by taking his hand and leading him up the stairs. As soon as he was sitting down, she began firing off questions so fast he struggled to keep up.

"Do you fly aeroplanes?"

"No."

"Have you ever killed a man?"

"Um... no... not yet..."

"Have you ever been out on a fishing boat?"

"Pardon?"

"Where are you from?"

"Wales."

"Have you ever been to Lowestoft? That's where I'm from."

"I can't say that I have."

"How many brothers and sisters do you have?"

"Three brothers, one sister."

"Do you have a child?"

Private Jones laughed. "No, I don't, I'm still one myself."

"Annie," Marnie scolded, "enough of the inquisition."

"It's alright," said Private Jones. "I'll be well prepared if the enemy ever captures me." He turned to Annie, telling her all about the farm he grew up on, his brothers who had joined up at the same time as him, and his mother, who didn't want any of her sons going to war. When he spoke of his sister, who drove an ambulance for the Red Cross, Marnie wished once again that she could do more to aid the war effort.

"How long do you expect you'll be in Padstow?" asked Richard, when he could finally get a word in.

"Possibly not much longer. There's talk they may ship my unit out to Southampton. I'd happily stay here forever if I could. We've been so welcomed by the local community and I've enjoyed working in partnership with the navy."

"All this talk of invasion," said Helen. "Do you think it will really happen?"

"I pray it won't," said Private Jones, "but we have to be prepared. With so much coastline, I'm afraid Cornwall would be just the type of place Hitler would look to invade."

Annie climbed onto Marnie's lap, her forehead creased and a thumb stuck in her mouth.

"Oh dear, Miss Annie. I hope I haven't frightened you? Have you heard the aeroplanes flying around?"

Annie nodded. "Sometimes they wake me up when I'm asleep. I don't like how noisy they are."

"Do you know what their job is?"

"No."

"Their job is to keep you all safe. They fly around checking no one's trying to get into Cornwall who shouldn't. They won't let anything happen, don't you worry. And there are soldiers like me, watching from the cliff top, and the navy monitoring the sea. Honestly, Annie, between all of us keeping watch, you've nothing to fear."

Right on cue, the sound of a plane on its way from the St. Eval airbase sounded overhead. It might be an added protection, but as the engine thrummed through the still autumn air, it reminded everyone around the table that life beyond the cottage walls was very uncertain, and only time would tell their fate.

Chapter 53

October, 1940

M arnie plastered a smile on her face and linked arms with Helen as they entered the hall. She'd finally relented to the pressure from other mothers and was attending her first whist drive. The shop had given her a good excuse to avoid the many committees she'd been roped into, but her lack of presence at fund-raising events was verging on embarrassing, and she hoped by attending this one she'd be left in peace for a while.

"You've remembered all I taught you?" asked Helen, lifting her hand to wave greetings to customers and friends.

"Let's hope so," said Marnie. "It was good of Richard to watch Annie for the evening."

"To tell the truth, I think he was glad. He's been looking exhausted today, and besides, all the gossip at these evenings grates on him. He'll have been glad of the excuse to miss a week."

Marnie laughed and followed Helen to a table. They found themselves paired with an elderly couple. Reading glasses perched on the edge of their noses, expressions serious. Marnie raised an eyebrow to Helen, jerked her head towards the opposing team and grimaced. Helen stifled a giggle.

Despite Marnie being a novice at the game, the pair won the first round and moved on to another table. The woman beside Marnie looked familiar, but she couldn't think where she'd seen her before. The other woman seemed to think the same, casting glances towards Marnie, her forehead creased.

"Where do I know you from?" asked Marnie.

"I was wondering if it was back in Lowestoft, but judging by your accent, that can't be right."

"Don't let my accent fool you," said Marnie. "I've lived in Lowestoft for the past twenty years."

"You live on The Grit?"

"Aye."

"Me too. That'll be where I've seen you. You must be from a fishing family. Is your husband here with you, or has he been called up?"

Marnie's eyes filled with tears, and she looked down at the table.

"Oh no, I'm so sorry, love. I know who you are now. You're Tom's missus, yes?"

Marnie thought back to all the times she'd resented being referred to as 'Tom's missus'. Now, she'd give anything for that to be true.

"I thought all the Lowestoft families had gone home?"

"They did, but when we heard about the war, we came back. My Bill's too old to join up, but he's joined the Home Guard here. Have you heard the army is using The Grit as a training base? I dread to think what state our house will be in once all this is over. Mind you, we've put in for one of those new council houses they're building in town. You know the ones?"

"Yes, I..."

A thundering sound outside interrupted their conversation. The room went quiet, then people dashed to the windows to see what was going on. The hall walls shook. A sense of panic overtook the room, cards left discarded on tables as men and women pushed back chairs and leapt to their feet.

"We have to get back," said Marnie.

"I'm not sure it's safe, maid. I hope I'm wrong, but that sounds like a bomber to me."

"I can't abandon Annie."

"Fine," said Helen, pulling on her coat. "Let's go." Helen grabbed Marnie's hand and pulled her to the door before they could be forced into the nearest shelter. They ran through the village, the noise deafening as a plane circled above their heads. The relief at reaching the cottage was short-lived, for the plane's whine was growing closer and closer.

Marnie threw open the back door to the cottage to find Annie alone in the kitchen, pulling on her boots.

"Annie? Whatever are you doing? Where's Uncle Richard?"

"In bed. I heard the noise and got scared. I was coming to find you."

"Why's Uncle Richard in bed, maid?" asked Helen, kneeling down and taking Annie's hands.

"He's poorly. He had a funny turn just after you left."

Helen let go of Annie's arms and raced up the stairs to her bedroom. Marnie pulled Annie close to her, covering her daughter's ears with her hands. She leaned over and snuffed out the solitary lamp Richard had lit. Light was too great a risk, even with blackout curtains.

"Let's play a game," Marnie said. "We'll hide under the kitchen table until the noise goes away."

"I don't like it," said Annie, snivelling as Marnie pushed her under the table.

Despite it being strong and sturdy, Marnie didn't fancy the table's chances against a bomb, but at that moment it was the best she could do. "Here," she said, pulling a handkerchief from her bag and handing it to Annie. "Dry your eyes, bairn. Mam's with you. The aeroplane will be on its way back to Germany before you know it. We'll be able to put the lamp on again soon."

Annie snuggled close to Marnie, her small body shaking as Marnie stroked her hair.

"Marnie?"

"Under here," said Marnie, as Helen ran into the dark room. "How's Richard?"

"He's got a terrible fever. He's talking nonsense. It sounds like he's been feeling ill all day but didn't want to worry me."

"Can you get him down here? We need to shelter."

"I can't. There's no way he can stand, and even between the two of us, we won't be able to lift him. And what am I going to do? Squash an ill man under a table or down a damp cellar? No, he needs to stay in bed."

"You come under here with us then."

"I won't leave him. If we go, we go together."

"Helen…"

"No, my mind's made up and they'll be no changing it."

Marnie sighed, but let her friend go. The noise rumbled on for what felt like an age. Annie was just dropping off on Marnie's shoulder when there was an almighty bang. The glass in the kitchen windows shattered, dust and plaster falling from the walls and ceiling as the house shook to its foundations.

Annie screamed and Marnie pulled her daughter closer, though whether it was Annie's shaking limbs or her own she was trying to still, she couldn't tell. Another tremendous explosion sounded and now it was Marnie who screamed. Annie sobbed loudly and Marnie tried to push her fear aside. If ever there was a time to prove herself as a mother, it was now. She couldn't give in to her own fear. She had to be strong for her daughter.

Chapter 54
October, 1940

Marnie counted six explosions before the sound of engines retreated. She heard more explosions but judged them to be further away and let herself relax a little. She cradled Annie for a further hour before deciding the immediate danger had passed.

"Come on, bairn. I think we're safe to go upstairs now. Let's get you into bed, then I can check on Aunt Helen and Uncle Richard."

Annie gripped Marnie's hand so tight her nails left marks. "I don't want to be by myself."

"Fair enough. We'll check on Uncle Richard together, then I'll stay with you upstairs."

Annie nodded, taking tentative steps towards the staircase. Too frightened to risk lighting a candle or lamp, Marnie felt her way up the stairs. Her fingers caught in cracks on the walls that earlier that evening had not been there. Wherever they had landed, the bombs had come close to hitting them. Thank God they'd escaped unscathed.

"Helen," whispered Marnie, knocking on Helen's bedroom door.

"Come in," came a whispered reply.

Marnie and Annie stepped into the room. Even in the darkness, they could make out the shape of Richard lying on the bed, Helen propped up beside him. "How is he?" asked Marnie.

"Much the same." Helen's voice shook, and Marnie sensed her friend was holding back tears.

"I think the bombers have gone," said Marnie. "I heard them move away, then more explosions further north."

"They could come back," said Helen. Marnie felt Annie resume her shaking.

"No, not tonight. They've made their point." Marnie wasn't sure who she was trying to convince. Should she stay under the table with Annie until daybreak? It wasn't as though it offered much protection. Perhaps she should go to one of the air-raid shelters? But that would mean leaving the house, and leaving Helen and Richard behind. No, they would have to take their chances and pray they were left in peace.

"We'll say goodnight," said Marnie, "but call me if there's anything else you need."

"Thank you," said Helen. She picked up a towel and stroked it against Richard's forehead.

"Come on," said Marnie, picking up Annie and hugging her. "It's way past your bedtime."

Annie gave a loud yawn, which Marnie hoped meant she would sleep, despite the events they had just lived through. Marnie carried Annie up to their bedroom and tucked bedsheets around her. Before she'd even kissed her daughter goodnight, Annie had fallen into a deep sleep.

Marnie's own lids were growing heavy when a crash in the kitchen caused her to sit bolt upright. She climbed out of bed with care, not wanting to disturb Annie, and pulled her dressing gown on over her clothes. She crept down the stairs, her ears straining for any sound. As she neared the kitchen, she could hear laboured breaths, and the occasional groan.

"Who's there?" Marnie asked as she entered the dark kitchen.

No answer came, and Marnie felt she had no choice but to turn on the lamp. The air was free of planes. A small glow of light should do no harm.

"Jack?" Jack stood leaning against the open kitchen door. Cold air rushed past him, causing Marnie to shiver despite the many layers she had on. "Jack? Whatever's the matter? Come in, close that door and sit down."

Jack wordlessly closed the door, stumbling to the table and throwing himself into a chair.

"Jack, you're scaring me. What's wrong? Were you hurt in the blast?"

Jack continued to stare straight ahead, incapable of speech. His hair stood up in a wild halo, his skin as pale as snow. "Richard," he said eventually. "I need Richard."

Marnie sat in a chair beside Jack and laid her palm across one of his shaking hands. "Jack, Richard's unwell. He'll not be leaving his bed tonight. Tell me what's happened. Is it to do with the bombs?"

Jack turned his face to Marnie, eyes both wild and drenched in sorrow. "My neighbours... my neighbours..."

"Aye," coaxed Marnie, "your neighbours. What about your neighbours, Jack?"

"I... I... should've been there. I could have helped. That poor child, that poor, poor lad."

"Jack," said Marnie, her tone changing from sympathetic to commanding. "You must tell me what is going on. Were your neighbours caught in the blast?"

Jack nodded, a single tear falling onto the table.

"The whole family?"

Jack nodded again, his mouth emitting a long groan before he threw his head into his hands.

"Where were you when this happened?"

"In the pub's cellar." His words were bitter, spat from his mouth.

"Jack," said Marnie, tightening her fingers around his hand. "If you were home when this happened, you couldn't have saved them. No one can be saved from the path of a bomb. In all likelihood, you would have lost your life too. Now, what did you need Richard for?"

"They've not yet found the bodies. The heat from the fire was too great for anyone to enter the building. Now some time has passed, I was hoping Richard would join me in the rescue mission."

"But surely there's no hope?"

"There's always hope."

"Fine. I'll come."

"No, Marnie..."

"I can't run into burning buildings or carry a man across my shoulders, but I can tend to the wounded... if there are any wounded..."

"All right," said Jack.

Marnie stood and pulled her coat over her dressing gown. She followed Jack out of the cottage and through the short walk to his home. Realisation dawned how close the bomb had landed and Marnie's legs turned to jelly. A short distance south, and it would be her and Annie lost beneath smouldering rubble. The thought left her sick to her stomach.

Jack stopped short, and Marnie almost tumbled into him. Even in the darkness, she could tell he was crying. She followed his line of sight and stifled a scream. The bomb had gashed a hole in the middle of a row of cottages. Rubble spilled onto the street, the night sky filling the space once taken by a roof. Everyday debris lay scattered across the road; a shoe, a spinning top, the grate from a fire.

Jack's hands gripped Marnie, and she had to steady him as two men emerged from the rubble. In one man's arms lay a body shrouded in a blanket. Given the size and ease with which it was carried, there was no mistaking it. The body the man held was that of a child.

Chapter 55

October, 1940

T he first dawn pastels were filling the sky. Around Marnie, men moved slowly, silently, as if in a dream. Some shovelled dirt, some scooped piles of rubble into wheelbarrows, some were still dousing the ashes where a home had once stood.

"Jack," said Marnie, tugging on his sleeve, "let's get back to Helen's cottage. Annie will wake soon, and I want to check on Richard."

Jack stared at the destruction, his eyes cloudy. Marnie wondered if he'd heard her.

"Jack? Come on, Jack, there's nothing to be done here." Marnie took his hand, his skin feathered with cuts, a hard layer of dried blood crusting above them. After the initial shock, he'd worked like a madman, joining the futile attempts at rescue that soon turned into recovery as a further two shrouded bodies were removed from the crumbling remains. "Jack?" Marnie tugged his hand. "Come on, Jack. Let's go. You need to rest."

Jack gave a small jump, as though he'd only just registered her presence. "I want to check on the cottage."

"But, Jack, it's too dangerous. You must wait until the building's secure."

Jack ignored Marnie's pleas, turning on his heel towards his front door.

"Jack," pleaded Marnie, running after him and trying to pull him away. Jack threw off her hand, turned the doorknob, and stepped inside.

Against her better judgment, Marnie followed Jack into his cottage. Despite the increasing morning light outside, darkness blanketed the rooms. Marnie covered her mouth with her sleeve, ash and dust causing her lungs to burn. She took a step forward, searching for Jack, who had faded into the gloom. The floor crunched beneath her feet. Marnie bent down, her hand settling on broken pieces of crockery strewn like straw in a barn.

"Jack?" Marnie squinted but couldn't see him. The thud of a boot and creak of wood told her he'd reached the stairs. "No, Jack, don't go up there. We don't know if the floor's sound, or the stairs."

Jack didn't reply, but Marnie heard the slow thud of boots moving higher.

"Jack, please come down."

Again, there was no response. Marnie kicked the remains of a plate in frustration and groped her way towards the staircase. She consoled herself that if the stairs could hold Jack's weight, they could hold hers.

Marnie found Jack in the middle of the room, illuminated by a pool of light flooding through a large hole in the roof. Around him lay slate tiles and splintered pieces of wood, several still smouldering. As Marnie stepped towards him, Jack collapsed to the ground. She reached him, wrapping her arms around him as he buried his face in her arm and let out loud, angry sobs. Marnie ran her fingers through his hair, and stroked his back, trying to comfort him just as she'd done for Annie as a baby.

Eventually the sobs stopped, and beneath her arms, Marnie felt Jack's body tense. He raised his head, inches from her own.

"Why?" he croaked.

"There isn't a reason, Jack. At least none that makes sense to ordinary, decent folk. It's evil, pure evil."

"A child, Marnie. A whole family, wiped out, like that." Jack clicked his fingers and Marnie saw anger flash in his eyes. His despair reached her, her chest tightening as the horror of what they'd witnessed sank in.

Jack's hands gripped Marnie's coat. His jaw clenched, his brow furrowed, his breaths coming fast and ragged. He let go of Marnie's coat and pulled her tight to him, burying his head in her hair. Marnie wrapped her arms around him, his body trembling.

"Come on, Jack. Let's get you back to Helen's."

As the fight left him, Jack's body deflated. Marnie helped him off the floor, holding an arm tight around his waist as he stumbled to his feet. She led him towards the stairs, not letting go of his arm as she walked a step ahead of him, scared he'd lose his balance and fall.

Marnie left the front door swinging open on its hinges as she hurried Jack away from the destruction and death filling the space around the cottage. Jack stumbled along the street like a drunkard, Marnie's arms aching from the effort of holding him up.

"Come on, nearly there."

Back at Helen and Richard's, Marnie propped Jack against a wall and opened the back door. She found Helen standing at the stove, stirring sweet-smelling liquid around in a pan.

"Oh thank God," said Helen. "I've been so worried."

"I've got Jack with me," said Marnie. She took Jack's hand and led him into the kitchen. His face was ghostly white, his limbs still trembling. Helen helped Marnie guide him to a chair. "I'll fetch the brandy," said Marnie. "How is Richard?"

"Very unwell. I wanted to give him lemon and honey for his throat, but thanks to the damned war, I'm having to make do with oranges. What happened?" asked Helen, pointing to Jack.

"Let me get some brandy, get Jack settled in the living room, then I'll explain," said Marnie.

Between them, the two women helped Jack climb the stairs. While Helen laid him out on the sofa, Marnie fetched all the blankets she could find. They bundled Jack up as best they could, but as he lifted the glass of brandy to his lips, its contents spilled, his hand unsteady thanks to the uncontrollable shivering that he seemed unable to still.

"Do you think he's coming down with the same illness as Richard?" asked Helen.

"No, this is the result of shock," said Marnie.

Jack finished his brandy and Marnie took the glass, placing a pillow beneath his head and instructing him to sleep.

"Let's go downstairs," said Helen, once Jack was settled. "You can tell me what's happened."

"Aye," said Marnie, "but I'm afraid it's an awful tale. This is a dark day for the town. A very dark day indeed."

Chapter 56
October, 1940

In the three days Jack had been staying with them, he hadn't uttered a word. Marnie thought he'd at least respond to Annie, but her attempts at cheering him up were met with a stony silence and she now steered clear of him. In fact, every member of the household avoided the living room. Jack hadn't washed since his arrival, and between the smell of his body and a lingering aroma of brandy, it was not an environment anyone relished spending time in.

"I've tried jollying him along," said Helen as she and Marnie sat eating their lunch. "But all he does is shout at me. I've got enough on my plate already without this. Not that I'm not sympathetic, but what good does all this moping around do?"

"I know," said Marnie, squeezing her friend's hand. "How is Richard today?"

"On the road to recovery. He ate a piece of toast this morning and his temperature has almost returned to normal."

"That's one positive."

"I haven't told him about the bomb yet. He'll be devastated and I worry it will set him back."

As they were talking, Jack thundered down the stairs, pulling a coat on over his dirty shirt.

"Where are you going?" asked Helen.

Jack ignored the question, marching across the room and slamming the door behind him. Helen sighed and threw her head in her hands.

"Listen, Helen. Let me worry about Jack. You concentrate on Richard and getting him better."

"Thank you," said Helen. "I don't know what I'd do without you."

*

Between running the shop singlehanded, entertaining Annie after school, and cooking dinner for everyone, by the time Marnie came down to the kitchen after settling Annie she was exhausted. The kettle was coming to the boil when a knock came on the door. Marnie opened it, finding a scowling Mrs Keswell on the doorstep.

"Oh, hello," said Marnie. "Is everything alright?"

"No," said Mrs Keswell, "it is not. I need to speak to Helen."

"She's upstairs with Richard, who is still poorly."

"Right, then I'll tell you. This is a town in mourning. The way that brother of hers is carrying on is disgraceful."

"Jack? What's he done?"

"Judging by his behaviour, I'd guess most of his day has been spent in the pub."

"What behaviour?"

"Singing in the street, urinating against houses, making a nuisance of himself and being extremely disrespectful given recent events."

"Where is he now?"

"Down by the harbour. I'm surprised you haven't heard him?"

Marnie grabbed her coat from the hook. "I'll deal with it." She pushed past Mrs Keswell and ran towards the harbour. Jack was standing on the harbour wall beside his boat, swaying back and forth and looking as though he was about to jump aboard. "Jack!"

Jack turned and Marnie rushed towards him, grabbing his sleeve just as he looked set to topple into the water.

"What on earth are you doing? I've just had Mrs Keswell at our door complaining about you."

"Mrs Keswell," said Jack with a harsh laugh. "Interfering old bat."

"That's as may be," said Marnie, pulling Jack away from the harbour, "but on this occasion she's right. Folk are in mourning, Jack. You going around the town singing your heart out is going to upset folk. Come on, let's get you home."

"Alright," said Jack, weaving from one side of the road to the other, in the opposite direction to Helen's cottage.

"Jack, where are you going?"

"Home," he said, pointing up the road before losing his balance and grabbing hold of a drainpipe to steady himself.

"That's not the way home."

"My home," he said with a slur.

Marnie sighed, running to catch him up. Despite his inebriated state, Jack was too strong to tame, and Marnie resorted to pleading, hoping her words would persuade him if she physically couldn't. By the time they reached Jack's cottage, Marnie was desperate, her tiredness leaving her fraught and exasperated.

Jack kicked open the front door and lurched towards where a half-drunk bottle of brandy stood covered in dust on the damaged kitchen counter. He grabbed it, flicking off the lid and began pouring it down his neck.

"Oh no you don't," said Marnie, reaching for the bottle. Jack held it above her head, giggling as she jumped and stretched in vain.

"I'll give you some to drink, but not if you're going to pour it away."

"Fine," said Marnie. She took the outstretched bottle. If she tried to tip it down the sink, she knew he'd be too quick for her. With a sigh, Marnie held the bottle to her lips and poured the brown liquid down her throat. She pulled the bottle away, coughing as it slipped down like molten lava.

Jack laughed. "Not keen on a nip of brandy? That's alright, I'll finish it myself."

Marnie reached out a hand, bending over to stop the coughing fit.

"You sure?"

Marnie nodded, accepting the offered bottle and raising it to her lips once more. Despite the foolishness of her actions, she worried that if she didn't dispose of the brandy herself, it would finish Jack off. She'd spent most of her life around sailors, but the state Jack was in, there was only one he'd give a run for their money; her father.

"Save some for me," said Jack, but Marnie kept swallowing, fighting against the nausea that threatened to bring the murky liquid straight back up again.

"There," she said, wiping her mouth and handing Jack the empty bottle.

"Why did you do that?"

"To stop you from killing yourself." Marnie grabbed hold of the back of a chair as the room spun. She rarely drank, and her body began an instant rebellion against the strong liquor.

"It's none of your business what I do."

"No, but I care about Helen, and what you drinking yourself to death might do to her. You're not the only one grieving, Jack. There's a whole town out there affected by what happened the other night."

"So says the woman who's made a habit of moping around ever since she got here."

"Sorry?"

"You, with your Tom this, Tom that. Anyone would think you're the first woman to lose a man to the sea the way you carry on."

Marnie stumbled back, stunned by the cruelty of his words. "I... I..."

Jack blinked, as though coming to his senses. "Oh, good Lord, Marnie, forgive me. That was an unforgivable thing to say."

"You're right," said Marnie, fighting back tears. "It was. You can be a hateful man, Jack Tristan." She stumbled her way towards the door, but Jack grabbed hold of her arm.

"I really am sorry. To make fun of your grief like that..."

Marnie rounded on him. "Aye, and you're a fine one to talk, drinking yourself silly rather than grieving with the community, shutting yourself away because of a twenty-year-old loss. Oh, yes, I know all about the woman you once loved, Helen told me. At least I try to get on with my life. At least I don't hide myself away, scared that the world will hurt me again."

By now, tears were flowing freely down Marnie's cheeks. She went to hit out at Jack, but he grabbed her wrists, pulling her towards him. "I'm sorry, I'm sorry. It's all this death... the war... I can't... I can't..."

They clung to each other, their thoughts blurred by the brandy, their souls aching from loss. Before Marnie knew what was happening, Jack shifted and his mouth met her own. His kisses were quick, urgent, as though trying to block out the reality all around them. Her mind blank, Marnie responded instinctively, matching Jack's urgent kisses, her hands gripping his clothes, sending all the feelings she couldn't articulate through her fingertips. They fell to the ground, hands tearing at clothes, cheeks slick with tears.

Later, Marnie could barely remember what had happened. All she knew was that in that moment, they'd been in some sort of trance, their minds buried beneath a mass of emotions that neither could speak out loud. They were desperate, afraid, angry, the physical release of pent-up fury providing a moment of brief respite.

It was over as quickly as it had begun, both flopping against the charred timbers of the floor, stunned. As rational thought crept back, Marnie fumbled with her clothes, ashamed.

"I'm sorry," whispered Jack.

"So am I. It was as much my fault as yours."

"Marnie..."

"No," said Marnie, sitting up and raising a palm. "No, Jack. We shall never speak of this. It was a moment of madness after a horrifying week. It wasn't us in this room, but exhausted, frightened shells of who we really are. I'm leaving now. I expect you'll be staying at Helen's again tonight, and I won't object. Things go back to how they were. This never happened."

Before Jack could reply, Marnie stumbled across the room and out of the door.

Chapter 57

October, 1940

Marnie squatted against the wall of the pub, the letter shaking in her hands. She opened it and read it again, the news no less brutal on a second reading.

"You all right, miss?" asked a passing soldier, making his way into the pub.

"Aye, thank you," said Marnie. "Just more bad news." She held the letter up as an explanation, and the soldier nodded.

"There's too much of it around these days. Do you need help to get home?"

"No, thank you. I need to make a telephone call. I'm just sitting here gathering the strength for it."

"All right then, miss. Well, you know where to find me if you need any help." He pointed towards the pub, threw her a smile, and stepped through the doorway.

Marnie pulled herself up to standing and dug around in her pocket for coins. With the telephone in her hand, she waited for the operator to put her through, her shoulders relaxing as she heard a familiar voice down the line.

"Hello?"

"Clara, it's Marnie."

"Marnie, so lovely to hear from you. Are you all right?"

"Not really. I've received some terrible news from Lowestoft."

"Oh no. What is it?"

"Kitty's eldest, Al, has died in France. He was only nineteen."

"Oh, good God. How's Kitty?"

"It's hard with only a letter to go on, but I can feel the pain in her words. It doesn't help that she's alone in her grief. Bobby won't talk about it. Kitty says he's not been the same since we lost Tom. I'm so worried about her, and feel so helpless being so far away."

"Of course you do. But you can't go back, Marnie. I saw Jimmy last week, and he brought me up to date with what's happening there. It's dreadful. You're safer staying put."

Marnie let out a joyless laugh. "I don't know about that. They bombed us last week. An entire family wiped out in a matter of minutes. It's all just too awful. And then..."

"Aye?"

"It's nothing."

"It sounds like something."

"Oh, Clara, I've done something so stupid, so selfish, and there's no one I can tell."

"You can tell me."

"I can't. It's too shameful."

"Marnie Hearn. Spit it out. Haven't we known each other long enough for you to know I'll not judge you?"

Marnie sighed, her fingers gripping tight to the telephone. "Something happened last week, a few days after the bombing. Something between me and Jack."

"Helen's brother?"

"Aye."

"Are you two courting? There'd be no shame in it. Tom's been gone a long time."

"No, no, we're not courting. He's proven a good friend, but a friend is all I see him as. It only happened because we were drunk, confused, addled with grief."

"What happened, Marnie?"

"We... we..."

"All the way?"

"Aye." Marnie's voice was quiet, as though the truth couldn't bear to escape her lips. "Clara, it was so disrespectful, with all that had happened... to... to..."

"But it doesn't sound like you engaged in some wild night of passion?"

"No, we didn't. Nothing like that. It was more of a need to be held. It was almost angry, I suppose. I don't know, I can't excuse it."

"Maybe not, but the war affects everyone differently. Not to mention the shock of what you'd witnessed. These are not normal times, Marnie, and so normal morals can't apply as they would in peacetime. Did you make a mistake? Aye. Are you paying for it? Aye. But what good will it do to keep berating yourself? Does anyone else know?"

"No, and they never can. Please, never tell Jimmy."

"Jimmy's not without his own secrets," said Clara. "But no, I won't tell him. How are things between you and Jack now?"

"I don't know. I haven't seen him. We're both too embarrassed. I worry he'll think I like him romantically. Oh goodness, I've made such a mess of things."

"That's enough," said Clara. "Put it out of your mind."

"Thank you for not judging me. How is everything there?"

"Better than Lowestoft or Padstow, by the sounds of it. Several families are waiting for news about their young men who are fighting, and a group of Local Defence Volunteers has been established. Ben's joined up and I can't tell you the worry that's caused to Da and Rachel. We've no news yet about where he's been posted. We're trying to press on with normal life the best we can. I saw your mam yesterday when I called in on Da. She's much the same as ever, and pleased Jimmy has been safely evacuated."

"How is Jimmy?"

"He's well, but worried about some evacuees. Some are thriving up there, but not all have been fortunate. He has suspicions about the treatment some of his pupils are receiving at the hands of their host families. They've moved others into children's homes with less than adequate supervision. What worries him even more are those children whose parents couldn't bear the separation and have taken them home. I've told him he can't fix all the world's problems, but you know what he's like. It helps that we can see each other regularly."

"I'm pleased you're able to support him. I'd better go as my money's running out, but send my love to Mam, and all the family. And thank you, Clara, yours was just the voice I needed to hear today."

"I'm not sure I've been much help, but you know you can call me anytime."

"I will do, goodbye."

Marnie put down the telephone, feeling calmer. She'd never forgive herself for what happened with Jack, but talking it through with Clara had at least salved some of the churning in her stomach. As Clara said, these were not ordinary times. She couldn't spend her whole life regretting one poor decision on one exceptional night. She had to move on from it, for Annie's sake, if not her own.

Chapter 58

November, 1940

Marnie woke with a gasp. Her heart was hammering so hard she worried it would escape her chest. For two straight weeks, the night she had given herself to Jack had replayed itself over and over as she slept. Once again, she woke to the burden of guilt and shame.

She still couldn't understand how it had happened. One minute she'd been fighting against Jack, the next... What happened next didn't bear thinking about.

She should never have gone looking for him. It wasn't her place to look out for him, to mother him. What an awful mess. And to think she'd been trying to help Helen. Marnie prayed Helen would never find out what had happened.

What was I thinking? Marnie asked herself for the thousandth time. The truth was, she hadn't been thinking, neither had he. Every moment since she had chastised herself for it. Every time she looked at Annie, she saw Tom. How could she have betrayed his memory in such a way?

Marnie sighed, pulled on her dressing gown, and with a wide yawn steeled herself to face the day. She met Richard in the kitchen, fully recovered from his illness and making a pot of tea.

"Good morning, Marnie."

"Is it?" she asked, flopping down in a chair.

"Another dreadful night's sleep?"

Marnie nodded. There was no point in hiding it. The first few nights of nightmares, Helen had rushed through at the sound of crying. Now Marnie was left alone. Both Helen and Richard believed her when she said the nightmares were about the bomb and its repercussions. After all, it wasn't a lie, even if she had omitted what those repercussions had been.

"Any plans for the day?"

"I thought I might take a walk, try to clear my head."

"Good idea. If you see Jack on your travels, can you ask him to call in? Helen's terribly worried about him. She can't understand why he's bunking down with a friend while he looks for a new home rather than staying here."

"I suppose he values his independence," said Marnie, knowing full well that was not the reason Jack had been avoiding Helen's home. Perhaps she should return to Lowestoft? If she got out of their hair, they could go back to being the family they once were. Jack could come and go freely without fear of bumping into her.

Later that day, with Annie at school and the shop quiet, Marnie found herself with a couple of hours to herself. Beyond her bedroom window, the winter sun shone down on the water of the harbour, salty jewels sparkling between the hulls of boats. The sky was a watery blue, devoid of cloud, the sun pouring uninterrupted from its centre.

Marnie placed a hand on the window. The chill of the glass reminded her they were in late autumn, the scene outside the window providing a misleading image of summer. Sunny days seemed so rare in these parts beyond summer, Marnie felt she must make the most of it. Hadn't she told Richard she might take a walk to clear her head? Marnie pulled on her thickest cardigan and went to find Helen.

"I'm heading out for a walk," Marnie said. "The day is too bright to be stuck indoors. Would you like to join me?"

Helen looked up from a book she was reading. "Not today, maid," she said.

Marnie frowned. Helen's eyes had none of their usual sparkle. Her face looked jaded, her eyes bloodshot.

"Is everything alright, Helen? Are you worried about Jack? I'm sure he's fine, just busy trying to find a new cottage."

"Yes, maid, I'm sure you're right. Don't mind me, I'm just having one of my sad days."

Marnie didn't know what to say to that. She'd never known Helen ever to be anything other than cheerful. At worst, Helen got a little tetchy, or worried about Jack.

"What have you got there?" asked Marnie, seeing a piece of blue wool poking out from Helen's closed palm.

"Oh, nothing. It's just me being silly."

Marnie crossed the room and sat at Helen's feet. "Helen, what is it? What's wrong?"

Helen laughed as tears brimmed in her eyes. "I'm being silly, that's all. I was searching in the cupboard for the Christmas box and came across this." She opened her palm to show a knitted baby's bootie. "I made these when Richard and I first wed. It's silly to have kept them all these years. I suppose I thought I could pass them on to someone, but I can neither bear to look at them nor to part with them. See, I told you I was being foolish."

"You're not being foolish at all," said Marnie, covering Helen's hand with her own. "Why don't I stay here with you? It seems you could do with a little company."

"No, maid. You go out and enjoy the day. I could do with an hour or two alone with my thoughts."

"If you're sure…" said Marnie, unwilling to leave her friend.

"Honestly, I'd rather be alone."

"Very well," said Marnie, standing up and grabbing her coat. "I'll be walking along the cliff top if you fancy some fresh air."

Helen gave Marnie a fragile smile. The winter sun's warmth stroked Marnie's skin as she walked away from the village, following the line of the estuary as it headed for the sea. Worry, grief and shame dissipated the further she walked, the beauty of the day making anything other than joy a struggle.

At the point the cliff descended to sand, Marnie stopped to remove her shoes and picked her way along the rock. Her toes tingled against the cold surface, but she pressed on, jumping from the final ledge, her feet sinking into icy grains of sand below. The beach was deserted, but Marnie followed the line of the cliff to a place where she knew she'd be undisturbed. She wanted solitude, with nothing other than gulls, sand dunes and wide open skies for company.

Rounding a large rock, Marnie stopped in her tracks. She would've turned back if he hadn't already spotted her.

"Marnie."

"Jack."

An awkward silence lay thick between them, neither knowing what to say to dislodge it. Eventually, it was Jack who broke the silence with a sigh.

"It's probably just as well we've met. We couldn't go on avoiding each other forever. Sit," he said, pointing to a shelf of rock beside him.

Marnie hesitated. She considered the easy option of turning and running home, but that would solve nothing. And wouldn't it help

Helen have her brother back? Marnie's shoulders slumped, and she trudged over to where Jack sat. Both stared out at the sea, neither able to look the other in the eye.

"We should probably talk about what happened," said Marnie, digging her toes into the sand.

"Yes. Perhaps I could say my piece first?"

Marnie nodded.

"For starters, I don't want you to take this to heart. You're a very attractive woman, any man can see that. I also think you're a wonderful person. That being said, I don't want to repeat what happened the other week. It wouldn't be fair on either of us. Please don't think it's anything against you. It's me. I'm not built to be in a partnership of any kind." To Jack's surprise, Marnie laughed. "What's so funny?"

"I'm sorry," said Marnie. "I'm not laughing at you. I'm laughing at the situation we find ourselves in."

"I've not hurt your feelings?"

"Quite the contrary," said Marnie. "Your words have brought nothing but relief."

"Really?"

Marnie nodded. "I've been summoning the courage to talk with you. I worried I'd given you the wrong impression, one you would have been justified in assuming. What happened resulted from heightened emotion, nothing more. I hate to say this, Jack. In fact, it pains me to say it."

"Good Lord, woman. Spit it out."

"I like you."

Now it was Jack's turn to laugh. "It pains you to admit you like me?"

"Aye, given you're a rude, arrogant, self-centred individual. But I've seen another side to you these past months, one I like. One I like, but don't love. You understand my meaning?"

"Completely. I feel exactly the same."

"Thank goodness for that. Perhaps if we'd met when we were younger, things might have been different, but my heart belongs to another, and it always will, even if I no longer have him by my side."

"We're a fine pair, aren't we," said Jack, throwing Marnie a sad smile. "Now we're clear that neither of us has any romantic intentions, can we go back to being friends?"

"Aye," said Marnie. "I'd like that. How about we begin our new friendship with a cup of tea? Helen's been dreadfully worried about you, especially given you've not been calling round."

Jack hung his head. "I'm sorry, I was..."

"Avoiding me?"

Jack gave a sheepish grin. "Yes..."

"And I was grateful for it, but now we've cleared the air, life can settle back to the way it was. Annie's missed you, too."

"And I her. How is the little madam?"

"As cheeky as ever," said Marnie, smiling. "You know, despite the war, despite losing Tom, I think our time in Padstow has been the making of her, the making of us. I've had to mother her in a way I never did when I had Tom to fall back on. You know she's excelling at the local school? They've moved her up a year. She even brought a friend home for tea last week. And to think she was so resistant to us coming here..."

"How long do you think you'll stay?"

"I don't know. News from Lowestoft isn't good and I fear that by going back I'd be placing Annie in more danger than she's currently in. That said, I sometimes long to be settled."

"You wouldn't think of settling here?"

"If it weren't for my brother and Tom's parents, perhaps I would. But I couldn't abandon them forever. It would be cruel after they've lost so much. Besides, as much as I now love it here, it isn't home, and I'm not sure it would ever feel that way."

"Well, friend, I'm glad we've got you for a while."

Marnie squeezed Jack's hand. "Aye, you're stuck with me for a while yet. Now, let's get back and find your sister and put her mind at rest."

The pair stood and made their way back across the sand. Marnie was relieved she'd cleared the air with Jack, but still felt some topics lay unresolved. What they'd witnessed that fateful night had left scars. She'd noticed when Jack smiled it didn't reach his eyes, and he'd aged in the few weeks since she'd last seen him. Silently, Marnie cursed the war and the destruction it wreaked.

Chapter 59

November, 1940

"That's the fifth morning in a row," said Helen, as Marnie walked out of the bathroom, wiping her mouth.

"It's just a bug," said Marnie, cursing beneath her breath. She thought she'd been discreet; clearly not discreet enough.

"Sit down," said Helen.

Marnie did as she was told and sat down at the kitchen table.

"Now listen here, maid. I'm worried about you. It's not normal to be ill for so long. A couple of days? Yes. Three even, but not five. Now, as I know you can't be with child, I think it's time we got the doctor to look at you."

Marnie's face burned with shame. She looked down at the table, picking at a splinter with her nail. It was time she was honest with Helen and herself. Annie had been poorly with some bug she'd picked up at school. It had given Marnie a little peace of mind. But now Annie was better, yet the sickness still gripped Marnie each morning. It was a sickness she recognised.

"Helen, I need to tell you something. You remember how Jack was after the bombings? You remember the evening I went out looking for him?"

"How could I ever forget?" said Helen, grim-faced.

"Something happened that night. Jack was in a terrible state. He'd been drinking all day and was threatening to drink even more when I followed him to his cottage. I ended up drinking far too much myself, just to keep the bottle away from him."

Helen nodded. "Carry on." Her tone was steely and quiet, like she knew what was coming.

"What we saw the night of the bombings, well, I think it damaged us both. When we found ourselves in his cottage a few days later, both having been drinking, both still in shock from what happened, we argued. Badly. We were both in a state, scared, hysterical, traumatised. Our anger turned to desperation, and we both needed a little human comfort. I didn't mean it to happen. Neither of us wanted it to happen and it's not happened again since. But... but..."

"Now you're left with the consequences of you and my brother's foolishness?"

"Aye," said Marnie quietly, glancing down at her stomach.

"You pair of fools," said Helen, her voice harder than Marnie had heard it before. "You selfish, ignorant fools."

"Helen..."

"No," said Helen, standing and grabbing her coat from the stand. "I need to speak to my brother."

Marnie jumped up and blocked the doorway with her body. "Please don't, Helen. Not yet. I need time to think."

"What's there to think about? You and Jack will have to marry quickly if we're to avoid a scandal."

"I won't marry Jack."

"What? Why?" Helen's fists were bunched, her face pale.

"Neither of us wants that. We weren't looking for love that night. It was a moment of insanity when our emotions got the better of us. We each regretted it as soon as it happened. Jack doesn't want a wife, and I don't want a husband. In my eyes, I already have one."

"Then what are you going to do, you stupid girl? The world may be changing, but attitudes haven't thawed that much."

"I haven't thought about it... I..."

"It doesn't seem like you do much thinking, does it?"

Helen turned on her heel and disappeared up the stairs, coat still on. Marnie slid to the floor, leaning against the door, her head in her hands. What was she going to do? She couldn't marry Jack. It would be for the wrong reasons and would leave each of them unhappy. Should she go back to Lowestoft? But that wouldn't work either. Tom's parents were wonderful, honest, and kind, but she couldn't see them welcoming her back if she were carrying another man's child. Angry tears slipped from Marnie's eyes and she pounded a fist against her forehead. Helen was right, she was stupid, so very stupid.

*

A week had passed, and a frosty atmosphere cloaked the house. It confused Richard, unsettled Annie, and devastated Marnie. She'd long thought of Helen as one of her closest friends, and the fact Helen refused to speak to her except in single syllables was unbearable.

"Can't you two just settle your differences? I don't know what's going on, but it's affecting everyone in this house, me included."

It had taken Marnie by surprise that Helen hadn't shared the news with Richard. She'd thought they shared everything. Marnie had dismissed Richard by saying something banal like *it will blow over*, but she could tell he was unconvinced.

With Helen refusing to discuss anything, Marnie took matters into her own hands and went to speak to Jack. As much as she'd like to, she couldn't put the moment off any longer.

After dropping Annie off at school, Marnie wandered down to the harbour, dragging her feet, delaying the inevitable. When she arrived at the water's edge, she found Jack in the engine house of his boat. He looked up when he saw her and smiled. Oil covered his hands, and a strip of black grease lay smudged across one cheek.

"This is a pleasant surprise," he said, then frowned when he noticed the expression on Marnie's face. "What is it? Are Helen and Richard all right?"

"Helen and Richard are fine," said Marnie, sitting herself down on a large metal box. "Jack, there's something I need to tell you."

"Uh oh."

"Yes, uh oh is about right. Now, I need you to listen and not fly off the handle."

"Alright," said Jack, wiping his hands on his trousers and sitting down opposite Marnie.

"I'm going to have a baby."

"What?" Jack sprang up, his hands flying to his head, spreading oil and muck through his hair. "But how?"

"You know how."

"But... but..."

"Listen, Jack. I'm not asking anything of you."

"But I'll have to marry you."

"No, you won't. I don't want that and neither do you."

"But you can't raise a child alone."

"There are a lot of things women can do alone, I think you'll find." Marnie's words were braver than she felt. Could she really raise another child on her own? She already had Annie and struggled with her. And then there was the shame. Marnie could cope with the shame the pregnancy would bring to her door, but what about Annie and her unborn child? Her actions would taint them. They'd live under a cloud of judgment.

"Marnie, you're not thinking clearly."

"Then tell me, if I wasn't expecting a child, would you want to marry me?"

"You know my feelings about marriage."

"Exactly. Jack, I love you as a friend, but you know anything more than that would make us both miserable."

Jack hung his head, unable to argue against the truth in Marnie's words. "Does Helen know?"

Marnie nodded.

"That explains the cold shoulder she's been giving me this past week."

"Aye, I rather think it does."

"Richard? Annie?"

"They know something's wrong, and it's only a matter of time before they find out what."

"What will we do?"

"I don't know... yet. Can you give me a little time? I'm sure I can think of a solution if I put my mind to it."

"Of course."

"Good. I suggest you don't tell anyone what we've spoken of."

Jack laughed. "Who do you think I'd tell? I like to keep my private business just that, private. The only person I'd talk to is my sister, and she knew before me."

"I'm sorry," said Marnie. "She knew something was wrong and was going to call the doctor. I had to tell her the truth."

"I understand. Is there anything I can do to help?"

Marnie sighed. "I think I need to decide on my own. But, Jack?"

"Yes."

"Do you want this baby?"

Jack looked at the floor. After a long pause, he answered. "As you know, I've never hankered after children of my own. But that said, I'm sure once this baby arrives I could love it. Perhaps in time I could learn to love you. After all, people marry for many reasons. It doesn't have to be for love."

Marnie shook her head. "That may be true, but it wouldn't work for us. Perhaps if we hadn't already experienced love, it could. But how could we marry, knowing what genuine love feels like?"

"It's not just about us now, though, is it?"

"No. Look, if you don't mind, I'll head off for a walk. I've a lot of thinking to do."

Chapter 60

December, 1940

Helen, Richard, and Jack sat down at the table, looking at Marnie with a mix of curiosity and apprehension. It was two weeks since Helen had learned about the baby, and a week since Marnie had relented and explained to Richard why the atmosphere in the cottage was so frosty. It had shocked him, but he took it better than Helen, who still couldn't muster more than monosyllabic greetings to her house guest and one-time friend.

"What's this about then?" asked Helen.

Alert to the tone of his wife's voice, Richard placed a hand over hers to calm her.

"I wanted to speak to you all together. About the baby."

Jack looked up in surprise. He'd honoured Marnie's wish to have time to think, but had assumed he'd be the first to know any decisions she made.

"I'm sorry, Jack, but I think this is the best way. It's clear my situation is affecting the lives of everyone in this house."

"Too right," said Richard, shaking his head.

"Well, I've been thinking of what to do. I think... I think I've found a solution that could benefit us all."

"Go on," said Helen, her eyes narrowed.

Marnie took a deep breath. "I can't keep this baby."

Helen sprang up out of her chair. Pointing to Marnie, she hissed, "it's not just your baby. What will you do, go to a backstreet hack and kill my flesh and blood? You'll have to get past me if that's your plan, missy."

"Sit down," said Marnie. Her voice was loud and clear. She held Helen's eye until her former friend took to her seat.

"As I was saying, I can't keep the baby... but you could."

Marnie looked round at the stunned faces in front of her.

"I... I don't understand," said Helen.

"I'm so sorry for how much my news has upset you. I've behaved badly, and you think less of me because of my actions. But there's more to your reaction than that. I know how you've longed for a child. It must break your heart to see me gain another one after only a misguided fumble."

Richard put a protective arm around his wife's shoulder. "Our situation has no bearing on this matter."

"It does," said Helen, her voice barely above a whisper. "Marnie's right. My own struggles to bear a child have led me to treat her terribly these past weeks. I don't judge you for your actions, maid. My reaction was born out of jealousy." Helen looked up at Marnie. "But that doesn't mean I'd take your child. A child should be with his or her mother."

"And father," added Richard.

"We'll not get married," said Jack. "We've discussed it and neither of us wants that."

"But it's the right thing to do for the child," said Helen, throwing her hands in the air. "You're such a stubborn pair, and if you don't mind me saying, selfish to boot. This isn't about what you do or don't want. It's about the child Marnie's carrying."

"Helen," said Marnie. "Ever since I arrived, I've seen the way you and Richard have been with Annie. I've seen what wonderful parents you'd make, given the chance. If Jack and I married, we'd both be unhappy, and that would do the child no good at all."

"But..."

"Please let me finish. At some point, I need to return to Lowestoft. I've family there, a life I've worked hard to build. I can hardly turn up on my in-laws' doorstep with another man's child, can I?"

"I'm sure they'd take you in."

"But it wouldn't be fair, on them, on me, on Annie, on the baby. Helen, I struggled so much with Marnie *Annie* when she was little, and I had Tom's help. There's no way I can do it all over again without him by my side. Whereas you," Marnie took Helen's hands in hers, "you'd make a wonderful mother."

"What do you think?" Helen asked Jack.

"I think Marnie's words hold a lot of truth. If you were to adopt my child, I could still be part of its life. It's Marnie who will suffer the loss, not me, so I think the decision should fall on her. I'll respect whichever path she chooses."

"This is ridiculous," said Richard, standing up. "We're too old to take on a baby. We never had the chance to be parents and we never will. Once the baby arrives, you'll fall in love, Marnie. You'll wonder why you ever suggested such a thing and leave Helen empty-handed and heart-broken. I won't let you do that to her. You'll need to find another solution. I'm sorry." He bent down to kiss Helen's cheek. "I'm going out for a walk to clear my head. I won't be long."

"He's right, you know," said Helen once the door had closed on Richard. "You'll give birth and fall head over heels for your son or daughter. The thought of giving them up will horrify you."

Marnie looked down at her hands. "I'm sure once my child makes its way into the world, I shall love it with all my heart. But that doesn't mean I'll change my mind. Please, don't dismiss the idea so quickly."

"Very well," said Helen. "We'll think about this some more. In the meantime, there are practical matters to consider."

"Such as?"

"There might not be many Lowestoft folk left in town, but there are some. If word gets out you're expecting, you'll have no choice but to marry Jack. The scandal would be too great for anything else."

"I have given that some thought," said Marnie. "If this pregnancy is like my last, I shan't be showing for quite some time. With Annie, it was only in the last couple of months my belly rounded to a noticeable degree. Could we make up some health complaint that keeps me away from prying eyes in those last few months?"

"I suppose we could..."

"And Annie keeps badgering me to let her walk home from school alone, so I wouldn't need to see the other mothers by the school gates."

"And what of Annie? She's bound to know something's amiss."

"I'll tell her the same story as everyone else. I'm ill and require bed rest. She's too young to guess the truth. When the baby comes, we can keep her out of the way. She need never know."

"I think you're underestimating your daughter," said Jack.

"Perhaps. But I don't see any other choice. Tell her the truth and she's bound to tell a school friend, who'll tell their mother, and before you know it, the news will spread around Padstow and make its way to Lowestoft."

"What a mess," said Helen.

"I'm sorry," said Marnie. "I never meant to bring so much trouble to your door."

"You're not solely to blame," said Helen, giving her brother a hard stare.

"Well, if that's all for tonight, I'll head on home," said Jack.

"Thank you," said Marnie, looking up and holding his gaze.

"For what?"

"For understanding. For honouring my wishes."

Jack threw Marnie a sad smile before turning and walking out of the door.

Chapter 61

December, 1940

M arnie woke on Christmas morning to Annie jumping up and down on their bed. "It's Christmas, Mummy! It's Christmas!"

"I'd never have guessed," said Marnie, pulling a pillow over her head. Whilst the sickness was easing, a deathly tiredness plagued her, in stark contrast to her daughter's boundless energy.

"Mummy," said Annie, pulling away the pillow. "Mummy, wake up. We need to see if Father Christmas has visited. Sandra's mummy said he won't be able to bring as much this year because of all the planes in the sky, but surely he's brought me something?"

Marnie made a mental note to thank Sandra's mother. Marnie had done her best with gifts, but between rationing and the small income from the shop they used to scrape by, it wasn't a bountiful year.

Annie leaped out of bed and Marnie eased her tired body from between the warm covers. "We'll see if you've a stocking under the tree," she said, "but you mustn't open anything until Richard and Helen are awake."

"But Daddy always let me open presents as soon as I woke up."

"Things are different now," said Marnie, "and Daddy would want you to be respectful of Helen and Richard's traditions whilst we're living in their house."

Annie pouted, but couldn't sustain a bad mood given the importance of the day. Marnie followed Annie down one flight of stairs and into the sitting room. There beneath the tree lay five small red stockings.

"Which one's mine?" asked Annie.

"They've all got names on, and you can read," said Marnie, "but my guess is yours is the biggest."

Annie pulled out a bulging stocking and began squishing it beneath her fingers. "Be careful," said Marnie. "You don't want to spoil whatever's in there."

"What's all this then?" asked a bleary-eyed Richard from the doorway.

"Uncle Richard, Father Christmas came last night!"

"Did he? I wondered if he'd find us in the blackout."

"Well, he did, and look," said Annie, holding up her stocking. "He's given me some gifts. Can I open them?"

"Let's have breakfast first, shall we?" said Richard. "I need a cup of tea before I can think straight. How do bacon and eggs sound?"

Annie's eyes widened. "It sounds better than porridge," she said, making Richard laugh.

Helen was next into the room. She wore an old floral dressing gown and had rollers in her hair from the night before. "You look funny, Aunt Helen," said Annie.

Helen sank into an armchair and yawned. "I know, Annie. But I want to look my best on Christmas Day. These," she said, patting the rollers, "will make my hair nice and curly."

"Do I need rollers?" asked Annie, pulling a strand of hair in front of her eyes.

"No, maid. Your hair is nice and curly on its own. You're lucky."

"Oh. Aunt Helen?"

"Yes?"

"Uncle Richard says we have to wait until we've had breakfast before we can open presents?"

"Uncle Richard's right," said Helen.

Annie sighed and replaced her stocking beneath the tree. "I'm going to help him make breakfast," she said. "Then it will be quicker."

As Annie left the room, Marnie turned to Helen. "Sorry," she said, "she's so impatient. Tom was always so soft on her. Last year she'd opened everything before we'd even had a cup of tea."

"You must miss him on days like these," said Helen.

"I miss him every day," said Marnie with a small smile, "but you're right, days like today are especially hard. He was out on the boat so much, but always home for Christmas, Easter and birthdays."

"We'll do our best to make today a happy one," said Helen.

"I know you will. But don't go to any special effort on our account."

"It's as much for us as you," said Helen. "You've no idea how wonderful it is to have a child in the house at Christmas." Helen flushed, realising she was straying into dangerous territory.

"Breakfast's ready," called Richard, saving the women from awkward conversation.

Marnie and Helen walked into the kitchen, savouring the smell of bacon and eggs.

"What a treat," said Helen. "Bacon and eggs and I'm not the one cooking them."

"I had a little help in the kitchen," said Richard, grinning down at Annie.

"Uncle Richard made the bacon, and I stirred the eggs," said Annie, puffing out her chest in pride.

No one around the table minded that the scrambled eggs were watery and the bacon overcooked. They savoured the chance to enjoy fresh food in relative peace, knowing that those in other parts of the country would not be so fortunate. Only the night before, they'd read the reports of the Blitz, of how it showed no sign of letting up for Christmas.

"Slow down, Annie," said Marnie, as Annie spooned enormous helpings of egg into her mouth.

"But I want to open my presents," said Annie, wiping scrambled egg from around her mouth.

Marnie sighed. "I hope you're going to be a little calmer once you've opened your stocking," she said, stifling a yawn. "This little pest was tossing and turning all night, too excited to sleep."

"I may be old," said Richard, "but I remember the excitement of Christmas morning well. We never had much, but Mother always cobbled together a stocking for us. I'd be up before dawn, desperate to open my gifts, just like you, Annie."

"Did your mother make you wait like you made me?"

"She did, and although I hated it, it made me appreciate my gifts more, and it ensured the day wasn't over too soon."

Annie sighed and folded her arms. Her foot tapped an impatient rhythm against the table leg, and her chair creaked as she wriggled and squirmed.

"Right," said Helen, laying down her knife and fork. "Looks like we're all finished here. How about a walk before we open our presents?"

Annie's mouth dropped open, her eyes wide in horror. Helen looked over at her and laughed. "I'm teasing, maid. Let's head upstairs and see what Father Christmas has brought us."

Annie jumped from her chair, grabbed hold of Marnie's hand, and dragged her to the stairs. Helen and Richard followed and they were all soon sitting around the Christmas tree.

"Let's take turns to open our gifts," said Marnie. She laughed as Annie's face folded into a frown. "Go on, you go first."

Annie dug her hand into a stocking and pulled out a rectangular, newspaper-covered gift.

"Careful with the paper," said Marnie. Annie nodded her head, her face serious as she carefully unfolded the wrapping. Her eyes lit up as she held a book aloft. "Can you read it?" asked Marnie.

"Yes, it's called *Joy Ride*," said Annie. "Look, Aunt Helen, it's about a girl and her horse."

"Oh yes," said Helen, taking the book and admiring it. "Perhaps you could read it to me later?"

"I'll read you a bedtime story," said Annie, causing the adults in the room to laugh. "Your turn, Aunt Helen."

Helen pulled a small package from her stocking.

"Not that one," said Annie. "I want you to open mine." She walked over to Helen and helped her select the right package.

"Oh my," said Helen as she unwrapped a cheerful red scarf. "This is wonderful. I hope it didn't cost you too much money?"

"I made it," said Annie, puffing out her chest in pride. She moved over to Richard and helped him select a squishy parcel. "This is also from me," said Annie.

Richard pulled a thick green scarf from its newspaper wrapping. "Goodness me, you have been busy." He wrapped the scarf around his neck, stood up and twirled around, causing Annie to roll on the floor giggling.

"Uncle Richard, you are silly."

"How about we let your mum open one now?" he said, sitting back in his chair.

Marnie pulled out a parcel and unwrapped it. "This is from us," said Helen. "Do you remember when it was taken?"

"May Day," said Marnie, smiling down at the photograph of them beside the harbour. "Such a happy day."

"It was," said Helen. "We thought it would be a good reminder of happy times. Richard made the frame."

"Thank you, both of you," said Marnie, gazing at the smiling sepia faces in her hands.

Half an hour later, Annie sat playing with a spinning top, the shell necklace Marnie had made for her draped around her neck. Helen and Richard wore their scarves, and Annie had insisted Marnie wore the mittens she had knitted for her despite the blazing fire in the hearth.

"I don't think we've done too badly," said Richard, thumbing through a local history book. "Considering all the restrictions and rationing in place."

"No. Thank you for the pencils you gave Annie. They'll keep her occupied for hours."

"We wanted Christmas to be as special as it could," said Helen, "despite all that's going on around us."

"Between the war and losing Tom, it would be easy to feel the world is a dark place," said Marnie. "But you two remind me that there is good in this world. There are people like you. I'll never be able to thank you for all you've done for us."

"It's our pleasure," said Richard, his voice gravelly with emotion. "Now, how about we get ourselves moving and off to church?"

Chapter 62

May, 1941

M arnie wrapped her hands around her stomach as she stood sideways in front of the mirror. A bump now protruded from her waist, and her breasts were fuller than usual. She'd felt the butterfly-winged flutter of new life within her, causing tears to spring to her eyes and doubts to form in her mind. The decision she'd made was not really a decision at all. What choice did she have?

Annie ran into the room and Marnie yanked down her blouse.

"You're getting fat," said Annie, wrapping her arms around Marnie's waist.

"It's part of the illness I told you about," said Marnie.

"You won't die like Daddy did, will you?" asked Annie.

"No, it's only a touch of something, nothing serious." Marnie cupped Annie's chin and tilted her head up. "I promise you, Annie, nothing bad is going to happen to me."

"Alright," said Annie. "Can I have some paper? I want to draw a picture for Nanny and Granddad."

"I'll fetch you some," said Marnie, grateful that Annie had accepted her explanation. Whilst she hated lying to her daughter, Marnie knew it was for the best. She could only imagine the taunts at school should news of her fall from grace reach the town gossips. Annie would suffer for Marnie's mistake, and she couldn't have that.

Due to a cold spring, the pregnancy was easy to hide. Shrouded as she was in layers of warm clothes, none of the regular customers noticed any difference in Marnie's appearance. The morning sickness had long since stopped, the tiredness was banished, and Marnie felt better than she had in a long time.

Helen and Richard had banned any talk about what would happen after the birth. Convinced Marnie would change her mind as soon as she held the baby in her arms, Richard made it clear he would not have Helen's hopes raised, only to be dashed again. Marnie wanted to reassure them. She knew her decision would not change, yet she kept quiet.

It was an ordinary Wednesday morning when the postman delivered a letter that would complicate Marnie's situation further.

Dear Marnie,

I hope you and my beautiful niece are well.

I'm afraid I'm writing to you with distressing news. You will have noticed Kitty hasn't written to you for a while, and she has asked me to write and explain.

A month ago, she received word that Stevie's regiment had been hit during a shelling in France. He was one of the few members to survive the attack, but it has left him with horrific injuries. He suffered awful burns and has lost one of his legs. After surgery and an extended hospital stay, the army has sent him to another hospital-cum-convalescent home on the south coast.

Kitty has left Lowestoft to be closer to him while he recovers. Bobby was relieved to see her leave. Things in Lowestoft have gone from bad to worse and everyone in the town is frightened of what is yet to come. I don't have an address for Kitty yet, but as soon as I do, I'll pass it on as I'm sure it would cheer her up no end to hear from you.

I'm sorry, Marnie, but that is not the only bad news I have to share. Roy went into hospital last week after suffering from a stroke. He's back home now but needs a lot of care, and Sally is struggling. With Kitty away, I've been allowed a temporary return to Lowestoft. I'm trying to help them more, but with the constant air raids and restrictions on entering the town, it's becoming harder and harder to support them. I've been granted a travel pass to enter the town, but by the time I've negotiated all the various checks, the time I have with Sally and Roy is more limited than ever. I'll stay as long as I'm able, at least until Kitty comes home.

I'm not asking you to come back. It's not safe for you and Annie here, but if you can think of anyone still in the town who could help, I'd be very grateful. Do you know if Sally and Roy have relatives elsewhere in the country? I've tried asking them and they've said no, but knowing how desperate they are to stay put, I can't be sure they're answering my questions truthfully.

You asked after Clara in your last letter. I'm pleased to report she is well, and the hotel continues to receive guests, which has come as a welcome surprise given world events. During my evacuation to Derbyshire, we grew used to seeing each other often and now I'm home, the separation is hard. But I'd rather we were separated, and she is safe.

If you can think of any solutions to Sally and Roy's situation, please let me know. Give Annie a big cuddle from me, Jimmy.

Marnie stared out of the window towards the harbour, turning the letter over in her hands. So lost was she in her thoughts, she didn't hear the soft knock on the door, or Helen enter the room.

"Marnie?"

Marnie jumped and spun around. "Oh, Helen, I'm sorry. I was away with the fairies."

"Is everything alright?"

Without uttering a word, Marnie handed the letter to Helen and perched on the end of the bed.

"Oh good Lord, maid," said Helen, folding the letter once she'd read it. "As if you don't have enough on your plate."

"I feel so terrible that I'm not there to help," said Marnie.

"What about Jimmy's suggestion of finding relatives for them to stay with? Do you know of anyone?"

"No, all the family I know of were in Lowestoft. Sally and Roy are the only surviving members of each of their families. Their siblings had children, but they left the town years back and I don't know how to find them. Tom was never in touch with any of his cousins."

"I'd offer to have them here, but it doesn't sound like your father-in-law would manage the stairs."

"That's very kind, Helen, but you're right about the stairs. And even if the stairs weren't a problem, you're already bursting at the seams having me and Annie here. I really don't know what to do. I can't take Annie back there. I'm not sure they'd even let a woman and child back into the town when most have been evacuated."

"No, of course not. I won't even entertain the thought of you going back. It's not safe."

Marnie sighed and buried her head in her hands. "If only this war weren't dragging on. There's no sign of things abating. The raids in London are horrifying, and don't suggest Hitler's in any mood to put a stop to things."

"You don't need to think of a solution this minute," said Helen. "Give yourself a day or two and someone may come to mind who could help you out."

"I hope so," said Marnie.

Later that afternoon, Marnie and Annie made up a package to send to Sally and Roy. In it was a letter from Marnie, a card from Annie, two of Annie's drawings, a scarf Annie had knitted and a selection of pressed flowers they'd been saving since the previous summer.

"I think Nanny and Granddad will be thrilled when our package arrives."

"I miss Nanny's cuddles and Granddad's stories," said Annie.

"I miss them too," said Marnie, pulling Annie closer. "When we next see them, they'll be so surprised by how tall you've grown."

"When will we see them?"

"When the war's over."

"When will the war be over?"

"I wish I knew," said Marnie. "But hopefully it will be soon."

Chapter 63

June, 1941

The months had passed quickly. Marnie was right in her prediction that the pregnancy wouldn't be obvious to onlookers for some time. It was at the end of her sixth month when she finally accepted that no amount of loose clothing could hide the round ball protruding from her middle. It was with sadness that she retired from working in the shop. She'd loved helping Helen and Richard improve the displays, find the best deals from suppliers, and greet the regular customers who crossed the threshold.

Now Marnie found herself with little to do. She could only leave the cottage after dark, and the days dragged, the hours lingering, reluctant to move from one to the next. Thank goodness she had her secret project. Jack had given her one of his old shirts as requested, and she'd cut a piece from the hem of her favourite dress. When Annie outgrew one of her summer blouses, Marnie squirreled the fabric away. When Helen caught her skirt on a shelf in the shop and tore it beyond repair, Marnie fished it out of the bin when no one was looking. Richard had been the trickiest person to scavenge from, but when Helen finally persuaded him to discard his old work trousers, Marnie was ready and waiting with an offer to dispose of them herself.

Now, with the baby stretching her skin, ready to come out any moment, Marnie's project was finally complete. She had shown Annie her handiwork before her daughter went to bed that night, but wanted to give it to Helen when they were alone.

Marnie headed downstairs, supporting her swollen belly with her hand, her project wrapped in tissue paper and tucked under her arm. She found Helen in the kitchen, making a cup of cocoa ready to take to bed.

"Goodness me, I'm surprised you can fit through the door," said Helen, studying Marnie's stomach as she waddled into the kitchen.

Marnie laughed. "It won't be long now," she said. She untucked the package from beneath her arm and held it out to Helen. "Helen, I've got something for you. I wondered if I'd ever get it finished, but with so much time on my hands lately, it's now complete."

"What's this for?" asked Helen, taking the soft, heavy package from Marnie.

"It's a thank-you. For everything you've done for me, for everything you've done for us."

"I don't need thanking," said Helen. "You've paid your way. It should be me thanking you for all your help in the shop. For your friendship."

"Aren't you going to open it?" asked Marnie. "You'd better open it at the table. It's big."

Helen sat at the table and carefully removed the string holding the newspaper in place. A look of confusion passed across her face as she stared down at the coloured fabric squares in her hands.

"Here," said Marnie, spreading the quilt across the table. "I'm no knitter, but at least I can sew."

Helen was quiet, her hand running from one square to the next. "Is this...?"

"Yes," laughed Marnie. "It's your old skirt."

"And this is from Annie's blouse?"

Marnie nodded. "This is from one of Jack's shirts," she said, pointing to a square. "Richard's old work trousers, my blouse. We're all there."

"But this is…"

"Our patchwork family. That's how I think of us. We may not be blood, but you're as much my family as Jimmy, Roy and Sally. And now, with this little one, we're linked by blood, aren't we?"

Helen brushed tears from her eyes. "I love it," she said. "But, Marnie?"

"Yes."

"This feels like goodbye."

Marnie smiled, but couldn't catch Helen's eye. "You're not getting rid of me just yet. But yes, it is a goodbye. I've been thinking a lot about what to do once this baby comes. I know you won't hear mention of it, but my feelings haven't changed about you having the baby. But this isn't just about the baby. The last few letters I've received from Lowestoft have left me so anxious. There's a forced jollity to them, but Roy's getting worse, Sally is struggling to cope, and Kitty is finding it harder and harder to get over and help them now she's back and forth to the hospital for Stevie, and Jimmy's back in Derbyshire. I've tried to find a solution. I wrote to my old friend Brenda from work, but the letter came back return to sender, so I assume she's been evacuated. Everyone else I thought of has left the town. I have to go back and help."

"But you can't! It's far too dangerous, for you and for Annie."

"I know. And that's why I need to ask something huge of you."

"What is it?"

"Would you keep Annie here, with you, until the war is over?"

"What?"

"I'm sorry. I knew it was too much to ask."

"No," said Helen, "it's not that. You know we love Annie like family. I'm worried about you, Marnie. I'm not sure you're thinking clearly."

"Thinking is all I've had time to do these past weeks. I hate the thought of leaving her, but to take her back to Lowestoft now would be madness."

"To go back yourself is madness."

"Then what should I do? What would you do, Helen, if you were me? Leave Sally and Roy with no help, grieving, ill, under constant threat of attack?"

Helen sighed. "No, I couldn't, but we're different, Marnie. You're a mother. If anything were to happen to you..."

"Annie would have you. And Richard, and Jack, and Jimmy and Clara. Between you all, you'd give her a happy life. I'm not saying I want to or am going to die, I'm just saying that everyone must make sacrifices. I wouldn't be the only woman in Britain living apart from her child."

"Children."

Marnie's hands instinctively went to her stomach. "I know it's asking a lot, too much, probably, to expect you to take in both my children..."

"Just as you wouldn't be the only woman separated from her children, we wouldn't be the only people taking in evacuees. The difference is that at least Annie knows us."

"So you'll do it?"

"I'll have to speak to Richard."

"Of course."

"Another thing, Marnie. Annie has been asking questions. She's not daft, she knows something's going on with you. She's a bright little button and keeps telling me you look like Aunt Kitty when she was going to have a baby. I don't think you can keep the baby a secret for much longer."

Marnie sighed. "It's for her own protection, her own reputation. I don't care a jot what people say about me, but I won't have my actions reflecting badly on my daughter. I've told her I have an illness that makes my stomach swell. As she gets older, I'm sure she'll put two and two together. But for now, I need to keep up the lie. It's too risky for her to know the truth."

"I'll speak to Richard about all of this in the morning. For now, though, get your rest. You'll need all your strength soon enough. Oh, and, Marnie?" Helen ran her hands over the patchwork quilt.

"Aye?"

"This really is beautiful," said Helen.

"Perhaps... perhaps Annie could keep it while I'm away. Then when the time is right for her to return to me, you could give it to the other child?"

Helen's eyes filled with tears. "I will. But you know, there's still time to change your mind. And if you don't, you can always visit."

"No," said Marnie. "I won't change my mind, and I won't visit. Give the child this, then I'll know I've left them with something. Goodnight, Helen."

"Goodnight." Helen watched Marnie waddle towards the stairs. Once Marnie was gone, Helen stroked her hands across the blanket, then wrapped it around herself. A patchwork family. The thought that part of her family would leave soon caused tears to spring to her eyes.

Chapter 64

July, 1941

Marnie gripped the bedsheets, her knuckles white, palms sweaty. How could she have forgotten the pain? How had her own mother done this so many times? An animalistic groan escaped her lips and Helen rushed to her, sweeping a damp cloth across Marnie's brow.

"Hush, maid. It will be over soon."

Marnie let the tears fall freely. *Over*. Helen was right. It would all be over soon, too soon, in so many ways. Her body tensed as a wave of pain crunched and twisted inside her. She welcomed the pain as an old friend. It was her penance, her punishment, her redemption. Marnie's back arched, fists clenched against sweat-drenched sheets, feet fighting with the blanket she had kicked off her body.

"Anything I can do?" came Richard's deep voice from behind the door.

"More hot water please, love. And a few more fresh towels."

"Right you are."

Marnie barely registered the comings and goings around her. She drew deeper into the depths of her being, the primal, hidden part of her soul which had allowed her to love, to dream, to make the biggest mistake of her life. Each wave of pain dragged her deeper, until the world around her blurred, her thoughts a mist of memories hidden beneath the blanket of suffering.

"It won't be long now, maid." Helen's voice broke through the fog, Marnie's bloodshot eyes turning to her. "Are you thirsty?"

Marnie nodded, and Helen held a cup to her chapped lips. The water slid down her parched throat like velvet across a palm. The relief lasted only seconds before another wave hit.

"I'm going to look," said Helen, placing the cup down on the dresser and lifting the sheets at the far end of the bed. "It's coming. I can see the head."

A cry sounded as Marnie followed her body's instructions and bore down on the pain.

"That's it, that's it, keep going, maid... now rest."

Rest? Marnie longed to close her eyes and let sleep overtake her. But she couldn't stop now. She gathered air in small laboured breaths, reaching for Helen's outstretched hand and gripping on to it for dear life.

"Right, this is it. I need you to gather all your strength for me, maid. When the next pain comes, I need lots of small pushes. We don't want any tearing, understand?"

"It's coming."

"Good. Now remember what I said."

Somehow, from somewhere, Marnie found the last of her reserves and, after five small gasps, felt something slide from between her legs. Her head flopped down against the pillow and she listened to the sounds of blankets being gathered, Helen's footsteps pacing back and forth across the floor.

"Come on, angel, come on."

Marnie lifted her head a fraction and saw Helen leaning over the dresser by the window, her hands roughly scrubbing at the parcel of cloth in front of her.

"Why is there no crying?" Marnie whispered.

"Be patient, it will come."

Marnie felt a tear slide down her cheek as Helen's face reddened, her rubbing of the child becoming harder, faster. Would this be the ultimate punishment? wondered Marnie. To bear this child, to have it torn from her body, only for it not to survive?

A sharp cry pierced the room, and Helen's whole body softened. She drew the parcel towards her and, in the watery morning light, her face shone with tears. Marnie barely registered her own sobbing as Helen crossed the room and, without speaking, laid the tiny bairn on Marnie's chest.

"You have a beautiful daughter," said Helen, her voice barely audible.

"A daughter?"

"Yes."

Marnie wrapped her arms around the child, her finger pulling back a corner of the blanket to reveal a mouth angry with cries, a shock of red hair fighting its way out of the blanket.

"Hush, little bairn," she said, putting her little finger to the baby's mouth. The child latched on to it, her crying ceased and a sense of calm filled the room.

"We're not quite done yet, maid. There's still the afterbirth to come."

Marnie nodded, handing the baby back to Helen, ready to finish the job. As soon as she left Marnie's chest, the child cried.

"She knows her mother," said Helen, gently placing the baby into a basket.

"I hope not," said Marnie, turning her face away, resolve fighting against love that seeped deep into her bones.

When all the mechanics of birth were over, the baby sleeping soundly in a basket downstairs, and the soiled sheets changed for fresh ones, Helen handed Marnie a cup of tea.

"How are you feeling?"

"Better now I've slept."

"Good."

"Where's Annie? Does she know what's happened?"

"We told her you're ill. She slept through most of it and is now at the neighbour's having breakfast and playing with her friends."

"What will I tell her?"

"That depends on what you want to do."

"It's not what I want to do, it's what I have to do. Helen, you know that."

"I thought once the baby came, your feelings might change."

"How could they change? How could I return to Sally and Roy with another man's child? It would destroy them."

"They're reasonable folk."

"They are, but this would break hearts which are only just beginning to heal. And besides, I'm a single parent now. I can just about manage with one bairn, but two?"

"Marnie..."

"No, Helen. My mind's made up. And even if my in-laws accepted the bairn and offered their help, I don't want it. You're a far better mam than me. You've seen how I struggle with Annie. I couldn't manage with two."

"But I'm not a mother, Marnie. You are. Take some more time to think about this, please."

"My mind is set and there'll be no changing it. The bairn is yours, Helen. She is your daughter. I will never lay claim to her, that I promise. Mind, I shall never even lay eyes on her again if I can help it."

Marnie turned her head from Helen, who sighed, recognising a stubborn woman when she saw one. "I shall not see that child abandoned. You know I won't. There is one thing you must give her, though."

"What?" Marnie turned her head a fraction, enough to see the sorrow, love, and frustration in Helen's eyes.

"Her name."

"Grace."

"You'd thought about it?"

"Aye, but I thought you'd like to name her, as she's your child now."

"Grace." Helen felt the name against her tongue, listened to how it sat on her heart. "I think Grace is the most wonderful name. A perfect name for a perfect little girl." Helen reached across and brushed a tear that was rolling down Marnie's cheek. "There's still the problem of Richard. I've yet to convince him. You know, he was certain once you saw your daughter, you would change your mind."

Marnie didn't answer. She simply pulled her blankets up around her chin and closed her eyes.

Helen sighed again, picked up the tepid cup of tea and left the room. She was not looking forward to confronting Richard on the child's future; however, when she wandered into the sitting room she found her husband in the rocking chair, the baby in his arms. Helen leaned against the door-frame and watched him. His large, rough hands stroked the baby's face. His eyes studied her movements, tucking in blankets, rocking her back and forth.

"I see you've met Grace," said Helen.

"Grace?" When Richard looked up, there were tears in his eyes. "How is Marnie? How does she feel about the child now she is here?"

"Marnie feels the same as before. There will be no changing her mind. And you? How do you feel now the baby is here?"

"Like I never want to let her go." A drop of water fell from Richard's eyes onto Grace's cheek. A tiny hand reached up and cleared it, as she snuffled and wiggled her head.

Helen walked over to her husband and put an arm around his shoulders. "Are we really going to do this?"

"Yes," he said. "I think we are. There is one thing, though."

"What is it?"

"I don't want to lay claim to another man's child. I will love Grace as a daughter, but she must call me Uncle, and you Aunt. You know how important honesty is to me. There'll be enough lies told as it is."

"And when Grace asks about her parents?"

"That will be up to Marnie and Jack. We'll honour their wishes."

"Very well. And the neighbours? What do we tell them?"

"That the baby was evacuated down to Cornwall. We could say she was born to a friend of Marnie's. After the war, presuming it ever ends, we could tell people her parents were dead so we're keeping her. Assuming Marnie and Jack agree to the charade."

Helen nodded. "Are you ready for this, my love? Are you ready to be a family?"

Richard held Grace with one arm and pulled his wife towards him with the other. "I'm ready," he said. "I think I've always been ready. I just didn't want to admit it."

"We'll have our work cut out," said Helen as Grace whimpered.

"That we will. But I think we're up to the job, don't you?"

"I do," said Helen. She leaned over Grace and kissed her husband.

Chapter 65

July, 1941

M arnie heard the unmistakable squawk of a new-born splinter-
ing the peace downstairs. It was her seventh day in bed and
she knew she'd have to face the world, and the baby, soon. After a long
discussion and Helen's failed attempts at persuasion, Marnie had had
nothing to do with the baby since its birth. Whilst she'd been prepared
for the emotional difficulty of such an approach, she hadn't realised
how much her body would protest at the separation.

Marnie felt like a teddy bear whose stuffing had become dislodged.
Her stomach sat like a bowl of dough, malleable yet painful to the
touch. On the third day in bed, her breasts became like two rocks
attached to her chest, but despite Helen's suggestion she use the milk
to feed the baby, Marnie had insisted on the use of powdered milk,
removing her own into a bowl.

Her heart, still fragile and chipped from Tom's death, threatened to
splinter into tiny pieces with each cry from her child. Beneath Marnie,
rags were soaked with blood.

"Mummy?" Annie's head poked round the bedroom door. "I've got
a cup of tea for you."

Marnie pulled herself up against the pillows. "Come in," she said.
She patted the bed beside her and Annie climbed up with care, her eyes
fixed on the cup in her hand.

"Are you feeling better now?" Annie asked.

"Aye, I am," said Marnie, trying to push down tears.

"Aunt Helen says it's time you got out of bed."

"Aunt Helen's usually right," said Marnie, managing a small smile. "Tell you what, how about I drink this tea, have a wash, get dressed, then you and I can play together for a while?"

Annie grinned. "Can we go for a walk? I've had enough of hearing that baby crying all the time."

Marnie wondered whether her legs could hold her weight after being idle for so long. "How about I get dressed and see how I feel?"

"Alright."

Marnie sipped her tea, and Annie fiddled with the blanket.

"Mummy?"

"Mmm?"

"Did that baby come from your tummy?"

Marnie spun her head around sharply. "What makes you say that?"

"Sandra told me babies come from mummies' tummies and your tummy got big."

"I already told you, I was poorly. But I'm getting better now."

"So, where did the baby come from?"

Marnie fought back tears. She hated lying to her daughter. She hated lying full stop. "You know children are leaving their parents to find safety elsewhere while the war is on?"

Annie frowned. "Evacuees, you mean."

"Aye."

"But I didn't have to leave you."

"No, that's because we came here before the war started."

"So, is the baby an evacuee?"

Marnie thought for a moment. "Aye. Aye, she is. She came from her mummy's tummy, but because of the war, her mummy couldn't look after her, so she's come to live with Helen and Richard."

"Oh. Will she stay here forever?"

Marnie couldn't bring herself to utter the word *yes*. "That will depend on the war," she said instead.

"Can we go for a walk now?"

"Let me finish my tea and have a wash first. Why don't you do some drawing while you wait?"

Annie jumped off the bed and went to find her pencil set. Marnie finished her tea and hauled her legs around and off the bed. She held on to the bed frame and tentatively pulled herself upright. Her legs felt like jelly, but after a minute or two, she felt confident enough to walk to the back of the door and put on her dressing gown.

Marnie climbed down the stairs slowly. After a week of inactivity, her head felt woozy and the last thing she needed was to fall.

"Oh, you're up," said Helen, as Marnie appeared in the kitchen.

Marnie kept her eyes to the ground, unable to look at the squirming bundle in Helen's arms. "Aye," she said. "I'm going to have a wash, then Annie wants to go for a walk."

"What a good idea," said Helen. "I can put Grace in her pram and come too."

Marnie couldn't find the words to tell Helen she wanted to be as far from Grace as was possible. Instead, she nodded and made her way to the bathroom.

Washed and dressed, Marnie surveyed herself in the mirror. Aside from her pale face, she really didn't look any different. To the outside world, she was the same woman. Inside, she couldn't be more changed.

It took an age to leave the house. Helen wouldn't step outside until Grace was covered and coddled within an inch of her life inside her pram. Marnie wanted to tell Helen that it was a warm day, with no need for hundreds of blankets, but knew better than to interfere. Any hint of Marnie taking an interest in Grace, and Helen would fret that Marnie regretted her decision.

When at last they left the house, it was to bright, warm sunshine. Helen negotiated the cumbersome pram across the market square and along the edge of the harbour. They'd only been walking a matter of minutes before Marnie's heart sank at the sight of Mrs Keswell.

"Oh, Mrs Hearn, how lovely to see you out and about. We've all been so worried after hearing you'd fallen ill."

"Thank you for your concern," said Marnie.

"And my, who is this glorious creature?"

Mrs Keswell leaned over the edge of the pram, stroking Grace's cheek.

"This is Grace," said Helen. "She's an evacuee."

"A very young evacuee, if you don't mind my saying. Where is her mother?"

Helen glanced down at Annie and mouthed to Mrs Keswell, *a victim of the Blitz*.

"Oh good Lord," said Mrs Keswell, clutching her chest. "The poor little mite. James heard from Richard that you were taking in a friend's child, but I didn't know the tragic circumstances behind it."

Marnie thought Mrs Keswell's horror was a little too forced.

"And you, Mrs Hearn? Are you recovering well?"

"I am," said Marnie.

"Well, there's nothing like new life in a house to put a spring in your step, is there?" asked Mrs Keswell, bending down to the pram once more. "What a fine head of hair the child has. She reminds me of your brother."

Helen flushed at Mrs Keswell's words. "If you don't mind, we'd best keep walking. I need to get this little one off to sleep."

"Of course, don't let me delay you," said Mrs Keswell. "I hope to see you at a whist drive once you're fully recovered." She addressed this last comment to Marnie, who nodded politely before striding off as fast as her battered and bruised body would allow.

"She knows," said Marnie, once they were a safe distance from the woman and Annie was distracted chasing a gull.

"Of course she knows," said Helen, laughing at the shock on Marnie's face. "Marnie, this is a small village. People aren't daft. First you disappear for months, then suddenly you're better and we have an extra child in the house. People are bound to talk."

Marnie felt gripped by panic. "But this is the worst outcome. If word reaches Lowestoft, it will destroy Sally and Roy. Annie will carry the shame, and as for... as for..."

"Grace will be fine. As will Annie. As will we all. Folk will gossip, yes, but we've given an explanation and we'll stick to it. Folk have far more to worry about than where a baby came from."

Marnie walked on in silence.

"How are you finding all this?" asked Helen. "It's not too late to change your mind."

Marnie turned to Helen and placed a hand on her arm. "It's hard," she said, "harder than I ever imagined it would be. But I've not changed my mind, Helen. You're a natural mother and Grace is lucky to have you."

"But she's your daughter."

"No," said Marnie, her voice raised. She took a deep breath and in a softer voice added, "She's yours. Yours and Richard's."

"But, Marnie..."

"No, Helen. I don't want you worrying I'll change my mind. I won't. Giving Grace away is the best thing I could do for her. My situation is precarious, yours isn't. You'll be able to give her everything I can't. I know you probably think I'm heartless by avoiding Grace, but it's the right thing, for me and for her."

"Aunt Helen, can we go to the beach?" asked Annie, running towards them with a bunch of wildflowers she'd collected.

"I can't get up there with the pram," said Helen, "and besides, there's barbed wire everywhere. Let's walk through the town instead."

Annie frowned.

"You'll find a lot more flowers in the churchyard than you would at the beach," said Helen.

"Alright," said Annie, skipping off, mollified.

"Is there any news on your return to Lowestoft?" asked Helen.

"Aye, I had a letter from Jimmy yesterday. He's secured permission for me to return to the town, not that he's happy about it. I should receive the paperwork I need within a week or two."

"I wish I could persuade you not to go," said Helen.

"Let's not go through that again," said Marnie.

"Does Annie know yet?"

"No, I'll tell her once I receive my papers. There's no need to worry her yet." Marnie watched as Annie skipped along the path. Why was every decision so hard? Why was she pulled in so many directions? Marnie sent up a silent prayer, that she was doing the right thing for both of her daughters.

Chapter 66

July, 1941

M arnie knelt down beside Annie, who was kicking her legs against the bed frame. "I promise, it won't be for long."

"But I don't want you to go."

"I know, but I have to. Granddad's poorly and Nanny can't care for him alone."

"What about Uncle Jimmy?"

"They've evacuated Uncle Jimmy to the north of England with children from his school."

"Then I should come too to help you."

"Oh, Annie, I wish you could. All the children have left Lowestoft while the war's on. You'd have no one to play with. And you'd miss your friends here, wouldn't you?"

Annie managed a grudging nod.

"Besides, Aunt Helen and Uncle Richard need your help with Grace."

"I don't like Grace."

"You don't?" asked Marnie, her heart hammering in her chest.

"All she does is cry."

"That will ease with time. You were the same when you were a baby. Soon she'll be able to smile, and I bet you'll do a fine job of making her laugh."

"When are you going back to Lowestoft?"

"Tomorrow."

Annie burst into loud, messy tears. Marnie pulled her close, rocking her back and forth like she'd done when she was a baby. Marnie thought back to only a few short years ago, when she would have jumped at the chance of time away from her daughter. Now, the thought was terrible, but there was nothing she could do about it.

When Annie's tears had reduced to little more than hiccups, Marnie set about her daughter's bedtime routine with something akin to reverence. With Annie in the bath, Marnie washed her daughter's hair, rubbing soap in with gentle hands, rinsing with jugs of water and noticing the way droplets pooled on Annie's curls before chasing each other off. She let Annie stay in the water until it was tepid. When Annie climbed out, Marnie wrapped her in a towel and pulled her onto her lap, breathing in the scent of her hair, feeling the softness of her daughter's skin.

Once in bed, Marnie told Annie more bedtime stories than usual. She spoke of a little girl growing up on an island. A young woman who'd fallen in love with a fisherman. Annie sat wide-eyed as Marnie described a wedding surrounded by family and friends, an island honeymoon and the joy the fisherman felt as his child was born into the world. Marnie spoke of a fisherman sailing among clouds in the sky, keeping a careful eye on his little girl, watching, loving her from afar.

Long after Annie had fallen asleep, Marnie found she was still talking. She spoke of hard times, good times, dreams the young couple had, adventures they'd planned.

Marnie realised her face was damp and wiped away tears with her sleeve. Mouth dry from talking, she crept out of the attic room and downstairs into the kitchen. She found Richard pacing up and down, baby Grace in his arms.

"Is Annie settled?" he asked.

"Aye," said Marnie. "She's upset at the thought of me leaving, so it took longer than usual."

"We'll take good care of her for you," said Richard. "Hopefully this war will be over soon and we can reunite children with their parents."

"Aye. How is Grace?"

"Come and see for yourself."

Marnie shook her head.

"Marnie, you're leaving tomorrow. What harm can it do?" Richard held Grace out to Marnie. Marnie stepped forward and Richard placed the baby in her arms.

"She's so light," said Marnie.

"I know. It's a wonder how something so small can make so much noise."

"How are you finding it?"

"What?"

"Being a father."

Richard tensed. "I'm not her father."

"You're as good as."

"I prefer to think of myself as her guardian. Jack's her father."

"He still hasn't seen her?"

"No. But he'll have to meet her, eventually."

"Richard, I'm so sorry for all the trouble I've brought to your door."

"Trouble? Look at the baby in your arms, Marnie. She may howl and scream, but she's a gift. You've given us the most precious gift anyone could give."

Marnie allowed herself to look down into her daughter's face. Grace was asleep, her lips pouting as though waiting for milk, her small cheeks lifting into what looked like a smile. "I think she's dreaming," said Marnie, battling against the rush of love swelling within her.

"Will you be alright for a moment if I pop to the bathroom?"

"Of course," said Marnie.

Richard left the room and Marnie stood rocking her daughter. Grace began to whimper and Marnie put a finger to her mouth, feeling tiny gums clamping around it as Grace calmed. "I wish you a life filled with love, Grace. Perhaps one day you'll forgive me for leaving you. Helen and Richard are good, kind people. They'll give you a wonderful life, I'm certain." Marnie leaned over and kissed Grace's forehead. "I love you, my beautiful girl," she said, her voice catching.

"Everything alright?" asked Richard as he came back into the kitchen.

"Aye. I might pop out for a quick walk," said Marnie, placing Grace back into Richard's arms. "I'd like to see the town properly one last time."

"Of course," said Richard.

Marnie forced a smile onto her face and let herself outside. With the door closed, she leaned against the cottage wall, tears falling silent and free as the loss sank in. From behind the window, she heard the running of a tap and the sound of a kettle being placed on the stove. Richard must be making up a bottle for Grace. Marnie couldn't risk being seen with a tear-streaked face, so took a deep breath, straightened her blouse, and headed towards the harbour.

The harbour was busy; a fishing boat had just come in, and the naval officers were milling around making adjustments to one of their ships. Keen to be alone with her thoughts, Marnie turned away from the harbour, meandering among the hotchpotch of stone cottages and shops.

With a deep sigh, Marnie turned upwards to a row of squat cottages. She hadn't visited Jack's home since his previous cottage had been condemned, but she couldn't leave without speaking to him. Marnie squared her shoulders and knocked on the door.

Marnie knocked a further three times before a dishevelled-looking Jack opened the door. His red hair stood up on end, the skin around his eyes sagged, and it didn't look as if he'd shaved for at least a week.

"Oh," he said.

Marnie gazed at Jack through narrowed eyes. Besides his appearance, his voice was gravelly, his breath stale as it reached her. She placed her hands on her hips. "Are you going to invite me in?"

He blew out air from pursed lips, then stepped aside for her to pass. Marnie couldn't hide her shock as she looked around the small sitting room. Dirty plates and cups lay scattered across the floor, balled-up blankets littered the sofa, and the closed windows had trapped rancid air between the walls.

Marnie marched over to the windows and threw them open.

"What are you doing?" asked Jack, finding his voice at last.

"It smells like a pigsty in here," said Marnie. "And it looks like one." She began collecting up the scattered dishes, carrying them over to a sink in the corner.

"Don't," said Jack.

"Don't?"

"It's not your place."

"No, you're right, it's not. But given there's no space for me to sit, and you seem in no mind to clear up, I'm left with little choice."

Jack grunted. He moved to an armchair, pushing a pile of newspapers onto the floor to make space. He rubbed his eyes and his face spread into a wide yawn.

"You haven't been sleeping?"

Jack shook his head.

"But you've been drinking plenty." Marnie frowned and kicked the empty bottles of ale littering the floor.

Jack nodded.

"And how's that going to help anything?"

"No one needs my help."

Marnie swallowed down her frustration, abandoned the dirty dishes, and threw the blankets onto the floor so she could sit down.

"What's going on, Jack?"

Jack threw out a brittle laugh. "What's going on? You know fine well what's going on."

"Grace."

"That's her name, is it?"

Marnie nodded. "I thought Helen would've told you."

"I've not seen her, despite her best effort to invade my space."

"She'll have been worrying about you. And that's the last thing she needs with a new baby, your baby, to care for."

"And yours," said Jack.

"Aye, and mine."

"Everyone knows," said Jack.

"About what?"

"You, me, the baby. You should hear what they've been saying in the pub."

"They don't know, they're guessing. It's your job to put a stop to such gossip."

"They say she looks just like me."

"She has red hair, but you're not the only man with red hair in the country."

"We should have married, like I said. Then the child wouldn't have grown up a bastard."

"Don't you ever call her that," snapped Marnie. "We've made a hard decision, but it will work out for the best. Helen and Richard deserve the chance to be parents, and they'll likely do a far better job than you or I." Marnie looked around the room once more. "You need to pull your socks up, Jack. If chaps in the pub are gossiping, their wives will be too, and you need to put a stop to it. Back up Helen's story that Grace is a refugee. Give her a fighting chance of having a normal life. And for goodness' sake, have a wash, tidy up, and stop drowning your sorrows in ale. Helen worries enough about you as it is."

"I've heard you're leaving."

"Aye. Tomorrow."

"Then it's easy for you to tell me what to do when you're running away."

"Running away?" Marnie gave a brittle laugh. "Have you any idea what I'm going back to? How much it hurts to have to leave Annie behind? What it's cost me to give Grace up? Of course you don't. It's so easy for a man. You do what you like and wash your hands of the consequences. So what if chaps in the pub are trying to rile you? You can carry on just as before, living as selfishly as ever. Don't expect my pity, Jack."

"I think you should leave now," said Jack, standing.

Marnie stood and walked across the room in silence. At the door, she turned. "I thought I'd misjudged you when I first arrived," she said, "but perhaps I was right all along. If you've any sense, you'll heed my words and put others first for once." With that, Marnie left the cottage, slamming the door behind her, angry not just at Jack but at herself. How could she have made such a mess of everything?

Chapter 67

July, 1941

The household was quiet as they sat in the kitchen eating breakfast, each lost in their own thoughts. Aside from the crunching of toast, the silence was only broken by Annie's occasional sniffs and sporadic grumbles from a sleeping Grace.

"I'll bring your bags down," said Richard, pushing back his chair. On the way to the stairs, he bent down to kiss Annie's head. The gesture brought tears to Marnie's eyes. She was lucky to have found such kind people to care for her daughters during these terrible times, but it didn't make the pain of separation any easier.

Helen jumped as the back door clicked. "Jack," she said, rushing to her brother. "You haven't been here in so long."

"Give over, Helen. It's only been a week or two." He untangled himself from Helen's arms and caught Marnie's eye. She smiled at the sight of him. All night she'd fretted that she'd been too harsh, but standing before her was a clean-shaven man in fresh clothes, not the vagabond she'd met the previous evening.

"Good morning, Jack," she said.

Jack walked over to the pram. "So this is the little mite I've heard so much about, is it?"

"She's called Grace," said Annie, climbing down from the table and standing with Jack beside the pram. "I have to help look after her while Mummy's away."

"And I'm sure you'll do a fine job," said Jack.

"I'm not doing the nappies though," said Annie. "They stink, and her poo keeps changing colour. At first it was black, now it's yellow."

"That's enough talk of toilet matters," scolded Helen.

Jack laughed and winked at Annie.

"Do you want to hold her?" asked Annie.

"Best wait, maid. Grace is asleep."

"No, she's not," said Annie, who had given the baby a surreptitious poke. Grace yelled, and Helen sighed.

Jack reached into Grace's pram and lifted her up onto his shoulder. She nuzzled into him, falling back to sleep in seconds. Marnie stifled a sob.

"You're a natural," said Helen, staring at her brother.

"I don't know about that," said Jack. "But, Helen, I'm here to help, any time you need it. I know little about babies, but from what I've heard, they're hard work. If you ever need a break..."

"You can join our team," said Annie. "We'll look after her together."

"I'd be delighted to join your team," said Jack. He turned to Marnie. "What time's your train?"

"In an hour. We'd best get going soon."

"Have you got all the paperwork you need?"

"Aye," said Marnie. "Kitty helped Jimmy to organise it all. It wasn't easy, getting permission to go back. They're trying to get women and children out of Lowestoft, not bring them back in."

"I'm sure your in-laws will be very grateful for your help."

"I hope so," said Marnie. She'd admitted her fears to no one. After the relative safety of Cornwall, she found it hard to imagine what she'd find when she stepped off the train. And before she reached Lowestoft, she'd have to navigate London. London, whose news of bombings had filled their newspapers for months. She sent up a silent prayer that she'd make it to Lowestoft in one piece.

"Here you are," said Richard, setting Marnie's suitcases down on the kitchen floor.

"Thank you, Richard."

"Perhaps we should make our way to the station," said Richard. "I know it's not far, but they'll need to check your paperwork and we don't want to risk missing the train. Who knows when the next one will be?"

"Come on," said Helen. "Jack, can you get Grace back into her pram for me?"

Jack transferred Grace to the pram with the care one might take over a precious family heirloom. He smoothed blankets over her, her tiny fist clamping around his finger. As she watched him, Marnie could see his face fill with love. She no longer doubted that Grace would have her father in her life, even if she only knew him as Uncle Jack. The look on his face told Marnie all she needed to know. He'd protect the child with his life.

"Right," said Richard, "let's go."

Before they'd even left the cottage, Annie gripped tight to Marnie's hand. With one last look around the place that had been a home, a refuge, Marnie closed the door behind her and on it, one of the most turbulent chapters in her life.

The tide was out, mud and sand glinting under the sun's rays, boats lying languidly, waiting for the water to come and right them once more. They walked past cottages and shops, Annie dragging her heels, keen to delay what was to come.

The station was quiet, a few soldiers and naval personnel milling about on the platform. Marnie waited at the ticket booth for her documents to be checked, and after a cursory glance, she joined the others on the platform.

They found themselves a bench to sit on, and the next half an hour passed in stilted small talk. Annie sat on Marnie's lap, her arms tight around her mother like a limpet clinging to a rock. Marnie wondered if she'd be able to prise her daughter away when the train finally arrived.

A whistle broke through their scattered snippets of conversation, and Marnie knew it was time. She stood, Annie in her arms, tears mingling as their cheeks pressed together.

"Be a good girl for Aunt Helen and Uncle Richard," said Marnie, "and know I shall think of you every minute of every day. You must be brave, my precious girl, but it won't be long until we're together again."

Annie nuzzled into Marnie's neck. Helen stepped forward and placed an arm around Marnie.

"You be careful up there, maid. We'll miss you."

"I'll miss you too. Thank you so much for all you've done for us." Marnie glanced down into the pram.

"Maid, it's nothing to what you've done for me. You've given me something I thought was lost, and in doing so, returned a piece of my heart I thought was broken forever. I'll do my best for her," said Helen, following Marnie's gaze towards the pram. "I'll do my best for both of them."

"I know you will. Annie, I need you to go to Aunt Helen now."

With expert hands, Helen took hold of Annie and prised her from Marnie's chest. "Come here, little one. It will be alright. You'll see

Mummy again soon." Annie fought against Helen, trying to get back to her mother. "No, you don't, maid," said Helen, her strong arms holding Annie in place. "You heard what Mummy said. You must be brave now."

"I don't want to be brave," cried Annie.

"Hush now, maid. Hush."

With Helen rubbing Annie's back, trying to calm her, Marnie stepped away towards Richard. "Thank you for everything," she said, offering a hand for him to shake.

"Don't be daft," he said, ignoring her hand and pulling her into a hug. "I'll miss you in the shop, so will the customers."

"I'll miss you too."

Richard let go of Marnie, and she turned to Jack. "Jack..."

As words failed her, Jack pulled her into him, holding her so tight she struggled to breathe. It turned out there was no need for words, their embrace saying all that was needed.

"Goodbye," Marnie said, turning back to the group. She bent over and kissed Annie's cheek. "I love you, my angel. I'll see you soon."

With Annie's cries ringing in her ears, Marnie turned her back on friends who had become family, and boarded the train. She found a seat among the servicemen heading home on leave, staring out of the window to hide her tears. What life waited for her in Lowestoft? How long would it be until Annie followed her home?

The train juddered, and Marnie took a deep breath, steeling herself for what was to come.

***

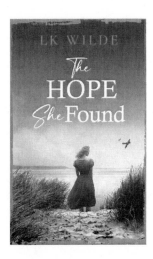

1941, Lowestoft

With her in-laws in desperate need of help, Marnie is forced to return to Suffolk, leaving her precious daughter Annie behind in Cornwall.

But Lowestoft is a very different town to the one she left. Ravaged by war, and a mere twenty miles from enemy lines, the seaside town she once loved now resembles a military base, and is firmly in Hitler's line of fire.

As she tries to rebuild her life amidst the rubble and horror of war, Marnie struggles to free herself from the grief and shame of past mistakes.

When naval officer Frank Merton moves into her home, he brings with him a vision of a brighter future, in which Marnie can find happiness.

But in order to move forward, Marnie must first confront the past. Can she forgive herself before it's too late? And with the end of war in sight, what kind of life will her daughter be coming home to?

Acknowledgements

When I wrote my debut novel *Silver Darlings*, I never imagined it would become a series, but Marnie was a character who caught my imagination. I wondered what had happened to her, after leaving the island of her childhood to care for the brother she adored in Lowestoft, and the only way to find out was to write her story! This book began life as a dual-timeline novel, but Marnie's story felt squeezed in that format, so I decided to give her a book of her own. That book expanded to two, and this is the first part of Marnie's story.

I've long been fascinated by the links between the fishing families of Lowestoft and Padstow, and although I only skim the surface of the topic in this book, I thoroughly enjoyed the research process, particularly my visits to the wonderful Padstow Museum. I can't recommend the museum highly enough. The volunteers provide visitors with a very warm welcome and a wealth of local knowledge. Whilst they patiently answered all my questions and let me borrow books for research, any errors or omissions in Padstow's history lie solely at my door.

In many ways credit for this book should go to a lovely friend and former colleague of mine called Nicky. She used to talk about her 'patchwork family' in the way some describe a 'blended family'. It was an image that stuck, and when I came to Marnie's story, the idea of a patchwork family, spread across the two locations of Padstow and Lowestoft, felt right.

Thanks are due to the team who've brought to the book the skills I lack – Jen and Jo for their editing advice, Jarmila Takac for the beautiful cover design, and Julia Gibbs for her expert proofreading skills. Thank you all!

Thank you to my family, to my boys Joe and Tom who despite their confusion as to which book I'm working on always take an interest. Thank you to Pete, for your patience and support when I doubt my abilities and have a 'wobble', and to Mum for everything you do for us all.

Lastly, thank you, dear reader, for picking up this book. It never ceases to amaze me that people actually read these stories that form in my head, and I'm grateful to each and every one of you. Laura x

Also By LK Wilde

People say you get one life, but I've lived three.

I was born Ellen Hardy in 1900, dragged up in Queen Caroline's Yard, Norwich. There was nothing royal about our yard, and Mum was no queen.

At six years old Mum sold me. I became Nellie Westrop, roaming the country in a showman's wagon, learning the art of the fair.

And I've been the infamous Queenie of Norwich, moving up in the world by any means, legal or not.

I've been heart broken, abandoned, bought and sold, but I've never, ever given up. After all, it's not where you start that's important, but where you end up.

Based on a true story, *Queenie of Norwich* is the compelling tale of one remarkable girl's journey to womanhood. Spanning the first half of the 20th century, Queenie's story is one of heartbreak

and triumph, love and loss and the power of family. It is a story
of redemption, and how, with grit and determination, anything
is possible.

**1840, Cornwall. The victim, the accused, and the wives left be-
hind. Welcome to the trial of the century...**

Based on a true story.

When merchant Nevell Norway is murdered, suspicion soon falls on
the Lightfoot brothers. The trial of the century begins, and two
women's lives change forever.

Sarah Norway must fight for the future of her children. Battling against
her inner demons, can Sarah unlock the strength she needs to move on
without Nevell?

Maria Lightfoot's future looks bleak, but she's a fighter. Determined to
rebuild her life, an unexpected friendship offers a glimmer of hope...

With their lives in turmoil, can Maria and Sarah overcome the fate of
their husbands? Or will they forever remain the wives left behind?

Book 1 in the Cornish feel-good *The House of Many Lives* series

Kate is stuck in a rut, She works a dead end job, lives in a grotty bedsit and still pines for the man who broke her heart.

When Kate inherits a house in a small Cornish town, she jumps at the chance of a fresh start. A surprise letter from her grandmother persuades Kate to open her home and her heart to strangers.

But with friends harbouring secrets, demanding house guests, and her past catching up with her- can Kate really move on? And will her broken heart finally find a home?

About the Author

Author and musician LK (Laura) Wilde was born in Norwich, but spent her teenage years living on a Northumbrian island. She left the island to study Music, and after a few years of wandering settled in Cornwall, where she raises her two crazy, delightful boys.

To keep in touch with Laura and receive a 'bonus bundle' of material, join her monthly Readers' Club newsletter at-

www.lkwilde.com

Or find her on social media- @lkwildeauthor

Finally, if you enjoyed *The Choice She Made*, please consider leaving a review or rating on Amazon. Reviews are so important to indie authors as they're the best way to help more people discover the book!

Made in United States
North Haven, CT
22 March 2024